"Neal Thompson's *The First Kennedys* is a riveting, beautifully written story and an important addition to our ongoing fascination with America's royal family. With captivating prose and breathtaking research, Thompson takes us on a remarkable journey from the blight-infested potato fields of Ireland to the unwelcoming, hardscrabble wharves and disease-ridden tenements of 1840s East Boston, where Bridget Murphy and Patrick Kennedy arrived to stake a claim to a new life. They joined millions of Irish immigrants who were at once reviled—white native-born Americans called them "maggots," "vicious," and "wretched"—but who also provided the desperately needed cheap labor for an expanding nation. The real hero of the story is Bridget—strong-willed, smart, and determined—who survived widowhood and climbed her way out of certain poverty to become a successful businesswoman, passing on her remarkable gifts of tenacity and confidence to generations of Kennedys. Settle in for a fascinating read!"

— Kate Clifford Larson, *New York Times* best-selling author of
Rosemary: The Hidden Kennedy Daughter

"Neal Thompson's *The First Kennedys* is both a profound portrait of the immigrant experience and an intimate look at the origins of an American dynasty. Deeply researched, intricately layered, and written in sparkling prose, this is narrative history at its finest."

— Karen Abbott, *New York Times* best-selling author of
The Ghosts of Eden Park and *Sin in the Second City*

"To understand the unforgettable stories of Jack and Bobby, Eunice, Ted, and the rest of their celebrated generation of Kennedys, we have to understand the stories of their extraordinary great-grandparents and grandparents. Now, thanks to Neal Thompson, we can. Read all about it in *The First Kennedys*."

— Larry Tye, *New York Times* best-selling author of
Bobby Kennedy: The Making of a Liberal Icon

"Bridget Kennedy, JFK's grandmother, achieved the American dream, but her story has been buried in patriarchal lore. No more. In this fascinating book, Neal Thompson gives Bridget her due—and in the process, makes us reconsider JFK's origin story."

— Alexis Coe, historian and *New York Times* best-selling author of
You Never Forget Your First: A Biography of George Washington

THE FIRST KENNEDYS

BOOKS BY NEAL THOMPSON

Kickflip Boys:
A Memoir of Freedom, Rebellion,
and the Chaos of Fatherhood

A Curious Man:
The Strange and Brilliant Life of Robert
"Believe It or Not!" Ripley

Driving with the Devil:
Southern Moonshine, Detroit Wheels,
and the Birth of NASCAR

Hurricane Season:
A Coach, His Team, and Their Triumph
in the Time of Katrina

Light This Candle:
The Life and Times of Alan Shepard,
America's First Spaceman

THE FIRST KENNEDYS

The Humble Roots of an American Dynasty

NEAL THOMPSON

MARINER BOOKS

Boston   New York

marinerbooks.com

Designed by Chloe Foster

Library of Congress Cataloging-in-Publication Data has been applied for.
ISBN 978-0-358-43769-7 (hardcover)
ISBN 978-0-358-43872-4 (ebook)
ISBN 978-0-358-57838-3 (audiobook)

1 2021
4500846066

Map (page viii) and family tree (page 283) by David Lindroth

Lines from "Sea Change" by Eavan Boland from *A Woman Without a Country*. Copyright © 2014 by Eavan Boland. Used by permission of Carcanet Press and W. W. Norton & Company.

Excerpt from *The Ungrateful Refugee: What Immigrants Never Tell You* by Dina Nayeri. Copyright © 2019 by Dina Nayeri. Used by permission of Canongate Books Ltd. through PLSclear and The Permissions Company, LLC, on behalf of Catapult.

In memory of the strong Irish women
who raised and shaped me:

My grandmother, Della (née Bridget)
My sister, Maura
My aunt, Patty
My mother, Pat

And to my wife—also strong, but Italian—Mary

Born in other countries, yet believing you could be happy
in this . . .

— THOMAS JEFFERSON

I was born in a place, or so it seemed
Where every inch of ground
Was a new fever or a field soaked
To its grassy roots with remembered hatreds.

— EAVAN BOLAND, "SEA CHANGE"

Immigrants, we get the job done.

— LIN-MANUEL MIRANDA, *Hamilton*

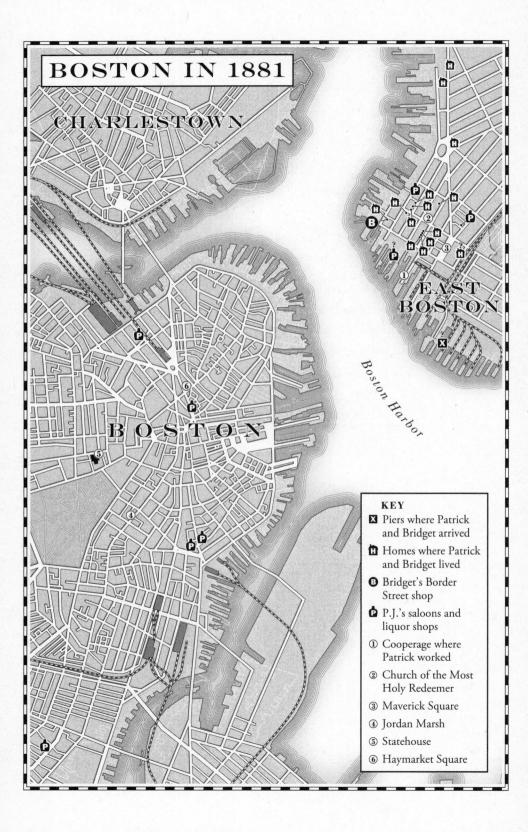

BOSTON IN 1881

CHARLESTOWN

BOSTON

EAST BOSTON

Boston Harbor

KEY

🗙 Piers where Patrick and Bridget arrived

🏠 Homes where Patrick and Bridget lived

Ⓑ Bridget's Border Street shop

🍺 P.J.'s saloons and liquor shops

① Cooperage where Patrick worked

② Church of the Most Holy Redeemer

③ Maverick Square

④ Jordan Marsh

⑤ Statehouse

⑥ Haymarket Square

CONTENTS

Introduction   xi

Prologue   1

PART I: BRIDGET THE REFUGEE

1. Bridget's Escape   7

2. Bridget at Sea   13

3. Bridget on the Farm   25

4. Bridget in the City   35

PART II: BRIDGET AND PATRICK

5. Bridget Goes to Work   47

6. Bridget Gets Married   56

7. Bridget the Mother   70

8. Bridget the Enemy   83

PART III: BRIDGET: ALONE

9. Bridget the Widow   99

10. Bridget the Servant   110

11. Bridget the Hairdresser   123

12. Bridget the Grocer   137

PART IV: BRIDGET AND P.J.

13. P.J. the Rascal   149

14. P.J. the Longshoreman   160

15. P.J. the Bartender   174

16. P.J. the Democrat   189

PART V: P.J.

17. P.J. the Legislator   205

18. P.J. the Senator   221

19. P.J. the Boss   238

20. P.J. the American   256

Epilogue: Joe and John   272

Family Tree   283

Acknowledgments and Author's Note   284

Notes and Sources   289

Select Bibliography   318

Index   324

INTRODUCTION

John Jr.

AT SUNSET ONE muggy summer night, a small plane ascends above New Jersey.

He'd wanted to leave earlier but got delayed. Then traffic. It's growing dark now as he and his wife and sister-in-law head north and east toward Massachusetts in his recently purchased low-wing Piper Saratoga. He isn't trained to fly at night, though. And he isn't medically fit, still limping on the ankle he'd injured in a paragliding crash; the cast had been removed just days ago.

It will become apparent soon enough: John F. Kennedy Jr. shouldn't be flying at all. An hour later, nearing Cape Cod in the moonless sky and hazy air, the plane dips, dips again, then dives straight into the Atlantic. Investigators will blame spatial disorientation. Others will blame hubris, confidence bordering on a sense of invincibility.

That day in 1999, when JFK's only son failed to arrive at his destination and his death seemed likely, my *Baltimore Sun* editors sent me to join the hordes of reporters who pounced on the well-to-do village of Hyannis Port to cover the story. I interviewed neighbors, relatives, the mailman. I sat through mass, where the family priest asked the unanswerable question: "Why are there calamities in life?" The same question had been posed at other Kennedy deaths, numerous and always newsworthy.

Walking through the historic seaside village, home of the Kennedys' waterfront compound since the 1920s and now littered with reporters' coffee cups, water bottles, and yesterday's newspapers, I visited the John F. Kennedy Memorial Park and the John F. Kennedy Hyannis Museum. There, visitors scribbled names and condolences in a guest book, including a husband and wife from Ireland: "We are saddened at this latest Kennedy tragedy."

When pieces of the plane were found off Martha's Vineyard, I was sipping a Jameson with a bartender who cried that she "felt like I just lost a family member." When they found the bodies —John, his wife, Carolyn, and her sister, Lauren—I stood behind barricades outside the family compound, which is tucked behind stone walls and white picket fences. A light rain began to fall. An American flag was lowered to half-staff. Ted Kennedy read a statement—"John was a shining light in all our lives"—and a week later he would eulogize his nephew, who "seemed to belong not only to our family, but to the American family. The whole world knew his name before he did."

John-John, son of an assassinated legend, nephew of another. He seemed like a decent if privileged guy, a journalist like me. My wife used to see him in Greenwich Village, running or Rollerblading, princely-handsome. I found myself wondering: Why are we still so connected to these reckless and beautiful Kennedys? What do they represent, especially to those of us with Irish blood? What do we *want* from them? And why do they keep *dying*?

Though I'd never nursed the default Irish American deification of the flawed and famous Kennedys—"America's royal family" and all that — I felt an unexpected sadness. Not so much at the apparent conclusion of Camelot but at the failed promise of a once-poor immigrant family.

Looking around at the lights and cameras, the tearful tourists trying to catch a glimpse of Ted, last of the famed sons, I also wondered, how and when and where and why did it all *start*? I knew the shorthand version: Joe Kennedy, the driven patriarch, the movie mogul and financier, the liquor importer and controversial ambassador who willed and bankrolled his sons to power. I also knew that Joe had lacked interest in his family's humble past. "We're Americans now," he'd insist. But how did the Kennedys *become* American? And who came first?

After filing my last story, I checked out of the "Cuddle and Bubble" motel and drove south to my wife and toddler sons. Passing through New Jersey, state of my birth, I came within a mile of my Irish grandparents' graves. His name was Patrick and hers was Bridget, though when she'd arrived at Ellis Island she gave the name Della. *Bridget* was too much of a stereotype, synonymous with *poor Irish maid.* Which is exactly how she began her life in America.

She'd been dead for a decade. He'd been gone more than half a century, having left her widowed and living in public housing with three kids, one of them my mother.

As I drove past on I-95 that day, leaving behind my grandparents and the grieving Kennedys and pondering the immigrant source of their story and mine, I felt something awaken.

Until then, while I rooted for Notre Dame (my father's alma mater), identified as Irish Catholic (easy enough in a town of Quinns, McCarthys, and Murphys), and attended *sixteen* years of Catholic school, I hadn't thought too deeply about my Irish roots, the Kennedys, or any of that. Having had a sister with Down syndrome, I did appreciate the family that helped create the Special Olympics, in which my sister competed. But not until JFK Jr.'s plunge into the Atlantic did something click.

That dead-Kennedy episode aroused my simmering Irishness. And though I didn't realize it at the time, that's when this book began.

Years later, amid the stirred-up cries to *build that wall* and *send them back,* my curiosity was reignited. I wanted to know more about the anti-immigrant low points in our history and found most of the nineteenth century packed with shameful examples: the anti-Catholic Know Nothings, the Chinese Exclusion Act, and the Immigration Restriction League, alongside the parallel efforts to keep Blacks enslaved and, even after Lincoln's Emancipation Proclamation and the turbulent period of Reconstruction, disenfranchised.

For much of that transformational century, the Irish were tops among America's feared and despised outsiders, coming to take your jobs and import their crime and their freaky religion.

As the grandson of immigrants, of those hopeful outsiders who often faced disdain or worse, I also sought to find inspiration in a story about America as a welcoming nation, of and for newcomers. In revisiting the Kennedys' origins, I've tried to understand how one family evolved, within a few generations, from loathsome invaders to one of the most powerful and beloved families in US history.

While plenty has been written about the twentieth-century Kennedys, none of it would have been possible without the heroic yet overlooked lives of a poor immigrant couple named Bridget and Patrick.

It all began 150 years before John Jr.'s death — in fact, just north of where he died — when his great-great-grandparents sailed into Boston Harbor, having left a country that couldn't sustain them to start anew in a city that didn't want them.

PROLOGUE

Cambridge, Massachusetts — November 23, 1858

BRIDGET MURPHY KENNEDY is burying her husband today. Boston doesn't want his Irish Catholic body in its soil, so she'll need to leave the city, travel west to the Catholic cemetery in Cambridge. Again.

He died at home, yesterday, after a slow surrender to tuberculosis, then known as consumption, a disease that *consumed* the body. Patrick Kennedy was thirty-five years old.

They'd been married nine years, having found each other after their respective escapes from a starving land. They'd had five children, buried one. They'd moved often, from cramped tenement to back-alley apartment, surrounded by more people in one block than they'd see in a month back on their farms in Ireland. Their entire world was now within walking distance of the docks where they'd landed, the docks where Patrick kept working—until he couldn't.

With no Catholic cemetery in East Boston, and only one in all of Boston, he'd have to be interred miles west at Cambridge Catholic Cemetery, one of the only local burial sites available for their kind.

Protestant Boston had done what it could to contain the Irish, corral the spread of their "evil popery." Preventing Irish funerals and burials had been a long-running goal of old-school Boston, whose Yanks didn't want the Irish walking *their* streets, spreading their sickness, their bad manners, their religion.

It's no easy commute to Cambridge from the island of East Boston, especially with four young kids in tow. The hours-long journey requires two water crossings. It's a journey Bridget made three years earlier, to bury her third child, her firstborn son.

John Francis Kennedy's brief life was hardly unique in its brevity. Irish immigrants' kids weren't expected to live past age five, a dismal survival rate. John had reached twenty months before an intestinal disorder known as cholera infantum, or summer diarrhea, took him — along with scores of other poor Irish kids that summer of 1855, when six in ten Boston deaths were children under the age of five. Consumption and cholera, typhus and smallpox, the fevers and diseases of the immigrant slums stalk Boston's air and water, flaring up like hotspots in a wildfire.

Her daughters have so far beaten the odds. Mary is now seven; Joanna just four days from her sixth birthday; Margaret, three. And in Bridget's arms is the youngest Kennedy, another son, named for his father: Patrick Joseph, ten months old. They call him P.J.

Mass was held early that day at East Boston's Church of the Most Holy Redeemer, a new house of worship built earlier that year beside its predecessor, St. Nicholas Church, which is being converted into a school for Irish Catholic girls like Bridget's daughters.

The pastor, James Fitton, offered a few kind words about Patrick, his work at the shipyards where he made barrels with Bridget's cousins, including Patrick Barron, the man who had introduced them and was standing there now, grieving beside Bridget.

The death of Patrick Kennedy earned no mention in the papers.

Just another dead Paddy among tens of thousands who'd been pouring into Boston—and Philadelphia, Baltimore, New York City, and New Orleans—over the past decade. It's a brittle-cold Tuesday with snow in the air as they start to make their way to the graveyard. The burial is scheduled for 2 p.m. A horse-drawn hearse carries the coffin, followed by carriages with Bridget and her children, then mourners on foot, a slow procession beyond Boston's city limits, a common sight. (Months later a train will plow through an Irish funeral procession, killing two women.)

The question has persisted for more than twenty years: where to put dead immigrants in a city that didn't want Irish or Catholics in its soil? City officials have passed laws and statutes to prevent Catholics from burying their dead in the mostly Protestant city. The city's lone Roman Catholic cemetery, St. Augustine Cemetery in South Boston, has been full for years. There is Bunker Hill Cemetery in nearby Charlestown, home of the infamous convent burning, whose town leaders rejected an incoming ship full of Famine Irish and generally shared the sentiments of their newspaper editor, William Whieldon: "Our country is literally being overrun with the miserable, wretched, vicious, and unclean paupers of the old country. They are not only introducing their wretchedness and disease among us but, if they ever recover from these plagues, they have a worse disease, which will overspread this country, their religion."

So, not Charlestown. Cambridge it would be. The decision had in fact been made three years earlier. A day after little John's death, Patrick had found a family plot there and paid six dollars for it, a grim investment, hoping he and Bridget wouldn't need it again soon.

John was the first Kennedy buried in the New World, the first not to be sunk into Irish turf. As his own death neared, Patrick was perhaps comforted to know he'd be lowered into the same American ground, to rest beside his son. His wife and children watch as the dirt covers his box.

With Patrick underground, Bridget and the others retrace their steps, back to East Boston. This is not the legacy she'd dreamed of on the deck of the ship that carried her here. She'll have to write to Patrick's parents, his brothers and sister back in Dunganstown, and to her own family in nearby Cloonagh.

Had it all been a mistake, thinking she could start a full new life in America? She has no choice now but to return to the job she took on when she'd arrived ten years earlier. She'll go back to serving others. A domestic. A biddy. A maid.

Her husband's death might have marked a tipping point into a tragic descent: into a lifetime as an overworked maid, watching as her daughters became servants too, and her son an underpaid dockworker, all of them destined to die young and poor among the reviled horde of refugees.

Instead, in a remarkable display of drive and resilience, over the next decade Bridget will march from strength to strength. She'll become a proper wage earner, an entrepreneur, and even a landlord, at a time when most women needed a husband's permission and a special license to open a business. She'll learn to sell things. She'll provide other immigrants with the supplies they need: flour, tea, milk, liquor. She'll develop skills to pass on to her son. She'll loan him money to launch his career, which in time will make him one of the wealthiest and most influential men on the island of East Boston. And by the end of her life she'll be recognized as "a woman of many noble and charitable traits." But first, before all of this, there was the irrevocable decision to cross an ocean, to escape toward the potentially grim unknown.

Part I

BRIDGET THE REFUGEE

Escape marks the first day of a refugee's life . . . You never forget the moment you were part of a shivering horde.

— DINA NAYERI, *The Ungrateful Refugee*

Ten years earlier . . .

1

Bridget's Escape

SHE STEPPED ONTO a mossy gangplank, looked back at her parents, sisters, cousins, and friends, a small herd of them. She knew she wouldn't return. Might never see them again. But she'd made her decision, and now it was time. What's done is done. Carrying all she owned, some food and supplies for the journey, she walked on up.

Unlike many others on board — and those on the hundreds of ships steadily draining Ireland of its stricken citizens — Bridget Murphy was not leaving home to escape starvation. The Great Irish Potato Famine, those dark years of hunger, evictions, and disease, had struck harder and deeper to the west. And though County Wexford was hardly spared, its crops often wrecked and its poorhouses always full, Bridget was no emaciated shell of a person in rags, subsisting on foraged nettles and donated grains. She was healthy and hopeful, a plucky twenty-something on the verge of a new life.

She was driven to this moment by a different kind of hunger, a craving to leave the safety of habit and family and fling herself among strangers toward a strange new land. Rather than be held down by the laws of a foreign oppressor (England), by the male-dominated norms of her peasant society, by the dour strictures of her religion, all of which had governed her life up to this point, she chose "a leap into the unknown," as her great-grandson would later put it. She joined a ship full of political refugees and other risk-takers "who dared to explore new frontiers."

The ship delivered her first to a port city doubled in population by flocks of Irish fugitives. Bridget's arrival in Liverpool, a hundred miles from Wexford as the crow flies but a days-long sail across the roiling Irish Sea and down the River Mersey, was like entering a manmade Mordor, a churning and raucous place spiked by smoke-stacks and ship masts. A middle ground between home and her destination, a type of purgatory, gloomy and dangerous, in the land of a queen, Victoria, who'd lorded over Ireland from afar, whose lawmakers dithered as Ireland went hungry.

Three out of four Irish Famine escapees will pass through this ashy industrial metropolis, more than 300,000 of them in 1847 alone, before boarding ships for America and Canada. Unprepared for its role as a human stockyard, the clotted burg became host to typhus and cholera, to lice and rats that invaded its squalid cellars and boardinghouses, to deaths by the thousands in its hospital wards.

Once one of the world's busiest slave-trading ports, Liverpool now traded in a new kind of human cargo. Famine victims arrived by steamer and packet ship from Cork, Wexford, New Ross, and Dublin, many looking every bit the part of the feared and reviled refugee: "half naked and starving," said one witness, "huddled together in a most disgraceful manner . . . covered with the dirt and filth of each other." Lives that had been full of hope were lost even before reaching Liverpool. One crowded steamer carried seventy-two dead—the captain had closed off the hatches during a storm and they'd suffocated. One little girl escaped through an opening, but her mother and five siblings perished. As one witness observed, "The pigs are looked after because they have some value, but not the emigrants."

Irish potato fields had rotted into sickening wastelands, and the mass emigration that started with a surge in 1846 had, by 1847, reached a full house-on-fire, run-for-your-lives stampede. Men and women who'd never ventured beyond the next town, who rarely saw more than a hundred humans together at church or the county fair, had flooded into the cauldron of Liverpool, desperate for a ship to Boston, New York, Baltimore, New Orleans, Quebec, *anywhere.*

After the simple life back home, hardly changed since medieval times, Bridget would have experienced a shock and a thrill at her first glimpse of Liverpool's hulking modernity. A thousand times larger than any village she'd known, the city hummed. A center of industry and technology, it teemed with a kaleidoscope of people from other lands, speaking in strange tongues. And it forced Bridget to confront a harsh revelation: other parts of the world had progressed while Ireland languished. There was so much she'd need to learn about the modern world.

For now, she had to focus on navigating Liverpool's dangerous lanes and staying safe for the few long days before her ship departed. Pamphlets like *Guide to Emigrants Going to U.S.A.* and *The Female Emigrant's Guide* offered advice and warnings: how to seek lodging and food, how to buy tickets, how to avoid the sleazy ship brokers and dock runners who preyed on naive or illiterate refugees, trying to sell them expired passage tickets or fleecing them of their meager savings.

Bridget witnessed the vile conditions facing tens of thousands of her fellow Irish. They crammed together, dozens to a room, in Liverpool's notoriously filthy subterranean dwellings, awaiting the next ship or begging for money to buy passage. The unlucky found themselves stuck in a Liverpool limbo, sick or penniless, wishing they'd stayed in Ireland. Hundreds of women were forced into prostitution.

In his semi-autobiographical 1849 novel, *Redburn: His First Voyage,* about a novice merchant seaman, Herman Melville described Liverpool's streets filled with hollow-eyed men and boys, starving and mummified-looking old women, and "young girls, incurably sick." Wrote Melville: "It seemed hard to believe that such an array of misery could be furnished by any town in the world."

Compared to Melville's sad yet sympathetic depiction, the American novelist Nathaniel Hawthorne — who lived in Liverpool, serving as US consul — was disgusted by the scene, referring to the desperate Irish "as numerous as maggots in cheese." Thomas Carlyle, the revered English author and historian who'd visited Ireland and witnessed streets filled with beggars and "human swinery," called the Irish of Liverpool "the sorest evil this country has to strive with."

The *Liverpool Mail* placed the blame at Queen Victoria's feet, acknowledging that "the scum of Ireland come to Liverpool and die in thousands . . . but whose fault is that?"

At the appointed hour, clutching a carryall containing her few possessions, Bridget joined the urgent crowds at the docks on the River Mersey. She walked up another gangplank, longer and steeper than the last, onto the slick passenger deck. After a frantic series of preparations — roll calls, checks for stowaways, families desperately searching the docks for last-minute arrivals — the ship lumbered down the river, the start of a dreary, dirty, deadly month at sea.

The crossing would be the boldest, riskiest thing Bridget had ever done. She had read in the papers about ships sinking, the sickness and death at sea, the odds of reaching America at all. Still, crossing an ocean seemed no more dangerous than staying on an island of putrid black fields.

Handbills at church and placards in the village had practically pushed her to make an escape. Time to admit defeat, they suggested —defeat to the English, to the Famine. Just *leave.* Newspaper ads —"Important to Emigrants for Boston!"—had listed dates of departure to Liverpool and a menu of "fast-sailing Packets" leaving from there to US cities.

And here she was, aboard one of those escape vessels, sailing west. She watched the land of her oppressors disappear, preferring this fragile wooden barrel and its watery arc to the life she would have faced, had she stayed in Ireland: at best, a farm wife; at worst, a victim and a statistic. Bridget, like other women, knew her country didn't want or need her, could barely feed and keep her, could promise her only a difficult, dreary existence. Accepting this sad truth fueled her flight.

As James Joyce would later put it, in terms applicable to generations of Irish but especially refugees like Bridget, "No one who has any self respect stays in Ireland." Self-respecting women escaped in greater numbers than the men, sometimes with sisters or cousins but often alone.

Many adventurous single women took advantage of the national tragedy to get out. Opportunities in mid-1800s Ireland were finite. Even without the Famine, farm life still promised tedium. Milk the cows. Feed the pigs. Sow the fields. Reap the harvest. Make the babies. Repeat and repeat. Bridget might've hoped to catch a good man's eye, ideally an older son who might inherit his father's farm. But then she'd need her parents' help to arrange the marriage, provide a dowry. Under the best of circumstances, she'd become only a tenant farmer's wife, tending to the hearth, the sheep, her children, and her man, the same as it had been for centuries.

But in America? In the land of freedom, whose eccentric founders had somehow managed to snub and trounce England, the enemy of Ireland? Whose revolutionaries had created a remarkable style of government called *democracy* — no kings or queens, lords or ladies, no ancient animosities? In this feisty and progressive country, activist women were now rallying for the right to vote and fighting slavery, agitating for workers' rights; they could now go to college, become teachers. In fact, some schools existed just for women, and an immigrant woman would soon graduate at the top of her medical school class to become the nation's first female MD. In a land like that, a refugee might just start over, reinvent herself, throw off her peasant cloak and customs to become someone wholly new.

Lady Jane Francesca Elgee, the fiery Irish nationalist poet (and later the mother of Oscar Wilde) who went by the pen name Speranza, taunted the British as "our murderers, the spoilers of our land" and described women like Bridget as Irish souls awakening. "Spread your broad wings brave and proudly," she wrote. "Arise, the dawn is breaking."

A generation of Bridgets chose to take a chance on a new dawn rather than wait for marriage in an ancient land run by church and queen. Many left home, wings wide, with a sense of adventure, optimism, and purpose, believing they could accomplish things in America that Ireland would surely have quashed. In Ireland, a woman was powerless, voiceless. In the United States of America, perhaps she'd find independence and a chance to speak her mind. Better to start anew, and afar.

If she could just survive the three thousand miles of open ocean.

Leaving Ireland, of course, was just the first step. As Bridget well knew.

2

Bridget at Sea

SHE WAS SQUEEZED with hundreds into a ship built for half as many. The crew allowed her out onto the top deck only during milder weather, so she spent most days below on the cramped steerage deck, stifling and dark. There, she found herself surrounded by sick and frightened strangers.

The Irish exodus had prompted the passage of new laws intended to protect the basic rights of overseas travelers. A ship was required to provide six pints of water a day per person, for drinking, washing and cooking, and a pound of food, which might consist of bread, rice, oatmeal, or perhaps just moldy biscuits; tea and sugar were doled out twice a week. For sleeping, there was a wooden bunk six feet long and less than two feet wide, which often had to be shared with another. But there was no guarantee that the crew would distribute water and food according to the requirements of the Passenger Acts. British ships were notorious for mistreating Irish passengers.

Many of Bridget's fellow travelers had been ill even before boarding; weak from hunger, they'd become infected with disease in Liverpool. Doctors tasked with inspecting passengers were sloppy or perfunctory in their duties, and the sick could easily hide their afflictions and slip onto the vessel. At sea, conditions were ideal for the spread of every disease—stagnant air due to the lack of ventilation, vomit and diarrhea soaking into the soggy wooden planks belowdecks because there were too few privies. Crewmen's reports described what Bridget saw for herself: bedraggled and "ghastly yellow looking spectres." Some did not have enough clothing to cover themselves.

Nothing could have prepared her for the horrors of the weeks-long wintertime crossing. Confined inside by the cold, she was forced to breathe fetid air, thick with the effluvia of hundreds of unwashed refugees, the rotting dregs of their meals, and their uncollected waste. Said a farmer leaving from Liverpool: "We thought we couldn't be worse off than we were. But now to our sorrow we know the differ."

Before reaching the open ocean, the ship passed near Ireland once more. A spell of cooperative weather might've allowed Bridget a brief pause at the rail for one last look north toward her homeland, her final glimpse of its browns and greens. Some passengers wailed as they watched their country disappear, while others wept for joy as they rounded the southern coast of Wexford, passing Hook Head lighthouse, sliding below the yawning bays leading north to Waterford and Cork, and finally past Cape Clear Island and out to the icy North Atlantic. How must Bridget have felt at this no-turning-back moment? Given her virtual anonymity among two million evacuees and the inconsistencies and imperfections of record keeping, in which the chronicles of men overshadow those of the women, the contours of her undoubtedly difficult crossing remain maddeningly faint, lost to the stony snub of history.

Bridget was too popular a name, the most common of Irish names for women. For centuries the legend of Saint Brigid of Kildare had inspired parents to name their girls Brigid, Bridget, Brid, Bridey, and other variants, including the diminutive Biddy.

Which meant that nearly every Famine ship carried its share of Bridgets and Biddies, often a dozen or more. Some passenger lists formed an alliterative poem of them: Biddy Beaman, Bridget Burke, Biddy Lawless, Bridget Briedy, Biddy Boyle. Among so many, it is hard to pinpoint the Bridget of our story, especially since her surname, Murphy, was the most common in Ireland. Also, passenger lists were notorious for gaps, misspellings, and other inaccuracies; they often omitted women entirely or listed some as just "Miss" or "Mrs."

Despite such obstacles, chroniclers of the Kennedys have explored various theories as to which vessel transported Bridget to America. Some suggest she traveled with a couple of sisters or perhaps her parents, or both, on the *Washington Irving* in 1849. But there's no record of a twenty-something Bridget Murphy (or someone with a similar name) aboard the *Washington Irving,* and of the Bridget Murphys who traveled to Boston in the late 1840s (some listed as Br., Brid, Brgt., or Biddy), none can be confirmed as *our* Bridget. Did she travel under a different family name — perhaps as Bridget Barron (her mother's maiden name) — as many Irish were known to do? Did she sail first to another city or to Canada, and then make her way to Boston?

She might've taken passage on the *St. Petersburg,* which left Liverpool in late 1847. Among its 250-plus passengers were a Biddy Murphy and a Catharine Murphy — roughly the same age as Bridget and her sister. More likely is the *Tarolinta;* its manifest lists a Biddy Murphy, age twenty-four, as well as a Patrick Barron Sr. and three sons, Patrick, John, and James — possibly Bridget's uncle and cousins on her mother's side, with whom she would live in Boston. (Of the *Tarolinta's* 199 passengers, 16 were named Bridget or Biddy.)

By the time of Bridget's crossing, the *St. Petersburg* was already known as an unlucky vessel. On a journey from Boston to Liverpool, it had sprung a leak and had to make emergency port in Providence for repairs. On a mid-1847 crossing, the ship's twenty-three-year-old captain slipped off the poop deck, fell to the deck below, and cracked his spine, expiring nine days later. Of the three hundred immigrants aboard, twenty-three died and scores fell deathly ill — "A singularly unfortunate passage," the *Boston Pilot* called it. On a subsequent crossing, forty-five would die of cholera.

Still, Bridget could've done worse than a ship like the *St. Petersburg,* whose history resembled that of hundreds of workhorse vessels that crisscrossed the Atlantic through the late 1840s. Owned by the Boston-based Enoch Train and Company, the *St. Petersburg* was part of an expanding fleet of ships that, after years of hauling cargo and cotton bales between Boston, Charleston, and New Orleans, were refitted to carry humans from Cork and Liverpool to America. Enoch Train advertised the *St. Petersburg* and other ships in Irish newspapers, promising a vessel "remarkable for size, strength, and swiftness," with comfortable berths and eight-foot-high steerage decks plus qualified doctors and an "able and humane" captain.

Whether she was on the *St. Petersburg,* the *Tarolinta,* or some other vessel, Bridget's Atlantic crossing can be imagined by means of the chillingly detailed tales left by many thousands of Irish who made the same journey. In the broader scope of history, the name of her particular ship matters less than what all such vessels were rightly dubbed: *coffin ships.*

Though trickles of Irish immigration to America had begun decades earlier, the Famine triggered a full-on draining. Those who could afford to, who saw what was coming, fled as soon as possible. Ships didn't instantly fill with the homeless and hungry; working-class carpenters, shoemakers, blacksmiths, tailors, butchers, masons, watchmakers, clerks, and coopers made up the earlier pas-

senger lists, along with those who toiled in the primary Irish occupation: *laborers.* Women were listed as wife or spinster, along with
the occasional seamstress, weaver, dressmaker, maid, or baker, but
most were categorized as *servants.*

By 1847, as starvation raged and evictions soared, panic
prompted all classes of Irish to flee. The vessels of their escape—
some, fittingly, were recently converted transatlantic slave ships—
advertised what they offered (food and speed) and what they didn't
(illness and death): "No Fever or Sickness on Board" and "Plenty
of Good Water and Breadstuffs." Some ships, like the *St. Petersburg,*
promised passengers even more than American maritime law required: thirty-five pounds of potatoes, fifteen pounds of bread, sixty
gallons of water, ten pounds each of oatmeal, peas, or beans, along
with boneless pork, rice and flour, a pint of vinegar.

The luckiest might make it to an American port (or to British
North America, as England's colonies in Canada were then known)
in four to six weeks. Eight to ten weeks was not uncommon.

Also common: disaster. Headlines in the *Freeman's Journal* in
Dublin, the *Irish-American* in New York, the *Illustrated London
News,* and other papers carried frequent and horrific reports on the
fate of Famine refugees. Ships had barely rounded the coast of Ireland before they were battered by hurricanes, shattered on shoals,
gouged by icebergs, or accidentally torched, like the *Ocean Monarch,*
which burned to the waterline soon after leaving Liverpool, killing
178; their bodies washed ashore for days. Another 109 died when
the *Maria* struck an iceberg: "A piercing shriek was heard from below but it was only for a few moments' duration, as the ship went
down immediately," said the *Liverpool Mercury.*

Ships were decimated by outbreaks of smallpox, typhus, lice,
and scurvy. Passengers and crew sustained frostbite or were swept
overboard. Stowaways emerged from casks or carpets, coughing up
blood and gasping for water. Before ships even reached the halfway

point, bodies were being tossed overboard. Ghostly faces bobbed and disappeared, their fish-picked bones gathering on the ocean floor, thousands of them, year over year . . . 98 dead on the *Henry Pottinger,* 106 on the *Bic,* 108 on the *Larch.* Of the 600 aboard the *Virginius,* 158 would be buried at sea; of the 427 on the *Agnes,* only 150 would survive.

A fiddler or pipe player might try to lighten the mood onboard with jigs and reels, and the heartiest might try a dance step or two. On calm days passengers mingled and talked, women knitted and sewed, men played cards, young couples flirted, children played games. They traded food, whiskey, stories. But for the most part, Bridget and her fellow passengers hunkered and prayed, hoping that tomorrow might bring a chance to cook some oatmeal at the always crowded top-deck fireplace; that tomorrow the captain might distribute more water; that tomorrow the crew might clean the overflowing privies, might pick up the scattered carcasses of chickens and pigs.

One westbound passenger would later describe Bridget's experience:

> Hundreds of poor people, men, women, and children of all ages huddled together without light, without air, wallowing in filth and breathing a fetid atmosphere, sick in body, dispirited in heart . . . The food is generally ill-selected and seldom sufficiently cooked . . . The supply of water, hardly enough for cooking and drinking, does not allow for washing. No moral restraint is attempted; the voice of prayer is never heard . . . I have known persons to remain for days together in their dark close berths, because they thus suffered less from hunger.

American ships were known to be safer and more sanitary than the cheaper, less well regulated British ships — some of them eighty years old or more — which yielded three times as many deaths, according to one count. Even Lord Clarendon, Britain's viceroy of Ireland at the time, would admit that conditions on British ships were "a calamity without parallel in the annals of history."

With doctors rarely available on board or poorly trained, thousands of pregnant women gave birth at sea, only to watch their ill-cared-for babies dropped overboard into the Atlantic.

On many ships, it became a daily ritual: corpses were wrapped in old canvas sailcloth, weighted with rocks, and "flung into the sea to be eaten up by them horrid sharks," as one passenger described it. When the sailcloth was gone, the dead were packed inside meal sacks. "One got used to it," an 1847 steerage passenger said, having witnessed the death of a couple and eight of their nine children. "Nothing but splash, splash, all day long."

Some ships completed most of the journey but then came up short. After a month at sea, the *St. John* from Galway was a day from reaching Boston when it got caught in a storm and slammed against the rocks at Cohasset Harbor. Of the 120 aboard, only a dozen survived. Henry David Thoreau traveled to witness the carnage, including the "swollen and mangled body of a drowned girl, who probably had intended to go out to service in some American family." Thoreau later wrote of seeing a mother and two or three children loaded into the same coffin, with "Bridget such-a-one" written on the lid in red chalk.

As she approached Boston, suspended between two lands with no solid earth beneath, our Bridget Murphy surely felt stirrings of doubt. Did an Irish farm girl have what it took to make it in a harsh and competitive city of more than 100,000 souls?

Standing on deck, she watched the gray shadows of New England form and grow closer, bolder. To the south, the tip of Cape

Cod curled its sand and rock like a giant *come here* finger. The smell of land reached her—"like the smell of a garden" is how the colonist John Winthrop described it in 1630, after his two months at sea.

The ship snaked through island-strewn Massachusetts Bay to Boston Harbor, followed by seabirds and led by pilot boats toward America's third-largest city, with its sky-poking church spires, crowded wharves, blocks of warehouses and smokestacked factories, its red-brick statehouse and recently completed Custom House. The home of America's founders finally took shape before Bridget's eager eyes. She passed near the famous spot where angry protestors, some disguised as Native Americans, had boarded ships sent by England's East India Company and tossed crates of tea into the harbor, igniting the revolution that would forge a nation.

For weeks she'd floated between old and new, and soon she'd step off the noxious vessel into an entirely new existence. As the ship neared shore, frantic preparations began, shattering the open sea's spell of monotony. Suddenly, it was happening . . .

If Bridget had picked up one of the guides distributed in Liverpool—such as *The Penny Emigrant's Guide to the United States and Canada,* which the *Waterford News* recommended for "every person who has an idea of exchanging the land of his birth for the free shores of America"—she might've known to expect bedlam during her final hours at sea.

To freshen themselves for the port inspectors, ships dumped weeks of accumulated trash overboard: mounds of filth-clotted straw and befouled bedding, barrels of effluent, rags and tattered clothes, and animal bones. Crewmen took roll calls and head counts, while hungry passengers with rubbery sea legs, itching to reach land and unite with family or friends, sometimes had to be restrained from leaping over the rails. The harbor boiled with activity: ferries and fishing boats and immigration officials scuttling between wharves and piers.

During the required stop at the recently opened Deer Island Quarantine Hospital, the port physician boarded to inspect passengers, mainly looking for typhus and selecting those to be removed and quarantined. Some of the unfortunates would be destined for the mass grave on that infamous island, which would collect hundreds of Irish bodies. Nearby stood housing for the city's juvenile delinquents, drunks, and derelicts — its own physician would die of imported typhus.

Medical inspectors often scuffled with sick passengers who'd survived the horrid crossing but now confronted strangers trying to prevent them from reaching their destination on the day they'd finally arrived. One witness described families being ripped apart: a husband "torn away forcibly" from his sick wife and kids, a widowed mother "dragged from her orphan children . . . rending the air with their shrieks," and "children snatched from their bereaved parents."

Thirty-one passengers were removed from the *Tarolinta* before it finally docked at East Boston in June 1847; twenty-six people were taken from the *St. Petersburg,* which landed the first week of 1848 after sixty-two days at sea — twice as long a trip as promised, running more than three weeks late. The *St. Petersburg*'s arrival earned a thirty-six-word brief in the *Boston Pilot,* and the *Tarolinta* earned thirty words — just two more of the daily washings-ashore of refugee Irish, two more ships completing a too-slow journey that littered the Atlantic with corpses. Of the 248 steerage passengers on the *St. Petersburg,* 25 had died and been tossed overboard. One in ten. Two babes were born at sea. Only three died on the *Tarolinta.*

At the pier, Bridget queued up to approach the men with their official papers and insistent questions. Asked for her occupation, she gave the answer most women on board did, the same one her immigrant sisters would, for decades to come. She declared herself a *servant*.

When Bridget finally stepped ashore — like most Liverpool passengers, she likely disembarked onto the waterlogged piers of East Boston — relief and joy were quickly jostled by chaotic and magical and disgusting scenes. Hustlers descended on shell-shocked newcomers, family members shouted for loved ones, horses and carriages weaved through streets jammed by tearful reunions, by beggars and pickpockets, doctors and dockworkers, police and priests, and the ever-lurking landlords (no getting away from them in America) advertising cheap rooms.

As had been the case in Liverpool, Bridget was approached by swindlers and runners, livery cabs, streetside food carts, employers seeking workers, and lonely men seeking companionship. But no words from an emigrant guide — how to rent a room, how to find work or a church — nor letters from kin who had previously immigrated could have prepared her for the Boston she met that first day. Just behind the wharfside circus that greeted every immigrant ship were the real streets of the city, the crowded shanties and tenements, the mud-packed lanes filled with garbage and horseshit, packs of dogs, and the occasional chicken or pig.

In a letter home, one Irish immigrant described the first moments on American soil: "The wharf of East Boston where we landed was of a miserable forbidding aspect. Dire poverty was to be seen all round, such wretched, horrible tenements with ragged, hungry looking dirty children playing in the ash heaps of a nearby railroad . . . Thinks I to myself, 'Is this the great country of peace and plenty? *This* is America?'"

As America got its first looks at the wide-eyed specimens of Famine Irish, America wasn't impressed either. One editorial writer

called it "lamentable to see the vast numbers of unfortunate creatures that are almost daily cast on our shores, penniless and without
physical energy to earn a day's living."

At the time of Bridget's arrival, nearly half of all immigrants to
the United States were Irish, tens of thousands of them arriving
each year since the Famine began. In Boston, more than twenty-five
thousand passengers would arrive on 921 ships in 1848, most from
Liverpool or a few other English ports, the rest from Cork, Dublin,
Limerick, or Galway. In all, 5,000 ships would carry more than a
million desperate and destitute Irish refugees westward through
the late 1840s.

Bridget had survived the Atlantic traverse and arrived healthy
enough to avoid quarantine and to walk unassisted down the gangplank, which put her amid bedraggled countrymen destined for
lives no less troubled than what they'd left behind. Now they were
bound for North End tenements and East Boston poorhouses, to be
"huddled together like brutes," as Boston's health inspector put it.
As one immigrant observed: "These wretched people were flying
from known misery into unknown and tenfold aggravated misfor-
tune."

At some point — that day? the next? — Bridget made a joyous connection with cousins from back home. Her mother had come from
a long line of Barrons, and Bridget had grown up alongside Barron
aunts, uncles, cousins, and others who lived on nearby farms.

The Barrons had been immigrating to Boston in ones and twos
since the 1820s and '30s. A few arrived just before Bridget, and
some may have traveled with her (if she was aboard the *Tarolinta*).
Others would continue to trickle in, and soon the bulk of the Barron family would be settled in Boston: Patrick and Mary Barron
(Bridget's aunt and uncle, who had owned the farm next door), at
least four of their children (Patrick, Thomas, James, Johanna), and

a few cousins (including Nicholas and Richard Aspell, both aspiring barrel makers).

Bridget's family had received letters from the Barrons already in America, and she would certainly have planned to connect with them the day she arrived, hoping to live with or at least near them in South Boston. She would stick with her tribe—both her immediate family and the broader family of Irish émigrés, a support network in a neighborhood of like-minded refugees.

As an eager, unwed, farm-to-city Irish woman, Bridget Murphy was hardly alone in gambling that America would promise freedom from the social and economic limits of a country in crisis. Thousands of single Irish women poured into America with the same idea, the same dream.

In fact, Irish women led the way west, outnumbering male émigrés in a female-dominated migration—making the Irish the only nineteenth-century immigrant group with more women than men. Most were unmarried, in their late teens or early twenties, and many traveled alone—choosing, like Bridget, to turn their back on a life of domestic toil and stubborn soil. Bridget was probably twenty-three when she arrived in Boston, although census records will later identify the year of her birth variously as 1825, 1827, or 1830. Her death certificate will list it as 1821, and her obituary as 1825. Most Irish at that time never knew their exact birthday.

She would miss her family, for sure. Perhaps she'd miss the squelchy bogs, the mewling lambs, the checkered fields of green, the gentle rains, and the evenings around the turf fire.

But she knew life on the farm held little promise.

She may have considered herself among the lucky ones.

3

Bridget on the Farm

AS IT HAD been for generations, life on the farm was simple, spare, and hard, even before the Famine wreaked its havoc.

Bridget and her siblings — two brothers (James, the eldest, and Edward, who died in childhood) and four sisters (Catherine, Ann, Johanna, and Margaret) — were raised in a one-room farmhouse, a lime-washed cottage of stone and mud. It measured thirty-six feet long by sixteen feet wide, with thatch for a roof, clay for a floor, and hay for bedding. Her parents, Richard and Mary, had worked their sixteen loamy acres for decades, having inherited the lease from Mary's father. (The land itself was not theirs; they were mere tenants.) Bridget's parents had met at a livestock fair, where Mary's mother sold a litter of pigs to Richard's father and an agreement was made to pair off the kids in marriage. Two of Bridget's sisters had left home to marry: Catherine to a nearby farmer named Nicholas Roche, with whom she'd have nine children, and Ann to a man named Patrick Kennedy, two decades her senior, whose farm was twice the size of the Murphys'.

With just one brother to help at home, Bridget and her two younger sisters took on the chores of sustenance and survival. Keep the peat fire stoked. Boil oats or cornmeal in milk for the morning stirabout. Feed the pig. Tend the sheep and the goat. Wash and mend clothes. Bake the oaten bread. Make soap. Harvest potatoes. Cut more peat. Slaughter a goose for supper.

Church on Sundays. The occasional dance, county fair, horse race. Sunny walks through the village of fewer than a hundred inhabitants, surrounded by jigsawed polygons of small farms, palettes of every shade of green and gray, spongy fields edged by hedges, clusters of gorse and heather, small pens encircling pigs and sheep, and the rare dog or horse.

Like most Irish lands, Bridget's town carried multiple names, depending on who was laying claim. The British Crown considered it part of the Barony of Shelburne, named for the Earl of Shelburne, whose family had received swaths of southeast Ireland as the spoils of war. The Dublin-based, English-run government of Ireland considered it part of the Electoral Division of Dunmain, in the Poor Law Union of New Ross, in the County of Wexford. To the Church of Ireland it was part of the parish of Owenduff, while the Catholic Church considered it the "half parish" of Gusserane, inside the parish of Tintern/Ballycullane.

Locals knew it as the townland of Cloonagh—Gaelic for "meadow"—just half a square mile of the country's lower-right corner, inland from Waterford and New Ross to the west and Wexford to the east. The midlands of County Wexford were boggy and mossy, sliced by old dirt paths, sluiced by dark-water streams, and decorated by the rubble of once-noble castles, churches and abbeys, neglected remnants of centuries of English assaults on Catholicism.

In a land of persistent rain and fog, gray mists sifted through the trees and across the Murphys' fields. The wet air soon to become thick with the rancid smell of ruin.

In the late summer of 1845, two years before Bridget's escape, a Wexford farmer walking his fields was overcome by a noxious odor.

The next day, he found every last potato plant wilted, the tubers splotched and slimy. The *Wexford Independent* reported that "a fatal malady has broken out among the potato crop," warning that eating infected potatoes "often proved fatal." The same devastation would blacken and putrefy fields across the country. Like every farm family, the Murphys waited and watched, hoping their vital and beloved crop—their primary source of sustenance—would somehow be spared.

Bridget and her parents and siblings consumed pounds and *pounds* of potatoes each week. Easy to grow and nutritious enough, potatoes made up a large proportion of their diet. Boiled, mashed and fried, stewed with buttermilk and cabbage, mixed into cakes and bread, potatoes made up a hefty portion of most Irish meals. In fact, some were *all* potato. Out of habit and because supplies of meat and other vegetables were scarce, some Irish, it was said, ate fifty of these tubers a day.

When times were good, they might cook the occasional goose or chicken, some mutton or beef, splurge on salmon or herring, or kill the family pig for pork steaks, sausages, or bacon. The Murphys grew other crops—barley, flax, beans, wheat, clover, turnips, and lowly fodder beets for the pig and sheep—but their soil, while more fertile than that of the rocky west, wasn't the healthiest. So, like all rural Irish families, they mainly grew and mostly ate spuds.

There were economic and political reasons for this too, and the heavy reliance on potatoes wasn't entirely by choice. Tenant farmers like Richard Murphy had to grow enough crops to sell and cover rent, since most Irish land belonged to its colonizer, England. The math foretold a devastating story: with a third of all agricultural land devoted to growing potatoes for food, if the potatoes sickened and died . . . so would the Irish.

Most of Ireland's potato crops failed again in 1846, and by the following year hardly a farm or family on the island had been spared, including the Murphys. An agriculture inspector touring Bridget's homeland deemed local crops a "total failure." And in a report he sniffed that farmers' love of the spud was partly to blame for the agricultural losses: "those poor industrious fellows . . . determined to persevere in their old but, I think, very mistaken mode of cultivation."

The real fault, however, lay in ancient socioeconomic imbalances. The Irish needed to grow and export food to England while subsisting largely on one vegetable, which was now dying. Also this: the Irish were tenants on what had once been their own land.

The backstory in a nutshell: England had conquered and reconquered Ireland over the centuries, and with Oliver Cromwell's victory over Irish Catholic rebels in 1653, the island was rolled by force into the British kingdom, along with Scotland and Wales. England doled out chunks of the verdant country to favored dukes, earls, lords, and viscounts, who hired middlemen to manage their "baronies." Those middlemen, landlords who often lived in England, rented land back to the previous owners: Irish farm families like the Murphys.

The country had since become the rural equivalent of a neglected tenement, subject to the rules and whims of the ultimate landlord, Queen Victoria, who seemed unconcerned whether her superintendent took care of the tenants. With its crumbling castles and "savage" citizens — the "vermin" that came along with the pretty green fields and folds — Ireland had become the unwanted stepchild of the aristocracy, "the one weak place in the solid fabric of British power . . . [a] blot upon the brightness of British honor," said Earl Grey, who oversaw England's colonies and who infamously shipped orphaned teen girls to Australia, ostensibly to ease overcrowded Irish workhouses but also to provide free domestic help to that British colony. Said Grey: "Ireland is our disgrace."

Publications like *Punch* mocked the suddenly starving Irish as ungrateful gorillas, scrawny and impudent, aboriginal and unruly. The *Times* of London was particularly harsh, blaming the Irish for their "indolence, improvidence, disorder, and consequent destitution." And the mothers carrying their dead children to a mass grave? The orphaned children trying to bury their parents in a pit? Not our fault and not our problem, *Punch* and Parliament mostly insisted. "We regard the potato blight as a blessing," the *Times* cruelly editorialized.

The assistant treasury secretary, Sir Charles Trevelyan, who oversaw all Famine relief efforts, felt that England shouldn't interfere too much with a blight that had been preordained from above. "God sent the calamity to teach the Irish a lesson," he said. The Irish journalist and activist John Mitchel later would offer this rebuttal: "The Almighty, indeed, sent the potato blight, but the English created the famine."

British authorities in Ireland continued to export the wheat, barley, oats, flour, beef, pigs, sheep, eggs, and butter produced by farmers like the Murphys. These provisions were loaded onto ships in Waterford and transported east, to Britain. Meanwhile in Ireland, the poor foraged on blackberries and lined up outside the workhouse.

England wanted Ireland to help itself. Reluctant to send food, provide direct funding, or allow the supplies raised for export to stay in the country and feed the locals, England instead put the Irish to work on public works projects, building roads that no one wanted or needed. By 1847, Parliament finally decided to feed the hungry, replacing public works projects with soup kitchens while passing the cost on to the landlords. But there was a catch. Soup kitchen meals were available only to those who didn't have a job and who held less than a quarter acre of land. Everyone else had to pay for the rations. (This was partly a scheme to reclaim small farms from peasant "cottier" farmers, the Irish equivalent of sharecroppers.) Some private soup kitchens attempted to help, but even those sometimes required the hungry to renounce the Catholic Church or sit through a Protestant religious service before they could eat. Catholics who gave in to such pressures were often denounced as *soupers*.

The choice was harsh: the Murphys could either give up their land to eat at the soup kitchens or coax sufficient sustenance from their stricken acres. By choosing to keep the farm, Bridget and her family were on their own, though at least they had a roof overhead. Many neighbors were less fortunate. Mass evictions became a particularly egregious side effect of England's handling of the Famine. Families that couldn't grow enough food to pay their rent were forced from their homes. Those who couldn't find space in the overcrowded poorhouses tugged a sack of belongings and slept outside by the road, beneath scavenged boards and branches.

One woman wrote to her landlord, "humbly requesting" food or a job or help in emigrating, after her father-in-law stole her goat, her only source of milk: "I have buried my husband and two children this month past and lost your rent by burying them."

Hundreds of thousands were rendered homeless and hungry. They roamed the countryside in search of work or food, spreading cholera and fever, which contributed as much to the death count as did the Famine and England's sluggish response to it. At one point, half the country was relying on public assistance of some kind. At its peak, the soup kitchens served three million meals a day. And the soup eaters were among the lucky ones. One farmer in the north of Ireland, writing to his niece in Boston, begged her to collect donations from friends. "It is a terrible time, the potatoes are totally gone," he wrote, bemoaning "this dreadful calamity that has befallen us at the hands of a despotic government." Everyone was on the verge of starvation, he wrote, and if evicted they would end up "with their mouths all green, striving to live on grass."

Those who were just getting by were tipped off their perch. Wages plunged or disappeared. Workhouses became scenes of desperation and chaos. Beggars and evictees filled the streets; the country was descending into madness. Stories spread of families sharing one lone meal per day, surviving on a single daily turnip apiece, missing meals entirely for days in a row, or resorting to eating the bitter mangel-wurzel beets meant for livestock.

The worst of it occurred west of Bridget's home, and news rolled east of families who ate snails, laurel berries, sycamore seeds and seaweed, who killed dogs to make soup. One family in nearby County Wicklow dug up a diseased cow to salvage strips of beef. Another Wicklow family found a dead rabbit, ate the meager but tainted meat, and died one by one within a week. Six sons of a widow in the town of Killarney were arrested for stealing a neighbor's sheep, cutting up the mutton, and hiding it beneath their hearthstone. The boys were shipped off to a penal colony and their mother died in the poorhouse.

Others were hanged for stealing food, and the papers in Wexford and New Ross carried news of residents organizing rallies, arming themselves, staging protests. The activists William Smith O'Brien, Thomas Francis Meagher, and John Mitchel—leaders of the Young Ireland nationalist movement—worked with the elder statesman Daniel O'Connell to repeal the oppressive Poor Laws, rallying for Irish independence and lobbying for stepped-up relief efforts. But despite the new aspirational tricolor Irish flag and the planting of hopeful seeds of independence, true political change eluded the rebels. (In fact, after a failed rebellion in mid-1848, O'Brien, Meagher, and others were arrested just west of Bridget's farm and imprisoned. Spared their initial sentence—to be quartered and decapitated—they were exiled to Tasmania.)

So, while the drumbeats of revolution pounded elsewhere—riots and uprisings in France, Germany, Hungary, Romania, Brazil

—those chanting for change in Ireland were silenced or deported. Meanwhile, stories of hunger, starvation, and theft devolved into stories of corpses and bones. One priest tallied his dead parishioners: "Mary Connell, found dead by a rick of turf . . . Bryan Flanagan, found dead by the road side . . . John Healy's two daughters . . ."

Graveyards could hardly keep up. Too often, the solution was a deep trench and a mass burial. In Skibbereen, bodies were piled into horrible troughs called "the pits." Behind the workhouse in Kilkenny, more than five hundred children were buried together, most of them under the age of six. Stories circulated of the near-dead being buried alive, of children trying to inter their parents under a pile of rocks, of mothers or fathers burying their entire family.

"All day long carts rumbled along carrying corpses," a survivor later recalled.

Bridget and her family avoided eviction—and the death sentence it often carried—thanks in part to their strange, mercurial land-lord, Jane Colclough Boyse.

The daughter of an English barrister, Boyse had married a wealthy landowner, Caesar Colclough, who died in 1842. She inherited his land, then married a lawyer named Thomas Boyse, and merged her dead husband's land with her new husband's County Wexford properties, creating a vast estate that contained the Murphys' farm.

Thomas Boyse, a playboy and bon vivant known for throwing parties and pursuing beautiful women, was also known for quietly providing aid to hungry tenant farmers and their families. Unlike other landed gentry, he also paid taxes and tithes out of his own pocket, instead of passing those costs on to tenants like the Murphys.

But his wife hated Ireland—"the climate disagreed with me,"

Jane Boyse would say years later, during a high-profile legal dispute over her estate. She left her second husband in 1846, months after they'd wed, and would spend the rest of her days in France or England, employing local agents to tend to her Irish properties and collect the rent. Though Boyse was "a person of very unamiable character and disposition," she and her ex-husband were "not regarded as being unduly tyrannical or unjust," one of her Wexford tenants said.

Having an absentee landlord with a somewhat charitable former husband meant Bridget and her family were spared eviction. They could scrimp and get by on the farm, growing just enough food to eat and to sell for rent, able to eke out an existence while others around them starved. Indeed, Bridget Murphy had it better than many other young women in Ireland. Some were abandoned by husbands, left alone with hungry kids, shipped off by their families to the notorious Magdalene asylums and laundries, or sent to England or Australia to earn money any way they could.

A lasting mythology grew up around these women. Books, artworks, journalism, and film would portray them as Famine's primary victims: weakened, bedraggled, clutching their starving children, incapable of saving themselves or their family. Apocryphal tales of "insane mothers" who ate their dead infants, of "hopeless famine-stricken old creatures" with wild seaweed-like hair, as *Freeman's* journal put it in 1851, would persist, as would the characterization of Irish men during the time of famine as rebels, thieves, and rogues. The truth: the Famine empowered women like Bridget, gave them a chance to fight back. They helped the sick and hungry, created private soup kitchens, opened secondhand clothing shops, collected and distributed blankets and shoes.

Or they embraced the chance to escape, to reject both the Famine and their apparent fate, choosing emigration as the best way to survive *an gorta mór,* "the great hunger." Bridget rebelled in her own way by joining a mass evacuation that caused some Irish towns to lose a third of their citizens, defeminizing swaths of countryside. The *Times* of London predicted that in no time, "a Celtic Irishman will be as rare in Connemara as is the red Indian on the shore of Manhattan."

Bridget opted for the uncertainty of adventure, the risk of a fresh start far from her doomed and unhappy homeland. As one observer wrote in 1846, the "natural vivacity and lightheartedness" of the Irish "has been starved out of them." Another said that "sport and pastimes disappeared. Poetry, music, and dancing stopped . . . The famine killed everything." By the time of Bridget's departure, Ireland's pre-Famine population of eight million had shrunk by more than a third. Most historians would blame the Famine for at least a million Irish deaths, on the scale of genocide. Another two million left for Europe, Canada, Australia, and the United States, in one of the largest mass migrations in global history.

Across the sea awaited the "bosom of America," which George Washington had envisioned as a welcome home for the opulent and the oppressed "of all Nations and Religions." "I had always hoped that this land might become a safe and agreeable asylum to the virtuous and persecuted part of mankind, to whatever nation they might belong," wrote America's first president (a slaveholder whose ideals concerning asylum clearly didn't apply to enslaved Africans).

Bridget Murphy in many ways matched Washington's description of the worthy immigrant — virtuous, oppressed, religious — but it remained to be seen whether the United States would be safe and agreeable.

Escaping Ireland, it turned out, was the easy part. Much harder would be surviving in a city hostile to the Irish, to Catholics, to women.

4

Bridget in the City

MANY OF THE rural Irish who left by ship in the late 1840s had one main goal: to reach Boston alive, to escape Ireland no matter what. Plans for what they'd actually *do* once they landed? Those details often came next.

For many, life in America began with a scramble to connect with relatives or friends who'd preceded them. Irish immigrants arriving in Boston grabbed the latest copy of the *Boston Pilot* and turned to the "Information Wanted" section, full of items from and about the disconnected diaspora. These advertisements, subsequently known as the "Searching for Missing Friends" ads, could be placed at a cost of one dollar for four weeks. They read like the collective anxieties of immigrants across time and place:

> "Any information, dead or alive, will thankfully be received at . . ."
> "Arrived in America about 2 years since, and not heard from . . ."
> "His brother, Patrick, is dangerously ill and is not expected to live."
> "Their mother, who is now in distress, is anxious to hear from them."

Thousands of such pleas appeared in the *Pilot* through the mid-nineteenth century, mostly from Famine escapees looking for

sons and daughters, long-lost siblings, coworkers, or errant husbands. When last heard from, these missing friends and relatives
reportedly had been "at work on the Railroad" or "employed in
Syracuse" or "in the American Hotel, in Burlington, Vt" or living
at Niagara Falls or in Maine, Cincinnati, Chicago. Sometimes there
were fears for the worst: "reported to have died of cholera."

> "has not been heard from, except a report that he lived in New
>   Jersey"
> "she walks with a prompt and active gait"
> "when last heard of was in Boston, and kept a store"

A woman from Donegal sought a shifty husband who "left me
and spent 230 dollars . . . He is 5 1/2 feet high, fair hair, cross eyed,
and a bend in one of his fingers and a scar in his hand and on the
back of his neck; he got blown up in East Boston at the foundry . . .
I was only 7 weeks married when he left me. I will give 18 dollars
to any one who will write me where he is."

Although there were plenty of notices in the *Pilot* from and for
Bridgets and Murphys, our Bridget was not among the seekers or
the sought through the late 1840s, likely because she managed to
quickly connect with family, the Barrons, and get settled.

Missed connections and disappearances didn't slow the flow of
enticing (if sometimes exaggerated) letters sent back to Ireland,
beckoning siblings, aunts, and cousins to New Orleans, New York,
Boston, and Baltimore—often overpromising on the conditions
they'd find in the "land of opportunity." One Famine immigrant,
Mary McCarthy, urged her family in Cork to "come you all together
courageously and bid adieu to that lovely place, the land of our
Birth." She enclosed twenty dollars and said her family would be
"fools" if they hesitated to "come to this plentiful country where no
man or woman ever hungered or ever will and where you will not
be seen naked."

McCarthy also added, accurately, "But I can assure you there are Dangers upon Dangers."

The dangers Bridget Murphy faced in those early days were constant and real.

On the one hand, there was the thrill of diving into an urban fantasia, a legendary and lively city, its streets lined with hotels, restaurants, banks, jeweler's shops, churches, saloons, candy stalls, pickle stalls, barbershops, and brothels, busy with people from all corners of the world, enlivened by street singers and magicians. Compared to Bridget's straw-roofed home, her farm and humble village, Boston, despite its cramped and dirty lodgings, was something of a wonderland.

On the other hand, the streets that Bridget navigated were also full of rotting garbage, raw sewage, dead animals, stray dogs, and skittish horses, their shit scooped up by roving wheelbarrow tenders. Public posters warned about the spread of cholera and typhus, and city health officials worried about the "wretched, dirty, and unhealthy condition of a great number of the dwelling houses, occupied by the Irish population."

The *Boston Pilot* newspaper (often known as the *Pilot,* and still published to this day), at times speaking as the self-appointed authority on what was best for fresh-off-the-boat Bridgets, cautioned against tenement living in port cities like Boston, scolding those who would "herd together in poverty and misery." Families sharing small rooms or cellar apartments were "inhaling disease and death in every breath of tainted air they draw," said one editorial, urging the Irish to stop clustering where they were easy prey to pestilence.

Patrick Donahoe, the *Pilot*'s Irish immigrant publisher, regularly admonished readers to avoid getting too comfortable in Boston. "To linger here is to destroy one's self — to throw away all the chances of bettering themselves they may have on this soil. Take our word for it and not remain in Boston a day longer than they can help it."

Whereas some Catholic priests wanted new immigrants to stay put in the city — with easier access to churches and like-minded parishioners — charitable organizations like Boston's Irish Emigrant Society encouraged a westward move toward open spaces and job prospects in the Heartland. But leaving Boston was hardly the safer bet. One Irish family traveling west through Pennsylvania, unprepared for a cold snap, tried to enter taverns along the route to warm themselves "but in every instance were refused admission." Two of their children froze to death. The *Pilot*'s headline: "Horrible!"

Donahoe's *Pilot,* although brash and biased, became a trusted voice among Irish immigrants and for many years published reports on weddings, obituaries, arrests, evictions, and other news from Ireland, attuned to the hardships back home. It also poked fun at Boston's elite and their discomfort with the incoming Irish, mocking "dear, delightful, bigoted New England," in the words of *Pilot* editor Thomas D'Arcy McGee.

Bossy and shrill, the *Pilot* repeatedly harped on the risky life in Boston's slums: "We really do not know any more miserable course for the emigrant to follow than that of settling down in the seaboard cities and expecting to be able to find employment and make a livelihood. It is a deplorable mistake. There is not employment here for half those who look for it, and the consequence is that Irish pauperism is beginning to look as dreadful here as in Ireland!"

But was any place really safe? America may have let Bridget and her people through the door — there were no federal laws to stop them — but the country made no promise that life would be easy. Weekly lists published by the city registrar, appearing beneath headlines such as "Deaths in Boston" or "Mortality of the Week" in the *Pilot,* showed a steady increase in deaths from the mid to late 1840s; some months set records of a thousand or more. As the *Pilot* pointed out, "The majority of those perishing on the seaboards are Irish." The mortality lists were indeed full of Mahoneys, Ryans, Killorans, Garveys, and Campbells.

The causes of death read like a tally of immigrant misery. Not just the sicknesses of the slums — cholera, consumption, scarlet fever, typhoid fever, dysentery — but drownings, gangrene, industrial accidents (Michael O'Neill caught in the gears at an iron foundry and "dreadfully mangled"), the occasional murder or suicide, including that of a despondent nineteen-year-old immigrant who cut her throat and was found in a shed by her father.

Meanwhile, as Bridget navigated her new city, she walked past the dirty, outstretched hands of child beggars, hundreds of whom roamed the streets — kids who seemed "literally born to die," according to one health official. The city's poorhouses were overrun, and on Deer Island, home of the quarantine hospital — with one ward dedicated to "women who have been broken down by a vicious course of life" — dozens were buried each week in paupers' graves. Plans were underway for a large new almshouse on the island, to accommodate the indigent Irish.

Boston police saw crimes soar in nearly every category, some types by more than 1,000 percent through the late 1840s, including aggravated assault, murder, attempted murder, prostitution, and the category that would come to define the Irish immigrant: public inebriation. Arrests for drunkenness rose in tandem with the growing number of liquor dealers and unlicensed home brewers.

So. For Bridget, what should have been a thrilling time of renewal and liberation was sullied by the suspicion that maybe she'd have been better off in Cloonagh, that life in America would be harsher than she'd imagined. Many immigrants read the *Pilot,* or had someone read it to them, and Bridget was likely familiar with its pages. We know she was able to read. The newspaper would have constantly reminded her that her journey was possibly incomplete. Preached its publisher, Donahoe, "Unless immigrants wish to starve, they must make their way from Boston and the other seaboard cities, into the interior."

And yet the Bridgets of Eire, these newly liberated and emboldened citizens of the globe, continued to rate crime-ridden, overcrowded, and unwelcoming Boston among their top destinations. Where plenty of haters and scammers were waiting for them.

Bridget's search for lodging and work began amid an oversaturated job market and increasing antagonism from native and longtime Bostonians, their patience with the influx of immigrants waning. Boston continued to absorb more Irish, including those who'd first traveled to Canada—or whose ships were turned away from Boston and sent to Halifax or St. John. These people were now finding their way south, skewing the city more Irish by the day.

Preying on greenhorns like Bridget were so-called "emigrant agents," hucksters offering help in finding an apartment, a train ticket out west, or a job to those willing to hand money to a stranger. To address the many cons aimed at gullible immigrants, the Irish Emigrant Society—one of several charitable organizations created to help outsiders avoid the pitfalls and hardships of life in America—developed its own bank, the Emigrant Savings Bank. This institution allowed Irish immigrants to deposit funds at one of its branches in Boston or New York, and family or friends back home in Ireland could make withdrawals.

But before Bridget could think of sending money back to her parents and siblings, which they were surely expecting, she needed a steady income.

Here again the *Pilot* weighed in, advising Bridget to seek employment somewhere other than a city of too few jobs and too much "human wretchedness, pauperism, and crime . . . in every respect like any old city of the old country." In stories like "A Few Words of Advice to Emigrants" the *Pilot* continued to beg immigrants to head inland, "where the prairies, towns, villages, mills, roads, canals, and farm-houses of Wisconsin, Iowa, Illinois, are waiting for the labor and industry of hundreds of thousands."

"We repeat—emphatically—that it would be wise for the people to stay and rot in Ireland as come to rot in Boston," insisted the *Pilot*. (Then again, the economic realities of journalism didn't prevent the *Pilot* from running ads for Liverpool-to-Boston crossings, often appearing in the same issue as its "stay in Ireland" pleas—sometimes on the same page.) For Bridget, and for all the incoming and struggling Irish, the mixed messages were alarming. In Ireland, if you were born poor, you were likely to die poor. Upward mobility was not a *thing*. In America, economic opportunity and advancement were the great hope and promise. But now the fine print was revealed: You can do well here, but not in this town. Try the next, or the next.

And where was Bridget amid the swindlers and beggars, the diseased and the dying? The same place all previous and future impoverished immigrants found themselves: in the scrum and near the bottom, in line for a job, at church for support, sharing a small room with too many others, skimming through newspapers for job listings, looking for her next meal, seeking a mate.

She may have found her way to one of the "intelligence offices," like the one run by Louisa May Alcott's mother, Abigail May, in the South End. Such agencies helped immigrants find jobs, food, and shelter; some were purely charitable, others more exploitative. A visitor to one intelligence office in 1850 found a crowd of women

seeking jobs as maids and remarked that they were "coarse, ignorant, unintelligent," but also full of "unshrinking self-assertion . . .
such rude, brawny womanhood!"

Despite the *Pilot*'s exhortations to abandon the crowded coast
and set out for greener pastures, Bridget already well knew what
rural life had to offer. By choosing to stay in Boston, preferring city
life to a return to the farm, she tied her future to Boston—a surly
teenager of a town, an immature metropolis, a city uncomfortably
in transition. A city that, in fact, didn't want her.

A hundred and fifty years before its starring role in the American
Revolution, Boston had been the swampy cradle of the Massachusetts Bay Colony, an outpost of English colonists seeking the freedom to practice their strict Protestant faith. Boston then became a
jumbled-together port village of fishermen, smugglers, preachers,
deck hands, and sailors, a pass-through for cotton, rum, tea—and
enslaved people. The post-revolutionary period and the early nineteenth century saw the mushrooming of textile mills and shoe factories, then banking and railroads, as Boston made a steady slog
toward big-city status. Islands and peninsulas, sluiced and divided
by inlets and brackish marshlands, were stitched together by roads
and bridges, railroads and ferries, and the low-lying mudflats were
filled in with the soil of lopped-off hilltops.

Boston had become home to America's keenest writers and
thinkers, who met to discuss poetry and politics at hallowed literary grounds such as the Boston Athenæum, frequented by notable
locals and visitors: Emerson, Thoreau, Alcott, Hawthorne, Longfellow, Margaret Fuller, and Samuel Howe. With fabled institutions
like the newly opened Boston Public Library and, across the river
in Cambridge, Harvard College, named for an immigrant minister,
Boston had gained a reputation as an intellectual nerve center, the
Athens of America. Charles Dickens had admired the city's "good

breeding" and observed in 1842 that Boston seemed "nearly per-fect."

Was it the "city set on the hill" that the Puritan leader John Winthrop first envisioned? Boston had reigned for a good long spell as "the hub of the solar system," as the author Oliver Wendell Holmes had called it. So much in its history seemed rebellious yet laudable, modern and exciting, home to suffragists, abolitionists, transcendentalists. Yet Boston was also profoundly traditional, in-sular, and old-fashioned, as set in its ways as the dear olde England that the settlers of Massachusetts Bay and Plymouth Colony had fled. Founded by devout, anti-Catholic Protestants, the city was still run by these inbred, Harvard-trained "Brahmins," as Holmes would dub them — a "harmless, inoffensive, untitled aristocracy." But as the lower-class O'Briens and Burkes, Barrons and Murphys, poured into the city, they began to find their Yankee neighbors were not so harmless or inoffensive.

Boston's persona had long been über-Protestant and anti-Cath-olic, but now the city was overrun by strangers like Bridget (plus streams of other immigrants, such as Germans, Italians, Poles, and Jews). It became a deeply conflicted and divided city.

As Bridget would learn, Boston hated the Irish, but the rich Brahmins wanted cheap help. Reluctantly, the city found that it needed these immigrants. And the Bridgets of Ireland were ready to oblige.

Determined to remain in Boston, Bridget Murphy found herself straddling two worlds: the slums where she lived and the shiny city where she aspired to work. She sought a job that seemed destined for her. The name Bridget was practically its calling card.

Part II

BRIDGET AND PATRICK

To become a refugee means that one's country has imploded, taking with it all the things that protect our humanity.
— VIET THANH NGUYEN

5

Bridget Goes to Work

TO HERALD THE start of spring, many Irish families celebrated Saint Brigid's Day, inspired by Ireland's female patron saint, Brigid of Kildare. Born into slavery in 451, Saint Brigid, named after the mythic goddess Brigit (the "exalted one," in old Irish), was said to have healed and fed Ireland's poor, performed miracles such as turning water into beer, causing a lustful man's eyes to explode in his head, and making the fetus of an unwed mother disappear, considered one of Ireland's first abortions. On Saint Brigid's Day, which falls on the ancient Celtic festival of Imbolc, children and musical troupes known as Biddy Boys went from door to door, collecting pennies for "poor Biddy." Families left food and drink on the front stoop for her; they wove four-armed "Brigid's crosses" from straw and hung them over doors to protect against evil spirits.

But once the namesakes of Brigid crossed the Atlantic, the heroic connotations of her name — Brigid the miracle worker, healer of the sick, patron saint of blacksmiths, dairymaids, fugitives, midwives, milkmaids, poets, the poor, and others — were replaced by an affiliation with servitude, submission, and humility. As Irish men laid rail lines, loaded cargo onto and off ships, built roads, dug sewers and canals, Irish women accepted the domestic versions of those physically demanding jobs. As maids, housecleaners, cooks, and laundresses, they scrubbed the floors, washed and mended the clothes, fed and otherwise tended Boston's blue bloods.

So common was the Irish maid named Bridget (as it was generally spelled at the time), the job and the name became interchangeable. Employers referred simply to *my Bridget* or *our Biddy.* They became a stereotype, ridiculed in literature and the press, depicted in cartoons and on stage as a bumbling, impudent, aproned caricature, an essential worker destined for a life of insult.

"As we can not dispense with her strong arms, we have to endure her ignorance, her uncouth manners, her varying caprices, and her rude tongue," *Harper's* magazine kvetched, decrying "Bridget's incompetency."

Bridget Murphy had spent her first twenty-plus years on a farm and was indeed unfamiliar with the expectations of a well-off city family and the domestic tasks required—cleaning wood floors and glass windows, taming the kitchens, minding the kids. Like many women who responded to ads for domestic help (at least the ads that didn't specifically exclude Irish applicants), Bridget would've learned on the job and under her employer's wary gaze.

Despite her lack of experience, Bridget was in other ways ideal for domestic work: young, physically fit, as yet untethered to man or child. Irish women in America often postponed marriage, content to stay single and earn an income well past the age at which women of other immigrant groups became wives and mothers. One post-Famine survey found that one in twenty-seven German immigrants in Boston was married; among the Irish it was one in fifty. Many women willingly delayed wedlock until thirty and priests discouraged early marriage, since it prevented women from earning money they could donate to the church or send to Ireland.

Most Irish maids lived with their employer, and living rent-free and eating cheaply helped them save money, even if their bed was in the basement or an attic or a windowless shoebox of a room shared with other domestic staff. "Nothing but a closet" was how one maid described her room. "In which there was neither light nor fresh air."

Whether Bridget worked as a live-in or day maid, her job plunged her into the middle class, offering a front-row view of daily life in a contemporary American household: sophisticated, stylish, and technologically modern, as if she'd been teleported decades into the future. She'd never seen such luxuries: chandeliers, fancy indoor washstands and basins, fine china and oriental rugs. Now she learned to clean and care for these remarkable objects.

Cooking at the smoky hearth of a peat fire turned out to be poor training for cooking on an American stove. Back home, meals had been bland and simple, dominated by spuds. But in Boston, Bridget tasted exotic fruits and vegetables: her first oranges and celery, strange lettuces, and the fanciest imports of the day, pineapples and bananas. Instead of growing, harvesting, canning, killing, and butchering, she simply bought provisions from grocers and shops.

But the work could be grueling and debasing. Most families employed a single "maid of all work," whose daily responsibilities included lighting the kitchen fire (which might burn wood or coal); fetching water from the nearest street pump (unless there was indoor plumbing, a rarity); emptying the previous night's chamber pots and slop jars; making the tea and breakfast; bringing fresh water, clean pitchers, and chamber pots to the bedrooms; making the beds; sweeping or scrubbing the floors; doing the laundry; polishing the silver; preparing dinner; clearing the table and cleaning the dishes. There might also be child-watching duties, window washing, or helping with dinner parties and afternoon teas.

The workday began by dawn—"Six o'clock is none too early,"

insisted one employer—and lasted twelve hours or more, often seven days a week. Some maids found they could get their chores done only by starting at five in the morning. Letters home reflected the grinding toil: "I am so tired and almost dead . . . Verry lonseom and down harted . . . Nothing but work all the time for us all . . . I feel very lonesome here."

Maids sustained burns and other injuries, and sometimes beatings. A maid in Connecticut, Bridget Kennedy, sued her employer for kicking her, beating her, and throwing a cat at her head, which the judge called "premeditated ugliness." He fined the employer six dollars.

While many maids were harassed by "malicious" and "contemptible" female employers, others were treated worse by the men, who might help themselves to the help. Sexual relations between biddies and their masters were not uncommon, nor were children sired by the man of the house. Attractive maids were known to be fired by a mistress for catching the husband's eye.

For her labors, Bridget would have earned two to four dollars a week. "It is not so very easey to get Muney heer," an immigrant maid (also named Bridget) wrote to her family in Ireland. "You have to work hard to make one pound."

Bridget Murphy and her fellow maids faced the insults and indignities that have confronted domestic servants across time. "We secretly acknowledged the disgusting nature of our job," a maid would write many decades later. "It was like the last job on earth . . . my unwitnessed existence, as I polished another's to make theirs appear perfect."

The Brothers Grimm depicted a similar life in their 1812 tale, *Cinderella:* "From morning until night she had to work hard . . . she had no bed to go to, but had to sleep by the hearth in the cinders. And as on that account she always looked dusty and dirty, they called her Cinderella." (In the Grimms' original German she was *Aschenputtel*, "ash girl" or "ash fool.")

By the time Bridget arrived, Boston had roughly 140,000 residents, nearly one in four of whom had been born in Ireland. And their numbers kept growing. Another 50,000 Irish immigrants would pour into Boston through the mid-1850s — most of them female, a hive of Irish womanhood.

By this time, one in three Boston families had live-in servants and others employed part-time help. Families might've preferred a nice English, Scottish, or Welsh lass, a reliably submissive Protestant, but the laws of supply and demand limited their options. Nearly three-quarters of the city's maids were Irish — upstart, untrained biddies like Bridget Murphy.

Though the job could be a demoralizing grind, it also provided access and insight. The ability to live among her superiors, invisibly at times, made Bridget a witness, an observer. As another maid later described the experience, "I'd see them, even if they weren't home, by the imprints left in their beds . . . I'd know them in a way few people did."

As Irish biddies became a more common presence on Boston's streets and in its homes, Bridget Murphy and her kind were increasingly maligned as ignorant, untamable, a nuisance. Bridget saw Boston's intolerance clearly stated in newsprint: "Wanted: a good, reliable woman to take the care of a boy 2 years old . . . good wages . . . no washing or ironing . . . positively no Irish need apply." Advertisements insisting that No Irish Need Apply were so common they earned their own acronym: NINA ads. Soon enough they were appearing in the papers of Boston, New York, New Orleans, and Chicago.

"Many families have positively refused to employ Irish servants at all, and especially those that are Roman Catholic," said the *Boston Daily Transcript,* in an 1852 series of stories called "Trouble in Families: Servants as They Are Nowadays." The *Pilot* railed against the "narrow-minded bigots" who discriminated against Irish domestic help in a country that considered itself Christian.

But Irish maids remained in high demand. Though they were poor and uneducated, they at least spoke English. And they were white. Boston was home to several antislavery organizations and abolitionist newspapers but in general wasn't ready to fully welcome free or formerly enslaved Black women into their homes. Fewer than two thousand Black people lived in pre–Civil War Boston, and while some Black women worked as domestic servants, they were far outnumbered by Irish Bridgets. Thus started the uneasy relationship between Boston's African American and Irish citizens, as they vied for low-wage jobs.

Irish biddies continued to be mocked for their unfamiliarity with certain kitchen utensils, their "ignorance and awkwardness," their thick accents and "Hibernian temper," their raw manners, and their religion. They were parodied in print as "Queen of the Kitchen" and "the funny, disorderly, hardworking but unpredictable servant girl." Yet they also displayed—laudably to each other, maddeningly to the Yankees—surprising reserves of assertiveness, "uppishness," and even arrogance. Some Bostonians didn't quite know what to make of them.

Mistresses and masters wanted their girls to be obedient, respectful, and invisible. Instead, they could be boisterous and curious, quick to joke and laugh, full of dark humor and cynical wit, unbowed by their lowly circumstances, saucy and stubborn. They'd demand days off (mainly for church or holy days). They'd refuse to do unpleasant jobs, at least not without more pay. If they became fed up with an abusive mistress, they'd quit midday and walk off.

Some prospective employers were miffed that young Irish women had the nerve to inquire about wages or living arrangements and, if unsatisfied with the answers, might turn down a job offer. Others grudgingly admired their virtues: "the affectionate nature of Bridget, her generosity in sending some money home to Irish relatives, her strong arms and self-esteem."

In a scathing and hilariously priggish piece in *Harper's* magazine, the writer Robert Tomes sputtered about the Irish Bridgets who were "both the necessity and plague of our homes."

> Born and bred in a mud-hovel, in the companionship of boorish peasants like herself . . . and the family pig. She can know nothing of the simplest elements of civilized life. Her knowledge of cookery is confined to the mixing of buttermilk and potatoes for the daily meal . . . The very utensils of the kitchen, beyond a soot-covered iron pot, are mysteries to her. In regard to washing and ironing, these are refinements we should no more expect her to have learned at home than to play on a piano or to dance the polka.

Bridget Murphy and other maids knew what their employers said about them. They gossiped about their mistresses after work, at the markets, and at church. And they'd often own up to their uppishness with pride. "I didn't want to do anything anybody told me," admitted one maid, whose employer had called her "an independent Irish hussy."

In an ambitious act of literary self-defense, a woman named Bridget penned a remarkable series of letters to the *Pilot,* describing life as an Irish maid in Boston. (She provided no last name, though it's tempting to imagine it was Murphy.) "I am a poor girl, and I work hard for my living in an American family," she wrote in the first of a half dozen letters—nearly ten thousand words in all, on some days filling half a newspaper page, expounding on both the dignity of labor and the "splendid misery" in some Boston homes.

"We could fill whole books with true accounts of what poor girls have to endure in these wicked times," she wrote. "They are so prejudiced against Irish Catholic girls and on that account charge 'em with faults they aint guilty of."

Addressing complaints about maids buying nice clothes, Bridget wrote: "We Irish girls have been called dirty, filthy, sluttish, and all sorts of hard names . . . Some of these mistresses of ours can't bear to see us dressing as people dress in this country, because they want to keep us down, like a distinct clan of people."

Bridget described watching her employer read these letters in the paper—fuming that "servants had no business to write letters" —unaware that the author was standing right beside her. "She said, in her smart way, that servants was overleaping all barriers, and unless some check was devised, society would fall to pieces. These rich women that have risen from poverty, and are always looking round for fear that we'll tread on the skirts of their dignity, make awful bad mistresses . . . They want to keep us ignorant, and then twit us with our ignorance, just as the English do with us at home."

Employers' scorn exposed a darker sentiment lurking in the hearts of Brahmin Boston, one that would soon boil over into full anti-Irish rage. Wrote Tomes, in *Harper's,* "If we do not do something toward civilizing Bridget and Patrick we may continue to live in fear of having our houses pulled down over our heads, or our throats cut every time the foreign element of our large cities is stirred to fermentation by some malicious demagogue."

Old-school Bostonians weren't prepared for the poor groveling victims of English oppression to react to the discrimination and scorn they now faced with a spirited resistance. While their male counterparts lost status in America, Bridgets and their sister maids began to gain agency of a kind that Irish society had withheld.

Their poise, wit, and sass made proper Boston squirm. 1
dies of Boston were becoming a force—Cinderellas "over\
all barriers."

For Bridget Murphy, the job would serve as a bridge to the future, not her life's vocation. She did not intend to spend her life in
service. She hadn't risked everything to become an "old maid."

Maids were sometimes given Thursday nights off (for dances)
and Sunday afternoons (for church). At these rare social occasions
Bridget would have worn her nicest clothes, nicer than anything
she'd owned in Ireland, and kept her eye out for a promising Irish
Catholic man—marrying a Protestant man was unthinkable at the
time. Thanks to her family (specifically her cousin, Patrick Barron)
she'd meet another Famine survivor from her home county.

A man with a job of his own. A man to start a life with.

His name was Patrick Kennedy.

6

Bridget Gets Married

PATRICK KENNEDY WAS a handsome twenty-five-year-old Wexford lad, born and raised on a rented farm outside the hilly village of Dunganstown. His parents, Mary Johanna and Patrick, raised four children there: sister Mary, brothers John and James, and Patrick, the youngest.

The modest two-acre farm abutted sixteen acres tended by Patrick's grandfather, conjoined properties that had been cared for by generations of Kennedys. By the time of the Famine it had grown to forty acres and sustained a growing brood: Patrick's brothers were both married with kids, and sister Mary would soon marry. They all lived and worked shoulder to shoulder. The main home was a long, low rectangle beneath a thatched roof, enclosed by thick white walls of stone, brick, and mud that were lime-washed once a year, a squat and sturdy structure not built for comfort but built to last. Its heavy front door stayed shut tight in winter but swayed open in summer.

As in many Irish homes, a peat fire smoldered day and night, season after season — in some homes it burned unextinguished for decades — and around that hearth the men sat on low benches, smoking their clay pipes as the women swung an iron pot on a hinge, into and out of the fire, cooking potatoes and stews and stirabout. The low-burning peat sent ribbons of earthy smoke up through a small chimney.

The Kennedy homestead sat amid a geometric landscape of farms, just east of the River Barrow, a patchwork of green bordered by stacked-stone walls, fences, and hedgerows. Nearby rose Slieve Coillte, wind-raked and gorse-covered, the hill where Irish rebels had camped after a bloody insurrection against British forces in 1798. (Patrick's ancestors fought at the ill-fated Battle of New Ross, where hundreds of rebels were tortured, hanged, burned, decapitated.) The highest point for miles around, Slieve Coillte offered views out to the widening river, down into Waterford Bay and on past centuries-old Hook Head lighthouse to the shimmery Atlantic.

Life in Dunganstown was humble, routine, familiar. Roughly two hundred souls lived in and around the village. The Kennedys attended Sunday mass at St. Brigid's Church a mile away and met with neighbors at livestock markets, fairs, and sometimes at a five-way crossroads known as The Hand. Like many Irish boys, Patrick likely played football (soccer) and the ancient, only-in-Ireland game of hurling, although most sports went quiet during the Famine. His schooling was basic, either occasional lessons with a priest at one of the illegal "hedge schools" — named for the secretive classes held in a cabin or cowshed, or tucked behind a hedge — or at one of the new national schools that started operating in the 1830s.

His days were spent mostly in service to animals and crops, keeping the peat fire stoked, pumping water from the well, feeding the livestock. Patrick sometimes traveled by foot or horse-drawn cart along the five crooked miles north to New Ross, a busy port town of sailors, fishmongers, and fishermen who pulled salmon and bream from the River Barrow. New Ross also moored the ships that carried away the Famine's escapees, and Patrick would have waved farewell as neighbors began the journey toward Liverpool and other foreign ports.

To cover the rent, the Kennedys grew wheat, barley, and other crops, and raised pigs and hens, which Patrick and his brothers sold at New Ross's markets or sometimes directly to their landlord. As one historian put it: "the money scarcely warm in Irish palms before it was returned to England."

It was that intractable relationship between Irish land and English landlords, between lessee and lessor, that would prompt Patrick's own departure from the only home he'd known.

Centuries before England conquered Ireland, the Kennedy family farm had belonged to the O'Cinneide clan, descendants of Irish royalty and King Brian Boru. The family name was eventually anglicized to O'Kennedy and then just Kennedy. Their ancestral land was now rented from a family called Glascott, Brits who owned hundreds of acres in County Wexford and leased hundreds more from another English landowning family, the Tottenhams, whose vast estate contained thousands of small farms across Wexford and surrounding counties. Charles Tottenham was a former member of the British Parliament, who during the Famine years served as high sheriff for County Wexford; William Glascott served as justice of the peace. As local law enforcement, Tottenham and Glascott could have easily evicted those who failed to pay rent, but they were known to be relatively sympathetic landlords.

While Patrick and his family could hardly avoid the effects of the Famine — they lost potato crops, subsisted on cabbage and beets, were kept from taking soup-kitchen relief by refusing to give up their land — they at least avoided eviction, which allowed them to maintain a stable if strained lifestyle.

As the youngest, Patrick knew his father's leased land would pass into the hands of an older brother, which meant he'd either work for his father and brothers as paid labor, leave home to find a wage-paying job, or find a small plot of his own to rent as a cottier farmer. (Except for a brief period of eviction, James and John would manage the Kennedy farm after their father's death and until their own.) From an early age, then, Patrick would have planned for— perhaps even dreamed of—a life beyond the borders of the farm. His first step in that direction was a job in town, one that might finance his hoped-for departure to America.

New Ross, with fifteen thousand residents, was home to a number of breweries and distilleries, including the century-old Crey-well's, which had been converted into the Cherry Brothers Brewery before the Famine. (A century later it would become a Guinness brewery.) The six-acre riverside complex included malthouses, corn and barley storage, a blacksmith shop, stables, and Mrs. Cherry's cottage. Also onsite was a cooperage where brothers Richard and William crafted their own barrels and where young Patrick be-gan working as a trainee cooper—a coveted position that promised him an advantage over his peers and his farmer brothers. (As long as he didn't get killed, that is. Years later the brewer Patrick Byrne fell into a vat of beer and drowned.)

Just upstream from the hustle of New Ross's quays, its tanneries, timber yards, and pubs, Patrick learned the ancient art of metic-ulously cleaving and carving wooden staves, warping and cinch-ing them tight with iron hoops to form casks and tubs for beer and whiskey, porters and ales. On the flanks of each one he fire-branded the name CHERRY BROS. The beverages were sold through-out Wexford and Waterford counties, advertised with the slogans "Cherry's Ale for the Cheery Gael" and "Cheers for Cherrys." Al-though a growing abstinence movement, led by the Irish Catho-lic priest Theobald Mathew, who preached against the "evil effects of drunkenness," had put a dent in southern Ireland's beer- and whiskey-making businesses, Cherry Brothers survived while other breweries and distilleries fell.

When the Famine struck, Patrick kept his head low, continued to learn his trade, saved his money, and refined his plans to emigrate. He would be the only one of his siblings to leave Ireland.

By the time he was ready to depart (mid-1848), hundreds in County Wexford had died of starvation and disease, thousands relied on public assistance, and the poorhouse in New Ross was overrun with women and children. The town leaders considered closing the bridge to adjacent County Kilkenny, to prevent the sick and starving from crossing into Wexford.

It was time to go. The rituals of departure were well established. Patrick would have stopped at St. Brigid's Church for a prayer and a blessing from the priest. He might've had one final sip from St. Brigid's Well; locals believed it had been blessed by the saint herself. He'd have bid goodbye to his coworkers at the brewery, then a tearful farewell to his family before leaving Ireland forever, his head a jumble of hope and fear.

It is believed that Patrick sailed first to Liverpool, possibly leaving right from the New Ross quays. According to family lore and historians' best guesses, Patrick chose as his vessel of escape the *Washington Irving,* an American packet ship owned by Enoch Train and Company.

As with Bridget Murphy's escape, the details of Patrick's crossing are obscured by his name, the most common in Ireland, along with other Saint Patrick–inspired variants: Pádraig, Padraic, Paddy, and the like. There's no definitive proof he was *the* Patrick Kennedy listed aboard the *Washington Irving,* and he might have sailed on another ship altogether. Many Pats, Patricks, Pat'ks, and P. Kennedys (as they were listed in ship manifests) sailed from Ireland or Liverpool to Boston in the late 1840s, and some sailed from New Ross to New Brunswick or Halifax, then made their way to the

United States. (Based on Patrick's application for naturalization in early 1853, he may have been a US resident by early 1848. His son would later say that his father could have emigrated as early as 1847.)

However he traveled, Patrick's coffin ship would have carried him along the southern Irish coast, along the path of so many countrymen before and since. If it was a clear day, he'd have looked north to find the swell of Slieve Coillte, one last look at the hilltop he'd climbed many times, soaked with the blood of his people. Though the *Wexford Independent* bemoaned the steady exodus of men like Patrick, the disdainful *Times* of London enjoyed seeing Ireland drained of more people, "gone with a vengeance . . . flying from the very midst of calamity into insufficient vessels . . . spreading death wherever they roam."

If the *Washington Irving* was Patrick's ship, he would have been delivered to America in a month, a trip faster and less deadly than most. One of the ship's 1848 crossings, which may have carried Patrick, saw only a single fatality, a forty-year-old woman buried at sea (days after another forty-year-old woman gave birth). Lists of passengers' occupations added another chapter to the story of the emptying of Ireland's working class; the steerage deck was jammed with blacksmiths, butchers, rope makers, weavers, tanners, shoemakers, dressmakers, wheelwrights, butlers—and a Patrick Kennedy listed as a "labourer."

His real occupation, as a cooper, would give him a slight advantage over the hordes of countrymen pouring into Boston, all big dreams but limited skills. And the barrel-making apprenticeship would yield other advantages. Once ashore, Patrick Kennedy sought out a former coworker from Cherry Brothers Brewery, an émigré from County Wexford named Patrick Barron, who would play a key role in helping Kennedy find a job—and a wife.

• • •

Had they known each other back home, meeting at a church picnic or a crossroads fair or the New Ross market? Had they been introduced by family, promised to each other? Were they lovers who secretly planned their escape together? Did they meet during a layover in Liverpool or, as a great-granddaughter would later suggest, aboard their coffin ship, maybe the *Washington Irving*, seeking each other out during the passage and meeting on deck to make plans for a future together? Theories have been floated over the years, the same questions asked but left unanswered, so it's unknown whether Patrick Kennedy was the love of Bridget Murphy's life, a familiar face from back home, a family friend, or just a reliable breadwinner who promised to be good to her. Most likely they made separate treacherous journeys and met in the churning pit of Boston.

They were nobodies who found each other. Just two refugees competing to make it in America alongside immigrants from around the globe. Whether they courted and married for love or convenience or through a family arrangement, no matter: they'd start a small life together, just blocks from the wharves where they'd arrived, never to return to Ireland. They also would never see more than a few square miles of their new country.

They married on a Wednesday afternoon, September 26, 1849, at the Cathedral of the Holy Cross, on Franklin Street in Boston's South End, near Bridget's aunt, uncle, and cousins. Designed by the famed Boston architect Charles Bulfinch and opened in 1803, Holy Cross had been the city's first Roman Catholic church and soon gained "cathedral status," led by Boston's first Catholic bishop, Jean-Louis Lefebvre de Cheverus. The simple brick church was named for the piece of wood, displayed in a glass case, that purportedly came from the cross on which Jesus was crucified. (The wood stayed on view until 2010, when it was stolen by a visitor.)

Beneath the bell tower and before the high wooden altar, the couple was joined by the blessings of the priest John J. Williams, a quiet son of Irish immigrants ordained four years earlier — "a tall, spare, tight-lipped young man . . . cautious, methodical, and dependable" — who would become Boston's first archbishop. On hand to witness the occasion were a few friends and family, all from back home, including the bridesmaid and best man, Ann McGowan and Patrick Barron, who had seemingly played the role of matchmaker. (Patrick Kennedy's mother and Bridget Murphy's mother, both named Mary, were each related to an arm of the Barron clan, possibly making Patrick and Bridget distant relatives.)

Bridget had been living with the Barrons in South Boston while Patrick had resided in a dollar-a-week room at a small boarding-house, with forty housemates sharing a single loo and a sink. After the wedding, the couple traveled north through the slums of the North End and over to Lewis Wharf, then took a ferry to the island of East Boston. There they moved into a crowded tenement on Liverpool Street — the first of many moves to come within a community overflowing with other hopeful Irish newcomers.

Two decades earlier, fewer than a dozen people lived on what was then called Noddle's Island, pastoral land that for centuries had been used for farming and grazing — and fighting. The island had hosted an early skirmish of the Revolutionary War, the Battle of Chelsea Creek, in which American rebels captured a British schooner, stole its artillery, and then torched the vessel, killing a few marines. A group of businessmen bought the island in the early 1830s and began developing the southern waterfront, naming streets after themselves (Sumner, White), after European cities (Liverpool, Paris, London), and after Revolutionary War battles (Princeton, Lexington, Saratoga). By 1836, Noddle's Island had been connected to other small islands as marshes and channels were backfilled with soil, creating the larger island of East Boston, which was annexed by the city of Boston. A lumber company came to town, then a sugar refinery, then the five-story Maverick House hotel. Frederick Law Olmsted designed a waterfront park (later buried beneath a runway at Logan Airport). The shipbuilder Samuel Hall founded the East Boston Ferry Company to transport folks across the harbor to Boston's North End.

The island's growth, and its coming role as a prominent ship-building and maritime hub, was due partly to the entrepreneurial zeal of an orphaned, widowed, and generally unfortunate man named Enoch Train. By the time twenty-five-year-old Train started his shipping company in the 1830s, he'd lost both parents and two siblings; he later lost his wife and two kids. Train launched Enoch Train and Company and the White Diamond Line, both offering passenger service between Liverpool and Boston. He invited the renowned shipbuilder Donald McKay to move his shipyard to East Boston, well timed for the coming mass exodus of Irish immigrants escaping the Famine. One of Train's first transatlantic ships was the *St. Petersburg* (which may have brought Bridget to America), and in 1845 McKay launched the *Washington Irving* (Patrick's purported transport).

Canadian carpenters and ship workers poured into town, and by 1849 East Boston's pre-Famine population had more than doubled to twelve thousand, on its way to doubling again over the next decade. The seaport attracted a colorful cast: sailmakers, fishermen, ferry operators, oystermen, stevedores, and saloonkeepers. Those with special skills, such as barrel makers, earned as much as two dollars a day, more than twice the day rate for common laborers.

Somewhat perversely, the Famine had fueled East Boston's growth, and Bridget and Patrick's new place of residence held out both peril and promise. Its tenements were shabby and crowded, but they ranged alongside the shipbuilding yards and bustling wharves that provided jobs like the one Patrick now walked to six days a week. Bridget would leave each morning to tend to her employer's home — likely riding the East Boston ferry to the city — while her husband devoted himself to a craft whose products held, among other commodities, the liquor that would one day contribute to his family's income.

Boston was becoming a city of whiskey making and whiskey drinkers, with at least fifteen hundred licensed taverns and "groggery" shops, mostly Irish owned and operated; many more unlicensed purveyors sold their potions out of grocery stores, restaurants, or their homes. Bridget may have considered herself fortunate to be married to a well-trained cooper whose skills were in demand. Patrick had the expertise to produce something useful, a product that a developing (and thirsty) city needed; it promised to keep him employed at a time when most Irish immigrant men wielded shovels and pickaxes, producing holes in the ground. Of Boston's nearly nine thousand unskilled laborers in 1850, eight in ten were Irish. There were only three hundred coopers, and less than a third of those were Irish.

Of the half dozen cooperage factories operating in East Boston, Patrick chose the boutique-sized Daniel Francis Cooperage and Brass Foundry, on Sumner Street. There he worked alongside other craftsmen, cutting, shaving, heating, and flexing planks — pine or cedar for the "dry" or "slack" barrels, aged oak for the "wet" — into staves that they then fabricated into bulged casks and bilge barrels, from the fifty-two-gallon tun to the half-sized pipe or butt barrel, to the quarter-sized hogshead, along with dye tubs, fermenting tubs, and water pails.

Coopering had a language of its own, employing specialized

tools with mysterious names: adzes, augers and borers, the chiv and the croze, crumming knives, roundshaves, and sun planes. Coopers would chime the cask, rivet the hoops, bore the bunghole. On request, Patrick and his crew would char the insides of oak barrels for aging whiskey and other spirits. Since Boston's earliest days, such barrels had been vital to the city's prosperity. Even John Winthrop had noted the need for good barrels, stating that "we have lost much by bad casks." During the peak shipbuilding years of the 1840s and '50s, East Boston's artisan coopers played a small but crucial role by supplying ships with tight, leakproof containers for brined meats, salted cod, whale oil, pickles, gunpowder, flour, and (important for both trade and a ship's crew) beer, ale, whiskey, and rum.

Patrick probably made just under two dollars a day, six days a week. By 1852, the Kennedys' annual income had reached $300 —still poverty level (about $10,000, in 2020 dollars), but at least better than what street sweepers, horse tenders, and stable boys took home. The job was also far safer than digging tunnels, hauling lumber and crates, or rolling the kegs made by Patrick and his coworkers onto and off the ships; these workers were "driven like horses, a slave for the Americans," as one Irish cellar digger wrote. One rail worker, who arose at four in the morning and worked until eight at night, was "often so tired that I wish God in his mercy would take me to himself . . . I have lost all ambition."

Many of Patrick's countrymen, ex-farmers not fully prepared for the risks of construction sites and factories, succumbed to horrific on-the-job injuries—men lost limbs on the railroad, fell off docks and drowned, got buried in a collapsed tunnel, got caught in machinery. Others worked or drank themselves to death, leaving behind a virtual epidemic of Irish widows. Always battling exhaustion and depression, some landed in the Massachusetts lunatic asylums. A city health inspector estimated that illness and injury shaved years off the average life span of an Irish immigrant male, that only the luckiest would survive much past their first decade in America.

In addition to workplace perils, tenement dwellers like the Kennedys lived under constant threat of disease, which could tear through a neighborhood like a tornado.

After years of lagging behind its big brother to the south, East Boston thrived, thanks to the machinery of immigration. The influx was transforming the island from backwater to port city.

In addition to its waterfront businesses — McKay's shipyard, the Cunard docks, the massive warehouses on Lewis Street, the Eastern Railroad depot, the ferries that ran every few minutes, shuttling thousands back and forth across the harbor — a newer East Boston was rising around Maverick Square, where churches, meeting halls, social clubs, saloons, and the new East Boston Savings Bank all clustered around the crown jewel, the luxurious Maverick House hotel.

In the hotel's shadow was the *other* East Boston. Bridget and Patrick had settled a few blocks away, on the west side of the island, amid a growing spread of two- and three-story tenement houses filled with working-class immigrants packed so tightly together, sometimes two or three families to an apartment, that health officials worried constantly about outbreaks of disease.

The Kennedys paid around six dollars a month for their Liverpool Street apartment. Those who couldn't afford an apartment paid one dollar a week to cram into a shared room, a warehouse chopped into cubbies, a dark and airless attic, or a cellar. Boston health officers had never seen anything like it and marveled that "the lamp of life" could burn in such circumstances, with families and strangers of all ages sleeping side by side by side, sometimes by the dozens, often with a single indoor privy or lone outhouse serving them all. Despite a few vague calls for tighter requirements for landlords and improved legal recourse for immigrants, health officials mostly moralized. "As might be expected," claimed the authors of one 1849 health report, "intemperance, lewdness, riot, and all the evil spirits . . . enter in and dwell there." Such living conditions were a tinderbox for illness. Smallpox, thought to have been eradicated from Boston, swept through its slums, as did an aggressive revival of consumption, plus a citywide cholera outbreak in 1849, which had prowled north from Philadelphia and New York.

In the early 1850s, the "Asiatic cholera" outbreak, as some scornfully nicknamed it (blaming the countries where it originated, China and India), exploded into a global pandemic, claiming victims across Asia, Europe, Africa, and Russia. It killed survivors of the Famine in Ireland, fourteen thousand in London, and many thousands in ports like Liverpool, where travelers passing through carried the disease with them to America.

In Boston, cholera gouged a deep scar through working-class neighborhoods during the hot summer months of 1849, before and after the Kennedys' wedding, especially in the North End, the South End, and parts of East Boston. Of its victims, numbering more than seven hundred, more than two-thirds were Irish immigrants living in tenements with contaminated water, poor drainage, and bad ventilation — plus jerry-built privies that were "constantly overflowing . . . a mass of pollution."

The deaths occurred "chiefly among the foreigners," said one appalled Boston doctor, calling the mostly Irish victims "intemperate subjects." On some city streets — including an especially crowded stretch along Liverpool Street — the death rate was one in seventeen. Circumstances like these prompted repeated exhortations in the *Pilot* — "It's not safe here! Go west!" — aimed at the semi-employable peasant ex-farmers now working as ditch diggers.

As a stably employed barrel maker, Patrick felt he could largely ignore the *Pilot*'s warnings, and he and his bride could stay put in their scrappy corner of Boston's immigrant-flooded island suburb. There on Liverpool Street — amid "hives of human beings" living in "abodes of fever," most of them "polluted with all manner of bad odors" — they would welcome their first child.

7

Bridget the Mother

SHE WORKED AS long as she could, her maid's uniform getting snug, until it was time to quit, stay home, and wait for the birth of her first child. Having a baby within ten months of her wedding day was typical for an Irish newlywed, but for Bridget the event came later: two years into her marriage, three into her American adventure. Her daughter arrived in midsummer 1851.

Opting not to burden her firstborn with a name that might brand her a biddy, she and Patrick called her Mary, after both their mothers. She was baptized the next day, a steamy Sunday in August, at St. Nicholas Church, East Boston's first (and, for years, only) Roman Catholic church, a few blocks from the Kennedys' home. Per Irish tradition, Bridget and Patrick likely hosted a christening party that afternoon, with the priest and Mary's godparents: Patrick Barron's sister, Johanna, and another East Boston barrel maker, Nicholas Aspell, a cousin of Patrick Barron.

Fifteen months later, the Kennedys welcomed another daughter, Joanna, and thirteen months after that, a son they called John, to be followed eighteen months later by another daughter, Margaret. Various family members stepped in as godparents, Barrons and Aspells, Doyles and Maloys, participants in the hundreds of christenings happening each year at East Boston's bustling St. Nicholas Church.

Bridget's youngest sister, also named Margaret, had left Ireland and was now living with the Kennedys, helping with the kids and serving as John's godmother. With her sister and cousins around to assist with child care, Bridget probably continued to work as a maid between pregnancies. Then again, the span between each child, while not quite the every-ten-months cadence of some prolific Irish families, was relatively brief.

Four children born in a four-year stretch (1851–55); only three would survive.

During those years of bringing American-born Kennedys into the world, Bridget and Patrick moved at least five times, from their first apartment on Liverpool Street, north to Meridian, east to Bremen, west to Eutaw, then to an alley at Marion and Monmouth, and eventually back to Liverpool—all within a half-mile square, all within walking distance of their church and Patrick's job at the waterfront.

The frequent moves, lugging the infants and their meager possessions from apartment to apartment, was the typical immigrant shuffle. Like their Irish neighbors, the Kennedys sought a slightly better home (and a more humane landlord) with each disruptive relocation, though a few things remained constant: not enough heat, too few windows, bad smells, rats and filth.

Though East Boston offered a bit more breathing room than the denser Irish slums of Boston's North End, it wasn't an especially welcoming haven for poor working families. Here, the Yankee landlord ruled, replacing the English landlord as gentry and lessor, the sometimes-ruthless rent collector. Boston landlords typically owned an entire building or a full block of adjacent row houses.

A city housing report said many were known to enforce "prompt payment under the threat, always rigidly executed, of immediate ejection."

The Kennedys' assorted homes varied little: a two- or three-story row house that was damp and cold in the winter and stifling in summer. Two to four families occupied each floor, with rickety stairs out back, leaky roofs, and a rear alley that sometimes turned into a stream of sewage. Tenement houses often shared a single sink, which drained into the alley, and one indoor privy or backyard outhouse served all occupants, who might number as many as a hundred. Some homes had neither sink nor indoor water nor privy, so residents got water from a pump or hydrant in the yard. During heavy rains, basement apartments, often housing two to three dozen immigrants, flooded with effluent.

Revealing a lack of sympathy toward families who had few options, health inspectors mostly blamed the Irish for these circumstances, brought on by "ignorance, carelessness, and generally loose and dirty habits which prevail among the occupants."

Tragic stories highlighted the struggles of young families still transitioning from farmhouse to tenement and settling imperfectly, sometimes carelessly, into unfamiliar urban homes. Just weeks before Bridget's second daughter, Joanna, was born, her neighbors, an Irish immigrant couple, had left their infant child asleep on the floor of their Maverick Street apartment to go out for a drink. They apparently left a candle or fire burning and, according to the police report, came back two hours later "in a state of intoxication, and found their child burnt to death."

All-too-common news items about Irish mishaps and deaths contributed to grand old Boston's growing frustration with the poverty, crime, and decay they felt immigrants had imported into the "once orderly and peaceful city of the Pilgrims," in the words of Ephraim Peabody, a Unitarian clergyman. Peabody likened the Irish influence over his venerable city to a "social revolution," even though poor newcomers like the Kennedys were more interested in jobs and safe housing than revolution.

The words of Peabody and others would grow louder and meaner into the 1850s, and Boston would become an increasingly inhospitable place for Irish families. Years before the Kennedys' arrival, two infamous anti-Catholic events had set the tone.

In 1834, rumors had spread that nuns and students at a convent outside Boston were being held against their will—possibly even sexually assaulted. (This story was debunked, but it presaged the scandals that would later haunt the Catholic Church, and its victims.) Dozens of men, riled by the rhetoric of bigoted preachers, marched on the convent and torched it.

Three years later, a clash in the North End between an Irish funeral procession and a volunteer fire crew exploded into a massive and deadly brawl. Responding to calls to "get the Irish," firemen and local working-class Yankees poured onto Broad Street, pummeling the outnumbered Irish with sticks, bricks, and knives, vandalizing and looting their homes. (The Broad Street Riot led to the creation of Boston's paid fire department and, the following year, its police department, the first such paid professional force in the United States.)

A decade later, just before Bridget and Patrick arrived, Boston entered a brief period of sympathy for the Irish and their plight. At the height of the Famine, wealthy Protestants held clothing drives and fundraisers and sent cash to the starving Irish. The Boston sea captain Robert Bennet Forbes sailed the USS *Jamestown* to Cork to deliver food and supplies in 1847, a deed that is considered America's first international humanitarian relief effort.

Although Boston and other cities had been willing to send food and money to a battered far-off land, they didn't actually want the Famine's victims as *neighbors*. Some Bostonians and their religious leaders had come to view the Irish as more than a nuisance: they were a threat.

The Protestant preacher Lyman Beecher, a fiery orator and prudish, twice-widowed father of thirteen (including the writer Harriet Beecher Stowe), had for years been warning his flock about the "tremendous tide" of "ignorant" and "corrupting" immigrants. Progressive in some ways (he was an abolitionist who promoted educational opportunities for women), Beecher filled his sermons with anti-immigrant dog whistles about "European paupers" who were a "danger to our liberties" and a threat to America's moral character.

"It is notorious that the Catholic immigrants to this country are generally of the class least enlightened," Beecher wrote in *A Plea for the West,* which called on the United States to "check the influx of immigrant paupers thrown upon our shores by the governments of Europe, corrupting our morals, quadrupling our taxation, and endangering the peace of our cities."

John Winthrop, the English immigrant cofounder of New England, had preached in 1630 that the settlers of the Massachusetts Bay Colony should act collectively "as a city upon a hill. The eyes of all people are upon us." (Ronald Reagan would regularly repurpose Winthrop's biblical reference, claiming that America's doors "were open to anyone with the will and the heart to get here.") But the city on a hill, while still a beacon of hope, was also becoming a city of hate.

Riled by Beecher's sermons and writings — with their menacing references to the "sword" of justice and to immigrants "filling our prisons and crowding our poorhouses" — the descendants of the original European refugees now wanted to shut America's doors, to wall off their stolen land. But on they came, more new-comers and their babies, pushing East Boston's population past the fifteen-thousand mark and tilting the island more "foreign" and Catholic by the day.

There was little in the way of legal constraint to stop the flow of unwanted Bridgets and Patricks — just a few state laws but no federal restrictions on immigration. Port officials had some discretion to detain those who were obvious paupers, carriers of disease, "lunatics," or "idiots." The rest? No documents required, and no quotas limiting their numbers.

Despite the regular moves to cheaper, safer, or larger apartments, Bridget and Patrick also experienced a sense of stability. Family, the Irish immigrant community, and the Catholic Church kept them and their young children anchored and socially connected.

By the mid-1850s, members of the growing Barron clan had moved up to East Boston to start their own families. The Kennedys remained especially close to Patrick Barron, who had married in 1851 and lived with his wife (also named Bridget) just a few blocks from the Kennedys. They'd raise eight kids in East Boston and the two Patricks would work together, along with cousins also employed as coopers.

Just a few years earlier, they'd all resided in the mud of an ancient and injured land. *All the news is famine and famine,* an Irish poet would later write.

But here in East Boston, they'd begun to create a new normal in their community of migrants. At St. Nicholas they'd see friends and coworkers, celebrate weddings, birthdays, and holy days. A group of parishioners started raising funds for a new church and there was even talk of developing a Catholic school for girls. On Sunday afternoons the men competed in boating and swimming races in the harbor, and families gathered for picnics at Maverick Square or Central Square.

Two oyster saloons had opened, one near the Lewis Street wharf and one a block from Maverick Square, where the Patricks (Kennedy and Barron) might stop for a drink after a day at the cooperage. There were now dry goods shops, fish shops, a bakery and a butcher, dress shops, apothecaries, millineries, shoe stores, and the grocery-groggery shops that sold whiskey as well as food and staples; all were gathering spots where the Bridgets (Kennedy and Barron) might shop and gossip with neighbors.

For the Kennedys and their kids, the epicenter of their expat lives was St. Nicholas Church, host to nuptials and baptisms and nurturing sermons, a place to sustain them during difficult times. This center of Catholic faith, oddly enough, had Protestant origins. Built in 1837 as the First Congregational Church, later known as the Maverick Church, it had been the first house of worship in all of East Boston.

Then the influx of Famine Irish caused Boston's Catholic population to soar. The *Boston Pilot* complained that "we are sadly off for want of churches. There is not half enough room for the people, who never attend church for the simple reason that they can never procure seats." Father John Bernard Fitzpatrick worked to build or expand churches that were "crowded to suffocation." When he learned the Maverick Church was for sale, he bought it from the Congregationalists for $5,000 in 1844 and renamed it St. Nicholas, in honor of the Turkish-born fourth-century Christian bishop who became a patron saint of sailors, fishermen, merchants, prostitutes, children, and brewers (among others), and whose generosity and gift-giving evolved into the story of Santa Claus. (Fitzpatrick became Boston's bishop in 1846, replacing Benedict J. Fenwick, who'd cofounded the *Pilot*.)

East Boston had other churches and meeting halls — Universalist, Episcopal, Baptist, Methodist, and Unitarian, along with Boston's first Jewish cemetery (Ohabei Shalom). But it was becoming largely an island of Irish Catholics. Across Boston, Bishop Fitzpatrick's flourishing flock would swell to fifty thousand parishioners. By the time John Kennedy was baptized there in 1854, services at St. Nicholas were standing room only. All four Kennedy kids would be baptized there, three by William Wiley, the sickly pastor who led them in prayer each Sunday. Assigned to St. Nicholas in 1851, Wiley got to know young couples like Bridget and Patrick and became part of their extended family. Less severe than most priests back in Ireland, Wiley was someone the Kennedys and others "loved and venerated, a teacher to whom you listened with eager delight, a counselor to whom you could freely open your in-most souls, a friend who would never betray you." In addition to conducting their baptisms and Sunday masses, Wiley officiated at their funerals and burials, which Bridget and Patrick found themselves attending all too regularly.

Among the first deaths in the Kennedy-Barron orbit was that of Bridget's cousin, Edward Barron, followed a year later by the passing of her uncle, Patrick Barron Sr., at age seventy-five; he left behind more than a dozen grandchildren. Bridget wrote home to give her mother the news that her brother had died — or, as was common, she might have asked Father Wiley to help compose the letter.

Despite the Barrons' deaths (with more to come — Bridget's aunt, Mary Barron, would die in 1856 at age seventy-five), the life expectancy of the Irish in Boston was slowly rising above that of Ireland. In addition to living longer, they kept multiplying. The report "Births and Deaths in Boston" showed that the city's population was growing faster than ever, thanks largely to the Irish and their prodigious baby-making. With immigrants like Bridget delivering more than half the city's newborns, Boston's Irish population grew by 200 percent from 1850 to 1855; the non-Irish population increased by just 15 percent.

The Irish were building their churches and carving out pocket enclaves nationwide — in New York, Philadelphia, Chicago, Baltimore, New Orleans, and even out west, in San Francisco. "The United States will become very Irish . . . on a colossal scale," the London *Times* had predicted a few years earlier. "We shall only have pushed the Celt westward."

The Celt was now firmly planted in America, and though some headed west (as Donahoe's *Pilot* implored them to do), many were content to keep taking their chances in Boston.

But the relationship between the Irish and their adopted city was fraying. They'd found their living spaces and their congregations but continued to face reminders that they weren't really wanted — not in this homogeneous Anglocentric city, hardened against infiltrators and determined to thwart the Irish and their suspicious religion.

In turn, the clannish Irish hunkered in their slums, insulated and wary, even as their priests urged them to assimilate and become more American. "This is our country now," said one *Pilot* editorial, advising readers to become naturalized citizens. "Ireland is only a recollection."

The Naturalization Act of 1798 (and other subsequent amendments) had allowed white males to become naturalized citizens after five years (down from fourteen) in the United States. Patrick Kennedy did so in 1853, and Patrick Barron followed in 1855. Bridget, meanwhile, remained a citizen by implication only; state and federal laws on citizenship applied only to the men.

Still, many Irish resisted citizenship and assimilation, as they had for decades. Boston's former mayor Theodore Lyman had called them "a race that will never be infused with our own . . . will always remain distinct and hostile."

The hostility was hardly without cause.

Hating and punishing Catholics (and other marginalized groups) had been an American pastime since colonial days. Lyman Beecher and Theodore Lyman were just the most recent megaphones for anti-Catholic and anti-*other* sentiments, their voices a steady hum that occasionally crescendoed into a roar, inciting violence.

Ann "Goody" Glover was one early example. Deported from Ireland during Cromwell's brutal occupation, Glover found work as a maid in Boston's North End. In 1688, her employer accused her of stealing laundry and fired her, and when the employer's kids began complaining of sharp pains and odd twitches, locals claimed the Irish maid had put a hex on them. The dispute caught the attention of the bewigged Puritan minister Cotton Mather, who called Glover an "idolatrous Roman Catholick" and a "scandalous old Irishwoman." Glover was arrested, tried for witchcraft, convicted, and hanged. Hearing her speak Gaelic, prosecutors said, was proof she was possessed of some sort of devil tongue. Four years later, egged on by Mather and other hard-line Puritans, nineteen additional "witches" were hanged in Salem (although most of those victims were descendants of English Puritans, not Catholics).

Anti-Catholic attitudes would prosper over the next two hundred years, as would calls from Protestant extremists to beware the Catholic "army," with its "nunneries" and "popery." Effigies of the pope were burned at "Pope Night" parties, which George Washington called "ridiculous and childish." The Puritans even banned Christmas celebrations, which were punishable by fine, and city schools would stay open on Christmas into the late nineteenth century.

Puritans had sought religious freedom for themselves—their very name came from a desire to "purify" the Church of England by removing all vestiges of Catholicism. But they did not extend this liberty to others. In fact, they terrorized perceived outsiders, and not just Catholics. Quakers were persecuted and hanged on Boston Common. Indigenous peoples—the Mohegans, Narragansetts, Wampanoags, Nipmucks, Mohawks, Algonquians, and Pocumtucs living on colonized lands that the British dubbed "New England" —were chased from their villages or massacred; the women and children were sometimes burned alive. After slaughtering many of the Pequots in Connecticut, the Puritans collected the survivors and sold them into slavery, a practice that would become common in future battles with Native Americans.

The Puritans embraced slavery, America's original sin. Though the institution was more widespread down south, the attitudes and ideas that allowed it to grow—self-righteousness, exceptionalism, white supremacy—thrived in New England, as did the enslavement of African and Native people. Less than twenty years after the Jamestown colony brought slavery to America, the original owner of Noddle's Island, Samuel Maverick, the namesake of Maverick Square, became one of Boston's first slaveholders in 1638.

George Washington might have imagined America's bosom open to "the oppressed and persecuted of all Nations and Religions," but the reverse was too often true: newcomers were oppressed, persecuted, or even enslaved in America. Other founders worried about opening the gates too wide. Ben Franklin fretted that "swarthy" Germans were "herding together" in Philadelphia rather than assimilating.

Over the century following Jefferson's penning of a declaration that all men were created equal and endowed with unalienable rights, the Irish in America were subjected to laws that restricted or banned outright their religion and their rights, much as the British-imposed Penal Laws had done back in Ireland. Into the nineteenth century, a flood of books, pamphlets, and newspapers screeched about a *Foreign Conspiracy Against the Liberties of the United States,* which was the title of a popular book written by the artist Samuel F. B. Morse, who also invented the telegraph and developed Morse code. Morse hoped his invention might make "one neighborhood of the whole country," except he didn't want Irish as neighbors and aggressively promoted a ban on Catholic immigration. (His electromagnetic dots and dashes were originally designed as a secret code that could be used to defeat a rumored plot to make "Popery" the law of the land.)

Hatred of Catholicism got baked into the school system. The widely used *New-England Primer* taught kids to read, write . . . and despise the "whore of Rome, and all her blasphemies." Catholic parents (and their priests) complained that such attitudes had infiltrated library books and novels, which portrayed the pope as rich and wicked, priests as "effeminate, licentious, and superstitious," and nuns as naughty. Most schools taught from the Protestant-preferred King James Bible, the British translation rejected by Catholics, which would in time contribute to the development of a separate Catholic school system.

The influential Unitarian minister Theodore Parker — like Beecher, a generally respected man whose antislavery views and words would later be cited by Abraham Lincoln and Martin Luther King Jr. — stoked the anti-Catholic fires, assailing Boston's Irish as "ignorant . . . idle, thriftless, poor, intemperate, and barbarian."

When Bishop Fenwick had created the *Boston Pilot* in 1829 (initially naming it *The Jesuit*), he wrote that his intent was to "explain, diffuse, and defend" Catholics and to combat "gross misrepresentations" that he felt had been "so cruelly heaped upon the Church."

He seemed to sense that more brutality was coming.

After the convent burning and the Broad Street Riot in the

1830s, other cities saw similar unrest as masses of Famine Irish moved west, fanning the flames of America's immigrant dread. Dozens were killed or injured outside Philadelphia during the so-called Bible Riots of 1844, which left churches and convents in charred ruins. New York's Bishop John Hughes hired armed guards to patrol outside his churches.

All of this surely terrified Bridget and Patrick, who feared for the safety of their toddler girls and infant boy. Violent episodes continued into the mid-1850s, and the Kennedys regularly witnessed the harassment of their people: Irish workers beaten on their way home from work, Irish saloons destroyed, Irish homes and churches vandalized or burned. Yankee extremists held protests and rallies, marched along Irish streets in East Boston, Charleston, and the North End, and called for the destruction of the paupers' hospital (which was full of immigrants) on Deer Island. Brahmin papers complained about emaciated immigrants begging for food, sleeping in doorways, and seeking medical help or charity — "completely uncontrollable," the *Boston Transcript* called them. Father Wiley and other priests visited Irish neighborhoods to soothe and comfort parishioners like Bridget and Patrick, urging them to stay alert and avoid being goaded into altercations.

But sometimes the altercations came anyway, as they did to East Boston in 1854.

8

Bridget the Enemy

ONE SUNDAY IN early May 1854, a menacing white-robed street preacher named John Orr, who blew a trumpet and called himself the "Angel Gabriel," came to the Kennedys' neighborhood, trailed by a chanting flock of Irish-haters.

Orr led a mob of protestors through the nearby town of Chelsea and then south across the bridge into East Boston, vandalizing Irish homes, smashing church windows, cheering and chanting. Orr's rowdy mob marched right past Bridget and Patrick's home on Eutaw Street, down Meridian Street and onto Maverick Square. Police prevented Orr from speaking there and chased him back north to Chelsea, where one of his followers climbed atop a church, tore the cross from the steeple, and threw it to the ground. The angry mob stomped it to pieces.

Spectacles like this had been going on for months, starting in New York and moving north into New England. Orr was often joined by an accordion player and the duo would stand on the steps of a church or city hall, shrieking about the Irish and the "evils of popery." They were often protected by gangs of youth from a secret paramilitary club called the "Wide Awakes," disgruntled working-class men drawn to the jingoistic sloganeering.

Typical of the pseudo-patriotic fetishes of such clubs — the Order of Free and Accepted Americans, the Order of the American Star — this lot wore funny hats and robes decorated with a star and the number 67, meant to represent George Washington's age when he died. Presumably unaware that Washington envisioned America as a "safe and agreeable asylum" for immigrants, they shouted, "Wide awake! Wide awake!" — a rallying cry designed to frighten Boston's Irish and muster others to the cause.

It was all dramatic and ridiculous, and Orr was often jeered — until things turned dangerous.

That evening in May, an infuriated Orr led his mob once more into East Boston, looking for "Irish settlements," chasing residents indoors, tossing bricks at their heads and through their windows, and eventually surrounding St. Nicholas Church.

Father Wiley and other Catholic priests had begged their parishioners to stay away from Orr's rallies. "Keep cool, keep away from all scenes of disturbance," counseled the *Pilot,* while the *Boston Herald* advised the Irish to "abstain from whiskey and violent demonstrations in the streets, and when the 'Angel Gabriel' or any other street brawler blows his horn, keep as far off from him as possible."

But many Irish found it hard to stay away from the bizarre trumpeter and his ruffians. Especially when Orr, his mobs, and his Wide Awakes threatened their churches.

The crowd around St. Nicholas swelled to more than a thousand — a mix of Orr's followers chanting to pull the church apart and Irish locals armed with bats and bricks. Stationed inside the church were a hundred parishioners, some with guns. The mayor finally sent police across by ferry to break things up and make arrests, and the incident slowly fizzled.

Orr's mob had marched past the Kennedys three times that day and night, and their kids surely witnessed the rioting. Bridget was pregnant at the time, and the chaos and violence must have terrified her and her children. It's unknown whether Patrick joined those defending St. Nicholas.

That summer, Orr traveled throughout New England, staging more rallies, getting arrested, but quickly being released. Inspired by Orr's example, rioters in Maine kidnapped a Catholic priest, painted him in hot tar, and decorated him in feathers, leaving him naked and unconscious on a pier. (The priest, John Bapst, was cleaned up with help from local Catholics, led mass the next day, and went on to become the first president of Boston College.)

Orr's ability to lead so many angry followers to the steps of their house of worship rattled the Kennedys and other St. Nicholas parishioners. In the *Pilot,* Donahoe called Orr a "lunatic" who needed to be locked up: "Orr is not insane. He is a shrewd fellow and an efficient tool and it is high time that his eccentricities were somewhat curbed."

Fanatics like Orr stoked an anti-immigrant machine that threatened to make Catholic-hating the law of the land. Its forces were coalescing into a national movement and a political party. Lyman Beecher preached that the tide had turned "and Catholicism forever in the Northeast must row upstream, carefully watched."

This was the world the Kennedy children were born into. Bridget and Patrick now knew that even some of their island neighbors wished them harm.

Though Orr was considered a trouble-maker and a kook, his message was becoming more mainstream. Even respectable citizens openly shared their concerns about the strangers washing ashore. A group of East Boston business leaders began meeting in secret to draft plans to keep the Irish and their "foreign influence" in check.

They'd been around for years: so-called benevolent societies, fraternal orders, and social clubs with names like the Supreme Order of the Star-Spangled Banner or the American Protestant Society. They launched newspapers and magazines: the *Signal,* the *Republican,* the *Protestant,* the *Order of United Americans,* the *Spirit of '76.* Membership was open to Protestants born in the United States — "native Americans," they called themselves — but anyone married to a Catholic was denied membership.

Claiming to be defenders of the Constitution and protectors of freedom, they insisted that Catholics could never be true patriots since their first allegiance was to the pope. At a time of war or national emergency, they couldn't be trusted. Some (like Morse) floated conspiracy theories: the Irish had come to America to infiltrate and contaminate it, part of a secret plot for a Catholic takeover.

Like adolescent boys playing games of spy, they created secret handshakes, passwords, and salutes. For example, the instructions for saluting the officers of Boston's Republican Liberty Guard were as follows: with right hand, make an "OK" symbol with thumb touching middle finger, then touch forefinger to right cheek. One Boston sect required members to identify themselves to comrades by tucking their right thumb in their vest pocket; the appropriate response was placing the left thumb in the vest pocket. One secret password exchange went like this: Q: "On what hill?" A: "Bunker Hill." Membership in such clubs soared in the mid-1850s, numbering an estimated one million souls who believed that only native-born Americans should run the show.

"Americans must rule America" was a favorite motto.

These groups were collectively referred to as the Know Nothings, a reference to their practice of denying that their group even existed; they professed to *know nothing.* Members aligned under the umbrella of the Native American Party, later called the American Party. The more devout among them were disaffected working-class urban dwellers worried about losing jobs to men like Patrick Kennedy. Complaints like theirs echo through America's anti-immigrant past and would continue well into the future: "they" were coming to take our jobs, "they" will depress wages, steal from us, spread their unholy religion, bring their drunkenness, their strange languages, foods, and smells — in short, these outsiders threatened "the American way of life." Preying on the economic fears of the poor, the Know Nothing publication *Almanac* asked readers: "Why are you poor?" Then answered its own question: "competition of foreign cheap labor."

The *Pilot* sometimes mocked dowdy, dotty old Boston; the former editor Thomas D'Arcy McGee called it an "eccentric museum." Another ex-editor, the angry, whiskey-swilling Irishman George Pepper, was more blunt, calling Boston's Yanks "that atrocious and impious band of sanguinary and ignorant fanatics."

Over the 225 years since the city's founding, some of its leaders had professed tolerance. John Winthrop had hoped America's settlers might "delight in each other, make other's conditions our own, rejoice together, mourn together, labor and suffer together." And the Massachusetts senator Charles Sumner once claimed that his home state welcomed the Irish as it did all immigrants and races: "He may be poor, weak, humble, or black — he may be of Caucasian, Jewish, Indian, or Ethiopian race — he may be of French, German, English, or Irish extraction; but before the Constitution of Massachusetts all these distinctions disappear . . ."

But the Know Nothings didn't see things that way, and now the *Pilot* began to fill with stories, editorials, and letters about "secret organizations" eager to burn churches and harm Irish residents, including "defenceless servant girls" like Bridget. Even the former mayor and Harvard president Josiah Quincy called the Know Nothings "birds of prey" and, in a letter to the *Pilot,* cautioned its readers that "the liberties of a people are never more certain in the path of destruction than when they trust themselves to the guidance of secret societies."

One particularly devout club of Know Nothings were Bridget and Patrick's neighbors, a group of Protestant East Boston business leaders who'd been meeting at secret locations since at least 1853 to discuss the "imminent peril of Freedom" that immigrants represented. By 1855 the East Boston chapter of the American Party had nearly eight hundred members and was led by Samuel W. Hall, son of a prominent shipbuilder and founder of the East Boston Ferry Company; he once ran the Sunday school at the Maverick Church (which had become St. Nicholas Church).

During their backroom meetings, Hall and other party leaders drafted a list of proposed laws they hoped to pass if Know Nothing candidates won upcoming elections. One called for an "absolute denial" of the powers of the "Papal Church" and demanded that anyone who believed otherwise (meaning Catholics) "shall not be permitted to hold any (federal) office."

Though the acronym *WASP* was not yet in use, the makeup of the Know Nothings was just that: white, Anglo-Saxon, Protestant. In addition to their zeal to suppress Catholicism and those who practiced it, they nursed a distrust of most lawmakers and hoped to carve out a place for themselves in national politics. The collapse of the Whig Party and the rise of the fledgling Republican Party gave the American Party an opening. In 1854, Know Nothing candidates swept elections across the United States, placing seven governors and nearly fifty congressmen in office. They were now poised to make life even harder for Catholic immigrants.

Some of their success resulted from voter suppression, fraud, and violence. The East Boston group authorized its treasurer to "procure and pay for 2500 votes." Elsewhere, Know Nothing gangs patrolled the polls, wielding clubs and pitchforks, demanding to see naturalization papers, and threatening those who looked or sounded foreign, inciting riots in Cincinnati, New Orleans, St. Louis, and Chicago. In Baltimore, a man named Charles Brown was gunned down by a Know Nothing thug outside his polling place, leading to an exchange of gunfire that killed five. The *Baltimore American* bemoaned the "guerilla warfare" tactics that the American Party used to prevent immigrants from voting.

In Louisville, Protestant rioters raided and torched a brewery, killing those trapped inside. Drunk on stolen brandy, they raged through the Irish district, known as Quinn's Row, setting fires and beating residents, including a priest, who was stoned to death. The *Louisville Times* described "barbarism which could not be surpassed by the wildest savages." One woman, running from the flames with an infant in her arms, was "followed by a hard-hearted wretch who . . . put the muzzle of the weapon to the child's head, *fired, and bespattered its brains over its mother's arms*," said the *Louisville Daily Journal,* which described men "roasted to death" and roundly scolded the American Party's "appetite for blood." Estimates ranged from twenty to a hundred dead in what was later called Bloody Monday.

Boston, meanwhile, managed to avoid this type of bloodshed in part thanks to public outreach by Bishop Fitzpatrick, his priests, and the *Pilot,* who all begged Catholics not to fight, but to *vote* — "as American citizens." Said the *Pilot:* "As the know-nothings will surely try to stir up riots at the polls, it will be well for us not to go in noisy squads, or to hang about the polls, but to deposit our votes quietly and then to go about our business . . . the know-nothings will adopt all manner of foul means to prevent us from exercising our right to vote."

A naturalized citizen, Patrick was eligible to vote, as was Patrick Barron. (Not Bridget, of course—and not in her lifetime.) But the votes of the Kennedy and Barron men were no match for the forces against them in 1855. While the ranks of Irish voters were rising in Boston, across New England hundreds of Know Nothing candidates were elected to state and local offices, with an especially strong showing in Massachusetts. There, the governor, the entire state senate, and all but four state representatives were Know Nothings, as was Boston's new mayor.

These lawmakers introduced a stream of anti-Catholic, anti-immigrant legislation. The Know Nothing–controlled legislature proposed that only native-born citizens be eligible for federal office; that only native-born Protestants represent the United States overseas; that no foreign-born resident be allowed to vote until he'd lived in the States for twenty-one years. One bill called for a literacy test for all voters. Another made the King James Bible required reading in state schools. Irish militia companies in Boston, the type of volunteer troops that had formed across the United States in the mid-1800s, were forced to disband. And in response to nativist cries to "send them back," Irish paupers were deported to Ireland or Liverpool.

Suddenly, the Kennedys had to worry that if they didn't maintain a certain level of income, the Know Nothings might ship them home. The Kennedy children inherited US citizenship from Patrick, but even naturalized citizens and their native-born kids were being targeted for deportation—sent "across the seas for the crime of being poor," said the *New York Irish-American.*

Some of these proposed laws would be voted down or overturned on technicalities—it turned out that many Know Nothing candidates were political novices unskilled at actually running things. And they began to attract plenty of opposition, including a clearly disgusted politician from Illinois who wrote to a friend:

> As a nation, we began by declaring that "*all men are created equal.*" We now practically read it, "all men are created equal, *except negroes.*" When the Know-Nothings get control, it will read "all men are created equal, except negroes, *and foreigners and catholics.*" When it comes to this I should prefer emigrating to some country where they make no pretence of loving liberty—to Russia, for instance, where despotism can be taken pure, and without the base alloy of hypocrisy.

In a subsequent letter, Senator Abraham Lincoln would write that by "tilting against foreigners," the Know Nothings in Massachusetts were dooming their chances of governing an increasingly foreign-born electorate.

Over the next few years, slavery would rightly become the primary political focus in the United States, and as the country raced toward war the Know Nothings' power, which reached a political peak (and a moral nadir) with the electoral victories of 1854 and 1855, would recede. Public support for the single-minded nativists would turn to disdain and even ridicule, especially as the newly formed Republican Party gained followers. The more blatant anti-immigrant posturing would retreat. The *Pilot* predicted, "Know-Nothingism Is in the Agonies of Death."

It wasn't dead, of course, just hibernating. Xenophobia had become an "American tradition," as one historian has put it, and it was destined to reappear, again and again, like a virus. In the meantime, as the nation came apart at the seams, the Kennedys grew more concerned with family matters than with politics.

• • •

In the middle of the scorching and tumultuous summer of 1855, Bridget gave birth to her third daughter, Margaret. Weeks later, her year-old son, John, became terribly sick.

It was an unusually hot summer, the heat contributing to outbreaks of yellow fever in the South, a cholera flare-up in Kansas, and scores of deaths from assorted fevers throughout New England. Although the *Pilot* had declared Boston "free from this disease" in late 1854, cholera made its way back to the city a year later, carried across the Atlantic from London.

Baby John developed an intestinal disorder that infected infants during warm weather—especially those exposed to tainted food or spoiled milk. Then known as cholera infantum, or summer diarrhea, it was common in the Irish slums, mainly among kids with poor diets. Working mothers weaned their infants off breast milk and fed them watered-down milk, sometimes mixed with cereal —a "gruel" that could quickly spoil in the heat.

Many cities saw surges of cholera infantum deaths each summer, up to a hundred per week in New York and at least a dozen each week in Boston. The affliction came on suddenly, with painful symptoms—diarrhea, vomiting, dehydration, fever, and rapid emaciation—that doctors struggled to treat. The cure was elusive. An improved diet and fresh milk sometimes helped, but for poor families those remedies were often out of reach. Infected children rarely survived more than a week; some became still, blue, and pulseless within hours of the onset of symptoms. A medical expert at the time said the brutal disease "thrives and fattens on filth, poverty, and impurities." Vexed doctors feared it was incurable and, per one medical report, "we ought to insist upon the public's learning that we cannot pull the stars from heaven."

There would be no stars pulled from heaven for Bridget's little boy. Helpless and horrified, she watched his condition worsen steadily until he grew quiet and still. In late September, two days before his parents' sixth wedding anniversary, he died. John Francis Kennedy was twenty months old.

Father Wiley, who had baptized John and his sisters, had died four months earlier; it's unknown whether someone else from St. Nicholas came to comfort Bridget and her daughters, or whether her faith gave her strength. Suddenly, she and Patrick had to make an awful decision: how and where to bury their only son.

Ads for coffins could be found easily enough in the back pages of the papers—often among ads for ships from Liverpool, Irish Emigrant Society meetings, jobs for immigrants, and the "Information Wanted" ads. But finding a suitable resting place was more difficult. Burying the dead had been a challenge for Irish Catholics back home too. Penal Laws prevented families from burying corpses in a churchyard, monastery, abbey, or convent that England had outlawed or destroyed.

In Boston, city officials had passed statutes to prevent Catholics from burying their dead in the city. The only Catholic cemetery was in South Boston, but authorities had closed it. (It would reopen later that year, after parishioners raised money to build a new fence, per city orders.) The next-closest option was two miles away, across the harbor in Charlestown, a city that had been particularly hostile to Catholics for two centuries.

The Kennedys selected a gravesite in Cambridge, not far from the renowned Harvard College. They paid six dollars for a family plot and baby John F. Kennedy was buried there on September 25, 1855, the day after he'd died at home.

They'd come so far and beaten so many odds. His death was a shocking, deflating blow. *Has anyone supposed it lucky to be born?* the poet Walt Whitman asked in "Song of Myself," published that year. As it had for years, the *Pilot* kept track of such losses. Deaths in Ireland continued to be more prominently displayed on page 2 or 4 of the weekly paper—dozens of names from Dublin, Wexford, Kerry, and Belfast—while Boston deaths were printed at the bottom of page 7 or 8, just before the clusters of coffin ads and "Information Wanted" posts.

The *Pilot* sometimes listed local passings by name, under the headline "Deaths in Boston." On September 29, the list included a "much beloved" eighty-eight-year-old doctor from Galway; a sixteen-year-old girl "too bright, too beautiful for earth"; and a "tender mother" who, at thirty-three, had "departed this transitory life." The day John Kennedy died, the *Pilot* also reported the death of a man named Henry Willard, who had just finished speaking at a Know Nothing meeting in Boston when he "dropped on the floor and instantly expired." Opined the *Pilot:* "But such is life. Today we are alive and tomorrow we are consigned to mother earth."

Baby John was not mentioned in print—paid obituaries cost a dollar—but he was included among the statistics. That same week, Boston saw 103 deaths, more than half of them children under the age of five, twenty of them felled by the cursed cholera infantum.

One of the victims was an Irish boy, Ambrose Joyce, who died at nine months, a week before John. His parents wrote a poem that was published in the *Pilot,* and its words captured what Bridget and Patrick were no doubt suffering.

> *A cloud upon my spirit rests, O'ershadowing it with gloom;*
> *For, oh! my boy, my darling boy—Lies mouldering in the tomb!*
> *He was so full of life and glee, So gentle and so fair—*
> *His little heart was filled with love—Can he be lying there?*
> *I loved thee as no tongue may tell, Thou wast my hope, my joy—*
> *And must I never see thee more, My precious angel boy?*

Two years later, Bridget was pregnant once more, carrying another son, another angel boy.

As his birth neared, bad news followed good. Her strong husband had gotten sick — coughing and feverish, chills and diarrhea.

Then East Boston's shipping industry took a hit. Work slowed. Incomes dropped.

Then Patrick got sicker.

Part III

BRIDGET: ALONE

I'm happy as I am, and love my liberty too well to be in a hurry to give it up for any mortal man.

— LOUISA MAY ALCOTT, *Good Wives*

9

Bridget the Widow

IN THE SMALL bedroom of their chilly Liverpool Street apartment, with newspapers and old stockings stuffed into window cracks to ward off winter's chill, with her sister and likely a midwife by her side, Bridget gave birth to her fifth child, her second son, who was destined to be raised and spoiled by three older sisters.

Two days later, on January 16, 1858, the boy was baptized at East Boston's recently built Church of the Most Holy Redeemer. Irish Catholic newborns were often baptized quickly: with the persistent risk of a premature death, parents wanted to be sure their child was cleansed of sin before it was too late. While Bridget recovered, Patrick or the boy's godparents likely rushed him to a side door at the church and the priest, Father Patrick Healy, said a quick prayer. With the hundreds of baptisms now being performed there each year, sometimes a brusque no-fuss affair was required. The unceremonious baptism welcomed into the world Patrick Joseph Kennedy. Neighbors would call him "Pat's boy." Bridget and Patrick would call him P.J.

That afternoon, the two-thousand-pound bell tolled from above the Kennedys' new church, which had finally replaced cramped little St. Nicholas and would accommodate the next generation of the island's still-growing flock of Catholics. But the church, its tolling bell, and the arrival of a new child all came at an otherwise precarious time for the Kennedys. They knew it wouldn't be easy in America, but the past few years had been rougher than expected: burying a child, facing down riots, and now Patrick's illness, which was getting worse.

Despite the persistent discrimination, the occasional violence, and the threats of anti-Catholic Know Nothing laws, it had also been a heady period for anyone tied to East Boston's shipbuilding industry. Immigrant barrel makers, rope makers, sailmakers, carpenters, riggers, spar and mast makers had enjoyed a years-long run of steady employment. Shipping and shipbuilding had boomed, weathering political and economic ups and downs, with more piers, wharves, and dry docks poking into the harbor and scores of waterfront businesses fringing the island: machine shops and iron foundries, timber mills and saloons. And the island was literally expanding — marshes and mudflats filled in with soil and stone, acre by acre.

With ten shipyards launching scores of ships each year into the mid-1850s, as well as yachts, fishing schooners, tugboats, and pile drivers, East Boston had become one of the busiest shipbuilding hubs in America. The *East Boston Advocate* bragged that the island was now "the workshop of Boston." To live in the beating heart of that thriving commercial machine, not a single potato field in sight, had been intoxicating for Bridget and Patrick. The world's largest and fastest ships were East Boston–built, some capable of reaching Liverpool in fourteen days. New vessels would slide down greased wooden rails into the harbor as the Kennedys and other families gathered for parties of cheese, biscuits, and rum punch. McKay's shipyard launched the *Flying Cloud* clipper, which set a record by sailing from New York to San Francisco, a distance of fifteen thousand miles, in just eighty-nine days — a record that would stand until 1989. McKay later launched the *Great Republic,* the world's largest wooden ship, inspiring Boston to declare a city holiday and close the schools. (Two months later, the *Great Republic* burned to the water-line and sank.)

Those ships and many more, large and small, needed lots of barrels. Patrick walked each morning to the waterside cooperage, working alongside his wife's cousins and their cousins, spending long days piecing together the casks, butts, and barrels that delivered flour, apples, vinegar, cider, wine, and ale around the globe. Trains heading west to California's gold miners carried barrels of absinthe, rum, grain, sugar, and salted cod; barrels packed with fish were in such demand that some coopers worked double duty as fish packers. At the railroad junction, men offloaded hundreds of barrels filled with Chicago beef; kegs full of nails, apples, potatoes, and honey; hermetically sealed barrels of oysters and cherries.

The good times had allowed Patrick to provide, if modestly, for his growing family. But then came the rise of steam-powered ships, which in the mid-1850s began replacing the sailing vessels. East Boston was slow to adapt. Enoch Train formed the Boston and European Steamship Company, planning to pivot to steamships. But then a global financial crisis rippled through all shipbuilding enterprises, forcing Train out of business. The Panic of 1857 was triggered in part by the Supreme Court's Dred Scott decision, which denied rights and citizenship to Black people and, by declaring the Missouri Compromise unconstitutional, allowed slavery to expand westward. The Panic caused railroads, banks, and insurance companies to collapse, and the effects spiraled through the markets in what the *New York Times* likened to a cholera outbreak. News spread through the electronic transmissions of the nativist Samuel Morse's thirteen-year-old telegraph network. Boston's economy tanked, and low-wage workers were among the first victims. Shipyards and related businesses were especially hard hit. Companies folded, wages were slashed by upwards of 30 percent, layoffs and unemployment became widespread.

Patrick kept his job—twelve-hour days, six days a week, striving for $10 a week—but his income rose and fell, always in flux, before and during the crisis. The family's annual earnings dropped from $300 in 1852 to $100 in 1856, according to an assessor's report. A year later, though, Patrick managed to save $400 in an account at the Provident Institution for Savings. He and Bridget had opened a family side business: a small neighborhood grocery shop in East Boston that brought in extra income. But due to his ill health and the Panic of 1857, the eager little shop would not survive.

Bridget may have tried to continue to work, although many Boston families fired their maids during the financial crisis, which lasted into 1858. Her sister Margaret, who'd been helping Bridget with babysitting, got married and moved out of the Kennedys' home, leaving Bridget without child-care support. Then, in the summer of 1857, Bridget's brother-in-law Nicholas Roche fell ill and died. The husband of Bridget's sister Catherine, who was still in Ireland with their other children, Nicholas had immigrated to East Boston three years earlier with his twelve-year-old daughter Mary, who moved in with the Kennedys after his death.

Nicholas Roche had succumbed to the most rampant disease of the day, which had now infected Patrick Kennedy: consumption.

From late 1857 into the summer of 1858, Boston's papers chronicled the disease's rampaging return to the slums. Ever attuned to the illnesses claiming its readers, the *Pilot* published dozens of articles, letters, and ads decrying the "vile destroyer of the parent's hopes; this fell monster, the devourer of mankind . . . thousands daily suffering from the early stages of this destroying malady." The *Pilot* reported that the percentage of deaths by consumption, sometimes a third of Boston's weekly fatalities, had doubled. (It's possible the *Pilot*'s particular interest in consumption stemmed from the personal loss experienced by its publisher, Patrick Donahoe, whose wife had died of that "destroying malady.")

The paper published ads from doctors, who pitched questionable treatments and medications such as tonsillectomy, doses of silver nitrate, calomel, antimony, or croton oil. Such ads and other stories about the disease would have caught Patrick Kennedy's eye, as would liquor makers' ads for tonics and cordials promising to "mitigate the evils of consumption."

We don't know exactly when or how Patrick contracted the disease, only that it was everywhere and hard to avoid. It spread through the air via its own impossible-to-suppress symptoms: coughing, sneezing, spitting. There was no known cure. Some people healed on their own (George Washington survived two bouts of consumption); many did not (James Monroe, Andrew Jackson). By the summer of 1858, Patrick's condition was deteriorating. He worked as long as he could, even with the hours too long, the wages never enough. But at the cooperage, he couldn't hide the violent coughing, the leathering of his skin, the flecks of blood on his chin. Couldn't hide the trips to the loo, the relentless diarrhea, signs of worse to come. Some episodes brought him to his knees, helpless fits of chest-rattling hawks, fevers and vomiting, coughing up phlegm and blood. He got so thin, disappearing a little more each day.

When the pain became too great, druggists offered palliatives — morphine and opium — to "lull the feelings of the patient," as their ads promised. It was a terrible way to die, slow and grueling. At some point, Patrick must have known, the realization washing over him: *I won't survive this. I'm done for.* It was just a matter of time before he'd be hauled off in a bag or a box. There would be no cure. And so it was. Patrick died at home, bits at a time and then, in November 1858, all at once.

Elsewhere in the neighborhood, others were similarly wasting away. It was the fate of the poor and the unemployed—"a cacophony of hacking coughs, bronchial rattles, asthmatic wheezes, consumptive croaks," an Irish American writer would later say of his neighborhood. Had Patrick crossed the Atlantic for *this?* To die shriveled and yellow—"the spoiling meat of him," as an Irish writer would put it—weak and helpless, in pain and ashamed?

Did he even get to hold his infant son? Or was he too weak, too dangerously contagious? With no means to pay for a hospital stay —and in truth, no useful thing a doctor could do now, not even at one of the city-built hospitals for "foreign diseased paupers"— Patrick's last days would have been spent prone and surrounded by his fearful family at 44 Liverpool Street, just an easy stroll away from the pier he'd strutted across, robust and ready, from the gangplank of a coffin ship.

Doctors estimated the average Irish immigrant's time span in America was fourteen years. Patrick had barely seen a decade; he was only thirty-five years old and furiously dying a quarter of a mile from where his hopeful new life had begun. Worse, dying at home meant his kids had to watch him rot and waste away, day by day, as his complexion turned from yellow to green to gray, the family offering wary embraces—*You'll be better soon, won't you, Da?*—and struggling to tamp down their confusion and fear.

He'd risked everything to get here, survived the Famine, the three-thousand-mile escape, the threatening chants and stones and bats of the Know Nothings. He'd found a woman to love, and together they'd kept four of their five kids alive, at least so far. Imagine them at his deathbed: Mary, the eldest at seven; Joanna, a year younger; Margaret, three; and baby P.J., just ten months. And hovering above them all the memory of baby John, three years gone. The Kennedy kids had seen the processions of coffins through their neighborhood, had seen other mothers and kids their age wailing for a young father felled by disease. Did they say their goodbyes? Kiss his cheek, press their skin against his? Or were they told not to touch, lest they inherit his sickness?

Scant details survive regarding Patrick's last days, his funeral, or his burial. A priest from Most Holy Redeemer would have been called to say a prayer over him, to perform last rites and anoint his forehead with holy oil. How his wife and children must have cried when the end finally came. The Barrons would have been there, Bridget's sister and brother-in-law, other close friends and family, all taking turns holding baby P.J. and comforting the girls.

It's unlikely Patrick received the traditional Irish wake, with his body laid out in the living room as loved ones told stories and wept into their whiskeys. Instead, fellow coopers likely came to the apartment to quietly pay respects, and may have collected coins to help Bridget buy food for the children, before Patrick's diseased body was wrapped and loaded and carted away.

Father James Fitton, now the pastor at Most Holy Redeemer, likely presided over a brief funeral mass before Patrick's pine coffin was loaded onto the bed of a horse-drawn hearse. In keeping with a city ordinance, the procession of the hearse and carriages of mourners would have moved at a slow pace, single file, watched over by a police officer to prevent rowdy conduct en route to the cemetery.

Like his infant son John, Patrick would not find eternal rest in the city of Boston. Except for the rare burial at the crowded St. Augustine Cemetery in South Boston (Donahoe was able to bury his wife there), most Catholics still could not inter their dead in city soil. And even St. Augustine Cemetery was occasionally closed by city officials, part of the battle waged for decades by those eager to shut that "public nuisance" for good.

"If the wishes of some persons were accomplished, the Catholics would soon be left without the right to bury at all, either in the city or out of it," Bishop Fitzpatrick wrote to city officials after it was discovered that smells coming from St. Augustine Cemetery, a source of public complaint, had been traced to a decomposing dog someone had buried in a hidden corner of the property. "The Catholics of Boston . . . have some reason to feel dissatisfied with the treatment they have received from time to time in relation to the burial of the dead."

While East Boston had cemeteries for members of other religious groups, including the first Jewish burial ground in Massachusetts (Ohabei Shalom), the island that had been a Know Nothing stronghold had no Catholic cemetery (and never would). Nor was the nearest Catholic cemetery, astride Bunker Hill in Charlestown, a viable option. Officials there had implemented a tax on burying Catholics. Plus, the cemetery had fallen into poor condition. In fact, the city had condemned a portion of the property to make way for a road project. Graves had to be dug up and the dead reinterred elsewhere.

So Bridget and her family and her priest once again made the miles-long journey west to Cambridge. Patrick Kennedy would be laid beside his boy, John, in the six-dollar family plot he'd purchased three years earlier, never expecting his burial would be the next. After two final water crossings—a ferry ride across Boston Harbor and the bridge across to Cambridge—he completed the "rapid the trot to the cemetery" that Whitman depicted in his poem "To Think of Time," published in *Leaves of Grass*.

> *. . . duly rattles the death-bell, the gate is pass'd, the new-dug grave is halted at, the living alight, the hearse uncloses,*
> *The coffin is pass'd out, lower'd and settled . . . the earth is swiftly shovel'd in . . .*
> *A minute—no one moves or speaks—it is done,*
> *He is decently put away—is there anything more?*

"May the Lord have mercy on his soul," Bridget and her children and the other mourners prayed, before making the sorrowful trek along snow-covered streets back to East Boston.

Patrick's headstone, if Bridget had been able to afford one, would have been etched with the date of her husband's death, November 22 — the same date that a century later would claim their great-grandson, John F. Kennedy.

During 1858, the year of Patrick Kennedy's last days, eight hundred Bostonians — half of them Irish — died of consumption. The disease literally consumed immigrant communities, proceeding, as one writer put it, "like a dark epic poem, slowly, solemnly, inexorably."

Depicted in art, opera, and literature through tragic figures — from Little Eva in Harriet Beecher Stowe's *Uncle Tom's Cabin* to Fantine in Victor Hugo's soon-to-be-published *Les Misérables* — consumption hardly made for a poetic departure. A year after Emily Brontë died of consumption, her sister Anne succumbed to the same fate. "A dreadful darkness closes in," Anne wrote at the end. "God's will be done." Years earlier, the eldest Brontë daughters, Maria and Elizabeth, had died of the same disease, as children.

Because doctors didn't yet know what caused consumption, nor how best to treat it, fear drove people to speculate. Some believed the illnesses of the immigrant class — consumption, cholera, scarlet fever, smallpox, typhus — were sent by God, the immigrants' due. Some speculations grew wilder. Late-1850s outbreaks of consumption led some in New England to blame *vampires*. Rumor spread through Massachusetts that consumption was contracted when the dead emerged from their graves at night and drank the blood of the living. The solution? Exhume the corpse, then burn the innards or cut off the head. Henry David Thoreau wrote: "I have just read of a family in Vermont who, several of its members having died of consumption, just burned the lungs & heart & liver of the last deceased, in order to prevent any more from having it."

"The savage in man is never quite eradicated," sighed Thoreau, five years before his own death—by consumption.

Boston counted seventy-two deaths the week Patrick Kennedy died, sixteen of them from consumption. The victims included two other men from East Boston, one of them a father of four who'd been bedridden for three months—"his life gradually wasted away under the influence of disease," said the *Pilot*.

Death by forty. It had become a cliché. The expected fate of the Irish grunt. Disease was hardly the only threat to his longevity. Men like Patrick had served as the whipped mules that made Boston's economic ascent possible. Like all beasts of burden, they were expected to do as they were told: work all day on the docks, in the rail yards, in the quarries and canals, the tunnels and trenches. All for a dollar a day, if they were lucky. No surprise they were so vulnerable to illness and injury. The Brahmin newspapers loved to feed readers titillating stories about Irish workers getting slaughtered on the job: *an Irishman drowned . . . crushed by a beam . . . twenty Irishmen buried alive . . . had both his arms cut off . . . mangled shockingly and cut in two.* The Irishman William Reynolds was ruined by the wheels of a gravel train months before Patrick's death, and a Yankee newspaper mocked Reynolds for being "angry about something and obstinately determined to punish himself." Brutally dead Irishmen had become *entertainment.* They were expendable and deserving of their fates, the papist louts. An entire generation of Boston children grew up rarely seeing a gray-haired Irishman.

Young P.J. would come to learn that many of his peers and playmates had been rendered fatherless through disease or fatal job-related injuries. Later still, he'd find that the men who, through policing and politics, were beginning to drag Irish Americans out of the ditches and into the middle class, had also lost fathers in boyhood. Men with names like Lomasney, Collins, Curley—and P.J.'s future in-law, Fitzgerald.

Which meant this: the boys destined to one day become the most powerful men in Boston in the late nineteenth century had been raised and influenced by strong, steely widowed mothers.

10

Bridget the Servant

SHE WAS IN her midtwenties when they'd wed. A decade later, he'd left her with mouths to feed—four scared and hungry kids, rent to pay, and little else.

Bridget Murphy Kennedy was now a thirty-something widow, surrounded by the sick and the poor, living amid those who still feared and hated her kind, blamed her for their city's woes, and ridiculed her religion.

Three weeks after Patrick's death in 1858, Bridget, her cousin Patrick Barron, and a neighborhood lawyer took the ferry to Boston to meet with a judge, who informed her that her husband's "estate" was worth nearly nothing. She already knew this much. It was not the merriest of Christmases, nor was P.J.'s first birthday, weeks later, the happiest of occasions.

Had she been proud of Patrick? Proud of a man who could build things that would outlive him? Had he been a good husband and father? Did she love him? Were they *happy?* All unanswerable. At least her husband's illness hadn't leapt the fence to claim what remained of her family. Losing another child the way she'd lost John years earlier—that might've been too much. Still, she knew her kids were hardly in the clear, with less than half of Boston's children expected to survive past age five at this time.

No one from Ireland could help. Life back home remained a struggle too, and no white knight would come to Bridget's rescue. Her husband's brothers were fighting to keep the family farm in Dunganstown, and a new blight was ruining that year's potato crops. Most of her own family, the Murphys, had been dispersed by the Famine and Ireland's slow recovery; two of her sisters and their children would eventually immigrate to Massachusetts, but that was a decade away.

Until then, Bridget would be largely on her own, though hardly alone in her aloneness. Just as dead-too-young Irishmen had become commonplace, the weary Irish widow with a brood in rags was now a stereotype, mocked in newspaper cartoons as a rosary-clutching fool. A decade past the worst of the Famine, women were still fleeing Ireland in greater numbers than men. That steady influx, along with the men's shorter life span, meant that women as breadwinners and single parents were becoming a dominant force among the Irish in Boston. This trend would persist as able-bodied Irishmen joined up to fight in the coming War Between the States.

For women in Bridget's situation, replacement husbands were scarce. A widowed mother with an infant boy and three little girls was not considered a catch. By choice or circumstance, Bridget never remarried.

Worse than not finding a new mate was the risk of losing her children to an orphanage, a Protestant foundling home, or one of the "orphan trains" carrying Irish kids and babies out west to be adopted by farm, prairie, or gold rush families. Groups like the Children's Aid Society, created in 1853 by an anti-Catholic humanitarian, scooped up thousands of homeless or orphaned kids—and sometimes flat-out kidnapped them. The orphan trains would stop at a village, where managers lined up their human cargo to let men and women poke, prod, and take their pick. Some aimed to give these children a good life; others wanted only free labor.

Missionaries and ministers prowled Boston's slums, luring children with promises of new clothes, plenty of food, and fields of green; some recruiters were convinced they were saving these kids from evil and an early grave, while others mainly wanted to rid their streets of Irish "scum."

"The city is dangerously and alarmingly overcome with a surplus of a mildewing population," a preacher from Boston's Children's Mission said in 1859. His organization, each year for the past six, had sent two hundred kids west, most of them Irish Catholic. He believed that these "children must be saved, and they cannot save themselves."

With four children and no husband, Bridget would have been a prime target for such do-gooders. Her kids, ages one through eight, were ideal candidates for the orphan trains.

And sometimes kids simply disappeared. Lizzie Morse, Bridget's twelve-year-old neighbor, was wearing a calico dress and black coat when she said goodbye to her mother one Monday morning, never to return. Noting that Lizzie looked more like fifteen years old, the *Boston Post* said that "grave fears are entertained lest designing persons have decoyed her away."

Bridget surely nursed her own doubts and fears in the early years after losing Patrick. Had it all been an absurd mistake? Did she have what it took to keep fighting on her own? Or had she come this far only to lose everything?

Many of Boston's excess children — first-generation Irish who'd lost one or both parents to disease or accident, drink or jail — were dispersed among a growing network of orphanages and other institutions. Some ended up in a uniform and a bunk bed at the New

England Home for Little Wanderers or at the Farm School for Indigent Boys. Others took to the streets, begging or stealing by day,
and by night sleeping in doorways, in boxes, beneath the trees in
city parks.

Ten days after Patrick's death, the *Pilot* carried a brief and increasingly typical article, beneath the headline "A Boy Wants a
Home." The story read: "A good healthy orphan boy wants parents
to adopt him. He is seven years old. Apply immediately to Patrick
Donahoe, at Pilot Office." Elsewhere in the same issue: "Several
orphan children want fathers and mothers to adopt them. Apply at
the Charity School, Channing Street, Boston." Another item, about
the upcoming Orphan's Fair fundraiser, carried this appeal: "Let
every parent, sister, or brother make the case of the orphans his or
her own."

As with other social, political, economic, or moral challenges,
Boston's unwanted boys and girls got caught in a tug-of-war between Protestants and Catholics. One well-known "child saver,"
Charles Loring Brace, who created the Children's Aid Society,
viewed Irish Catholics as drunks and "scum" and Irish street kids
as "vagabond, ignorant, ungoverned children." He considered it his
duty to rescue them from wretched and immoral circumstances.
"Evangelical child-savers," as one author would call them, believed
it was an *obligation* to snatch children from Catholic parents and
reform them anew, ideally as Protestants. In turn, some Irish — and
their priests — viewed these uninvited efforts as "a Protestant plot
to destroy their faith."

Catholic priests and Irish charitable organizations tried to create
their own safety network: St. Vincent's Orphan Asylum, Boston
Female Asylum, the Home for Destitute Catholic Children, the
House of the Angel Guardian. The last of these was the brainchild
of Father George Haskins, who worked with homeless and troubled kids in East Boston and the North End and often persuaded

city officials to let him take boys into his home, rather than send them to city institutions. He raised money to build the House of the Angel Guardian, open to homeless as well as "stubborn and wayward boys . . . boys beyond parental control." For five dollars a month—or just one dollar for widows like Bridget—a boy could receive "discipline that is kind and paternal," according to ads for the home.

When efforts at rehabilitation or adoption failed, or when space ran out at Haskins's home or other Boston facilities, a boy might end up on dreaded Deer Island. The very name stirred up visions of whippings, gruel, and hard labor.

Boston had a history of putting its more disreputable institutions on an island. Deer Island had previously hosted the quarantine hospital, which was the first (and often last) stop in America for many incoming Famine Irish. It was now home to the Boston Asylum and Farm School for Indigent Boys, an almshouse, a lunatic asylum, and assorted penal facilities, including the House of Reformation for Juvenile Delinquents and two especially hardcore facilities: the House of Correction and the House of Industry.

Before the deluge of Irish immigrants, Boston officials would invite foreign VIPs to tour the modern and reformist facilities on Deer Island. Dickens came in 1842 and watched inmates sing songs "in praise of Liberty," though he found it an odd and "rather aggravating theme for prisoners."

And that was before the island became downright Dickensian.

After a series of fires, attempted escapes, and budget cuts, the city basically gave up on separating ten-year-old orphans from twenty-year-old convicts. The various side-by-side "houses" blended together, the Farm School sharing space with the House of Reformation as the distinction between *indigent* and *criminal* faded. In 1859, two boys tried to set fire to the Farm School, and in retaliation the wardens, unable to tell one boy from another, put the entire population on lockdown for weeks. Other boys, sentenced for mere truancy, were "treated worse than brutes; injured for life, and even suffered to die, through the neglect or cruelty of some of the officers in charge," according to one investigation.

Catholic priests complained that they weren't allowed to visit Catholics on Deer Island, whose authorities favored Protestant ministers. The *Pilot* called it an "organized scheme for stealing Catholic children. The object is to make the children Protestants." (Father Haskins, who served in East Boston through the mid-1850s, would become the first Catholic priest allowed to visit the House of Industry.)

Most Irish immigrants knew someone who'd suffered or died on the dreaded Deer Island. And Bridget and her son would soon enough become well acquainted with the brutality and anti-Catholic restrictions on that island, that dark blot in the harbor.

The constant struggle to keep her kids safe and under the same roof would require, Bridget realized, a new plan. Keeping the fatherless Kennedy family intact called for both a humbling return to the workforce and a desperate search for affordable child care. Both efforts were complicated by a downturn in the hiring of maids, due to the ongoing financial crisis.

As she sought a return to the biddy's life — maid, laundress, nanny, or cook — Bridget found the odds still stacked against her. She was an immigrant. A woman. And a widow. Entering her second decade in America, she seemed destined to join other women in Boston's economic basement: Germans, African Americans, Italians, Poles, Jews, and Scandinavians. Their numbers were slowly rising, all of them "fated to remain a massive lump in the community, undigested, undigestible," as one historian has put it.

She wasn't fully welcome in Yankee homes, since many matrons still preferred native-born Protestant servants. Advertisements that

Bridget found in the papers continued to flatly state this bias: "Positively no Irish" and "none but Protestants need apply."

Even before the Civil War, Black people who had been freed and those who'd escaped slavery had been migrating north, and many found domestic work as butlers or maids. Chinese men and teens no longer needed in gold-bust California moved east to work in Yankee homes, where employers found them to be neat, clean, and obedient. Years earlier, Irish maids had faced less competition for the low-rung jobs. But now, without her husband's income, Bridget must have felt the discriminatory ads cutting deeper — not just hurtful but an economic threat.

The *Pilot*'s editors complained about the persistent "No Irish Need Apply" ads. One editorial vented: "It seems to us that none but a narrow-minded bigot would allow his animosity to get the better of his judgment, even if he were not well-disposed towards Irish men." Another column encouraged such bigots to "learn common sense . . . It would not be very pleasant to read in foreign papers, 'No Yankee need apply.'"

Bridgets were still viewed as "totally ignorant of housewifery," as *Harper's Weekly* put it in 1857. And some employers were "sick of the Irish . . . sick of all the race," as one Massachusetts matron wrote in her diary, praying that she might find "some good Protestant girls." Untrained for any other career, Bridget had to brush aside the bigotry and attempt a return to the humbling servitude of domestic work. If it felt like a setback or a dent in her dignity, now was not the time to dwell on such feelings. As Bridget and subsequent generations of immigrant maids would concede, *what choice did she have?* A maid named Hannah Collins, writing to her family, summarized the dream of every biddy: "I hope someday will come when I won't have to work so hard."

This time, however, Bridget Kennedy caught a break. By persistence or happenstance, she managed to land an enviable new job, just blocks from home. Instead of commuting by ferry to Boston, she could stroll to work. Her niece Mary (her sister Catherine's teen daughter) was now living with the Kennedys, babysitting the younger girls and P.J., freeing Bridget to work longer hours. As the household's only earner, she'd need all the hours she could get.

Her new place of employment, a five-minute walk to Maverick Square, welcomed her inside one of the largest and most extravagant buildings to rise above the streets of East Boston.

Named for the island's slaveholding founder, Samuel Maverick, Maverick Square had become East Boston's commercial and social hub, a landscaped oval green surrounded by clothing stores, pharmacies, cigar shops, and saloons. It was the civic heart of the neighborhood, home to churches, newspaper offices, and Lyceum Hall, which hosted lectures, debates, and concerts. The ferry landing that took islanders across to Boston was at the south end of the square, as was the towering Boston Sugar Refinery, famed for inventing granulated sugar.

And on the western flank loomed the legendary Maverick House, a hotel and meeting place with views of Boston, its western suburbs, and Bunker Hill. The original wood-framed building, built in 1833, had burned in the 1840s. An investor purchased the whole block and built rows of brick buildings, tenement houses, shops, offices, and a new hotel, also named Maverick House, which continued the tradition of serving elaborate meals prepared by eminent chefs and selections from a well-stocked collection of wines. A staff of forty waiters tended to diners.

Maverick Square and the Maverick House remained strongholds of Brahmin luxury and taste, an oasis amid the spread of immigrant neighborhoods. The Maverick House was run for years by Major Jabez Barton, a flamboyant proprietor who treated guests like royalty, "attentive to all their wants." President Zachary Taylor was once a guest. Renowned ship captains and navy men from around the globe stayed at the Maverick while their ships were moored at the docks. Major Barton famously hosted rounds of a drinking game called Snap Dragon, in which players tried to pluck raisins from a bowl of liquor that had been set afire.

A year before P.J.'s birth, another fire burned down the Maverick House and the rest of the block—Bridget and Patrick surely witnessed the conflagration. A year later, an even more luxurious new structure arose in its place.

Was Bridget there the night in February 1858, when the Sturtevant House Hotel was unveiled to the public? Opening night featured a gala and a lecture by George S. Hillard, a lawyer and businessman (and future US district attorney) who congratulated East Boston's elite on their "tasty and convenient" new assemblage of frescoed drawing rooms, high-ceilinged apartments, airy lecture halls, and well-stocked saloons. (Hillard and his wife, vocal abolitionists, were later found to be longtime harborers of fugitive slaves; their downtown Boston home served as a stop on the Underground Railroad.)

The six-story brick hotel, which locals continued to refer to as the Maverick House, boasted 350 rooms, a dining hall the size of a ship's deck, a women-only dining section (modeled after the "women's ordinary" at the famed Tremont House), a thousand-square-foot billiards room, and a bowling alley in the attic. The third-floor meeting hall was designed for concerts and lectures like Hillard's opening-night talk, which attracted six hundred attendees.

The man behind the $100,000 project was a fifty-something entrepreneur from a family of deep-rooted Boston Puritans, a man who loved flowers and trees and whose fortunes were seemingly unscathed by the Panic of 1857 and its aftermath.

By the time of Patrick Kennedy's death, Noah Sturtevant had built or bought a soap and candle factory, a linseed oil refinery, a sperm oil factory, a coal company, and more. His various enterprises, including Sturtevant's Wharf on East Boston's western flank and part ownership in two banks, had made Sturtevant one of Boston's wealthiest men.

We don't know when Bridget Kennedy first walked through the doors of Sturtevant's new hotel, but by 1860 she was among its scores of employees: domestics, porters, chefs, waiters, clerks, and housemaids like Bridget. Sturtevant House was also home to full-time boarders, lawyers, dentists, accountants, and bookkeepers. Some were registered simply as "gentlemen," and a few were quite wealthy: a lawyer from Maine, with assets of $23,000; a dry goods broker from Vermont worth $45,000.

Bridget, on the other hand, was worth less than $100 — at least on paper.

By 1860, she and her kids were living in yet another new place on Liverpool Street, a few doors from the house where Patrick died and just blocks from Bridget's first apartment. They'd moved so often over the years, though never far, always sticking within the familiar radius of Holy Redeemer and the Maverick House, the mudflats and shipyards, the ferry terminal and the warehouses and the rows of Irish slums.

Bridget's personal effects were valued at seventy-five dollars, according to that year's census. The same census showed that Bridget had taken in newcomers. In addition to her four kids, ages two through nine, the small apartment now included her teenage niece, Mary, and a six-year-old boy, Michael O'Brien (likely the son of a relative, possibly orphaned, who would in time become P.J.'s friend, tenant, and employee).

More than seventy-two thousand Irish now lived in Boston, rising toward half the population. Into the latter decades of the nineteenth century, most Irish women would continue to work as biddies, serving others while striving to learn the ropes of the middle

class. They gleaned lessons from their Yankee employers—in manners, literacy, culture, finances—and practiced what they learned
in their own homes, which would propel their slow ascent from
distrusted immigrant to authentic American. But for Famine Irish
women like Bridget, early to arrive and a decade or two older than
the Irish single lasses now washing ashore, life as a servant seemed
fated. They were destined to toil for someone else's family, then
watch their own girls become biddies and their sons go off to dig
ditches or work at the docks till their bodies quit at forty. That was
the destiny of the Famine Irish and their children.

But a new paradigm was developing, as emboldened women—
Irish and others—pushed against their limits.

A decade earlier, as an eighteen-year-old whose family had fallen
on hard times, Louisa May Alcott briefly worked as a maid. "Eager to be independent," Alcott hoped the experiment in servitude
would teach her something about the value of work. Her mother,
then running an "intelligence office" in the South End, helped find
Louisa a job at the rundown, rat-infested home of the dour "Reverend Josephus" and his siblings. After a few weeks of scrubbing
floors, carrying buckets from the well, shoveling snow, mending
stockings, cutting wood, lighting fires, and cleaning out the ashes
—"like a true Cinderella," Alcott wrote—all romantic delusions
were dispelled. Her hands had become "chapped, grimy, chill-
blained." She tossed off her cap and apron and left her scolding
employer, earning just four dollars for seven weeks of work. She
later called it one of her bitterest moments, one that would in-
form much of her life and subsequent writing. "I am not afraid of
storms," Amy March would say in *Little Women,* "for I am learning
how to sail my ship."

That was clearly Bridget Kennedy's plan—to "paddle my own
canoe," as Alcott put it in her diary. Bridget was determined not to
become an old maid, ruined by age and toil, like those she'd seen in

her dozen years of on-and-off domestic service. She'd been observing and studying, waiting for the right moment to break free. She wouldn't remain subservient much longer.

A quarter of a century earlier, during his travels through America, the French diplomat Alexis de Tocqueville had observed that the "lackey" need not stay a lackey for life. In aristocratic societies (England or France), servants were born to serve and to die doing exactly that, sentenced to "permanent inequality . . . obscurity, poverty, obedience for life." But in America, Tocqueville marveled, "servants are not only equal among themselves, but . . . equals of their masters." Which meant, said the incredulous Frenchman (who died of consumption five months after Patrick Kennedy did), "at any moment a servant may become a master."

Immigrant Irish women had been servile and obedient by necessity but hardly by temperament. A cartoon on the cover of *Puck* captured the public's view of the "uppity" Irish maid. A strong-armed woman, with head held high and broken plates at her feet, shakes a fist at a petite and pleading matron as a pot of water boils over and smoke pours from the oven. The caption: "The Irish Declaration of Independence that we are all familiar with."

Many biddies saw themselves in precisely that way, often living up to the stereotype of being impertinent, witty, strong — and rebellious. During her stints as a maid, Bridget must have been devising a plan to become her own master, to draft her own *declaration* . . . refusing to accept her lot, to remain stuck in servility. In America, Irish men often experienced decline — in their income, their control over the home, their overall sense of authority. They were downgraded from rebel farmers to ditchdiggers and grunts. But the women? Grunts back in Ireland, they'd become legitimate breadwinners in America, tasting an agency and freedom that they'd rarely experienced in their homeland, and likely never would have.

As men like her husband had worked outdoors amid noise and sawdust and sweat, Bridget had worked in fancy homes and was now employed in an elegant hotel. Despite the "No Irish" warnings, she'd found employers willing to hire a poor Irish maid, and she'd served them well.

But she'd wanted something more — less demanding work, better pay, and more promise. An unmarried, nonvoting, noncitizen servant in a land founded by "fathers," she felt stirred to step out of the muck. Her next step toward a better life for herself and her kids was a modest one. She decided to leave her job at East Boston's crown jewel, among "the most elegant and splendid edifices in New England," as one journalist described Sturtevant House.

She turned away from cleaning Yankees' homes and their hotel rooms and chose instead to style their hair. For a few pennies more per day.

Meanwhile, America was tearing itself in two.

11

Bridget the Hairdresser

THE CIVIL WAR wasn't her fight. Bridget didn't send a husband
or brother or son to join one of the Irish regiments. Her cousins
were too old to enlist, her daughters too young to become nurses
or volunteers. She saw many uniformed East Boston men march off
to the fight, but the war didn't directly affect her or her immediate
family—except maybe to cull the options for a possible husband
and leave more fatherless boys on the streets of East Boston.

At this turning point in American history, Bridget remained
mostly concerned with her job status and her family's survival,
matters that were always in jeopardy. For example, in December
1861, eight months after the fighting began, Bridget's employer,
Noah Sturtevant, was killed while traveling to his country farm
north of Boston. His horse got spooked at a railroad crossing and
bolted into the path of a train, dragging Sturtevant's carriage onto
the tracks.

At Sturtevant House, in the hallways, kitchens, salons, and par-
lors, staff and guests mourned their founder and patron, who left
behind a grieving household: wife, four children, three grandchildren, and three Irish maids. The *New York Times* called him "one
of the oldest and most prominent merchants of Boston," and the

Pilot praised the "wealthy and well-known citizen of East Boston." Across the island, flags were flown at half-mast.

Bridget seemed to take Sturtevant's death as a sign. Some time afterward, and perhaps prompted by it, she left her job at Sturtevant House, a career pivot that would further distance her from the caricatured Irish biddy. Once again, a boat would deliver her across water to a new phase of life.

East Boston's old-timey ferry system had evolved since the 1830s. The East Boston Ferry Company had reincorporated (Sturtevant was a director) and expanded its operations in the mid-1850s, followed by the launch of the new People's Ferry. The rival ferries introduced new boats and upgraded wharves, offering multiple routes and a half dozen crossings per hour, dawn to midnight. Commuters didn't quite view them as ferries of the *people,* however, and complained that the two-cent fare was "discriminatory and oppressive."

For Bridget, the ferry was a lifeline. A few days a week, she floated across toward the lights of Boston, joining packs of commuters on their daily back-and-forth ritual. Five minutes after leaving her island, she'd disembark at Sargent's Wharf, stroll south toward Washington and Avon Streets, later called "the busiest corner on Boston's busiest street." There, she'd enter the glass front doors of the multilevel Jordan Marsh store, to begin her day of washing, cutting, and styling the hair of well-off Boston ladies.

With her three girls on the verge of their teen years, Bridget would have tended to her share of female hair. She may have cut the hair of her sister maids before that, and perhaps done so for neighbors at her house, as many immigrants did, to earn side income. Whatever combination of skill and luck had led her to Jordan Marsh, she and her scissors were now entrusted with the locks atop some of the best-known heads in Boston.

Her new employer had risen from hardscrabble beginnings. He'd left his Maine home, fourteen and fatherless, and came to Boston to work as an errand runner at a dry goods store, later moving up to clerk. Eben Dyer Jordan opened his own shop in 1841, selling linen, yarn, and ribbons near the North End docks. His first customer was a young woman who arrived before dawn to buy a yard of red ribbon, and Jordan discovered that if he opened by 5 a.m., he'd catch the flow of foot traffic from the ferries and steamers. Marshall Field, his Chicago-based peer, later said he'd never met a more "enterprising, progressive or honorable man" than Jordan.

In 1851, Jordan partnered with Benjamin Marsh, who ran a nearby shop. Marsh's brother Charles came aboard and they formed Jordan, Marsh and Company, a beloved Boston institution and one of the nation's first "departmentalized" stores, expanding from silks and ribbons to selling kitchen goods, picture frames, books, clothing, stationery, carpets, and toys. By 1861, they'd outgrown their North End roots and moved into an expansive new home on Washington Street.

There, in the women's department, Bridget shampooed, trimmed, curled, dyed, and braided women's tresses, sometimes embellishing them with frizettes or wigs. In time, she would be named the department's chief hairdresser. No employee records from the era survive, so it's not known when Bridget started, how much she earned, and how she got to Jordan Marsh in the first place. Perhaps she had worked as a maid for the Jordan or Marsh family or for one of their friends. (By 1860, Jordan was worth more than $50,000 and employed four live-in maids, three of them Irish. He was known for his own unique hairstyle: enormous unruly tufts of gray sideburns, which he tugged on when nervous or impatient.) Or maybe Bridget met Jordan or someone he knew at Sturtevant House. Jordan or Marsh may have seen something in Bridget, by then in her midthirties, and offered her a slot at their new store.

But why take a risk on *her*? And what propelled Bridget to try for more than a biddy's due? What made her think she could defy the odds, keep and raise her kids, strive to become more than a lackey? It speaks to her drive that within a few years of widowhood, she had put aside both her mourning clothes and her maid's uniform to become a big-city wage earner, commuting with the hoi polloi into the heart of downtown Boston.

However it came to be, Bridget would study much more than hair at Jordan Marsh.

The five-story store was among the first to offer services and entertainment — a bakery and soda fountain, art and antique exhibits, music and fashion shows — in addition to customer-friendly practices like store credit and a "smile and take it back" guarantee. Like the first amusement park, the first baseball and football games, and other nineteenth-century American innovations, Jordan Marsh was one of those institutions that made anything seem possible. Even the *Pilot* praised "this energetic firm" and its mission to "benefit their patrons by a most liberal reduction in prices."

As Bridget walked to her station in the women's department, she passed silks and housewares, the latest styles from Europe. Her customers waited in the Ladies Parlor or the in-store library, reading magazines and newspapers or taking advantage of the free stationery to write letters. Bridget got a client settled in her chair and made small talk, breezily asking about the news, the weather, or the family, perhaps mentioning the war. She became an expert listener and used what she heard to convince customers that they needed things they didn't know they needed. She also abided by the principle her boss always emphasized: the customer was always right. Eben Jordan reminded every employee that a happy customer was the best advertisement. "Satisfy her at any cost," he said. "She is the boss."

From Jordan and her coworkers, Bridget learned about sales tactics, pricing, and public relations. From her clients, she absorbed the latest on fashion, food, and politics. She saw how the other half lived, once again witnessing the middle class in action. Another one of Eben Jordan's mottoes clearly struck a chord: "The better you serve your customers, the better you serve yourself." During her time at Jordan Marsh, Bridget would discover much about herself, about becoming her own boss, and about that uniquely American transition: from servant to master.

But as 1862 began, much of the talk at Jordan Marsh and elsewhere concerned more urgent topics: the escalating war with the South and its primary cause — slavery.

For Irish immigrants, the prospect of battle with the slaveholding states was a complicated issue. On the one hand, many Irish wanted to stand behind the nation that had given them a home after the Famine, slanting their loyalties heavily toward the Union. On the other hand, for those who'd been in America for little more than a decade, fighting to end slavery raised uneasy questions — and their religious leaders only confused matters.

Bridget might've viewed the situation like this: the Irish opposed slavery as morally wrong but were hesitant to support abolition if the Constitution implicitly allowed slaveholding and if war threatened to break apart the country. Another possibility is less flattering: the Irish didn't want to compete with formerly enslaved people for jobs.

We don't know what Bridget was thinking at the time, but many Irish, in Boston and beyond, wrestled with these and other questions: Should they fight? Why — and for whom? And whose voices should guide their decisions? Should they aspire to live up to the words of Frederick Douglass, born enslaved, who had visited Ireland during the Famine and extolled the Irish as "warm-hearted, generous, and sympathizing with the oppressed everywhere"? Then again, Douglass had grown frustrated with the Irish in America, who now seemed to "hate and despise the colored people," believing "the cruel lie . . . that our adversity is essential to their prosperity."

Should the Irish line up behind their bishops—Fitzpatrick in Boston, Hughes in New York—who for years tried to avoid appearing proslavery while stubbornly opposing abolition? Hughes once editorialized that although slavery was a "calamity," it was protected by the Constitution and therefore best left alone. He went so far as to suggest that enslaved people from Africa were possibly better off now, living in a more *Christian* land. (A historian has rightly called this "one of the most perfect pieces of idiocy ever penned by a Northern Catholic who insisted he was not a pro-slavery man.")

Patrick Donahoe's *Pilot* also wavered, which must've maddened readers like Bridget, who were seeking clarity. The newspaper decried slavery "in the abstract," calling it "a curse and blight upon the land." But it had been slow to adopt an antislavery stance, even after the Supreme Court's 1857 Dred Scott decision denied rights and citizenship to Black people, essentially endorsing America's "peculiar institution." Even the Catholic Church's official *History of the Archdiocese of Boston* would later call the *Pilot*'s passive support for slavery "shocking" and "regrettable."

The *Pilot* had tried to convince readers that abolitionists like William Lloyd Garrison, the Massachusetts-born publisher of the Boston-based newspaper the *Liberator,* were a danger to immigrants' fragile economic status. By 1861, as war came to seem inevitable, the *Pilot* stated its view more bluntly: if the enslaved people are freed, they'll take your jobs. "This is a simple truth. The white men of the free states do not wish to labor side by side with the Negro."

Irish refugees should have united in solidarity with enslaved Black people, and many abolitionists had long hoped to lure immigrants to their cause. As Garrison put it, the Irish came to America to "escape from the chains of British tyranny," after all, and now had an obligation to help end the "diabolical system of American slavery."

Decades earlier, the Irish lawyer and statesman Daniel O'Connell had been a hero of the antislavery movement, calling on his fellow Irish to "treat the colored people as your equal." He was quoted often in antislavery pamphlets and in Garrison's newspaper, whose name was a nod to O'Connell and his nickname, "The Liberator." (The *Boston Pilot,* also inspired by O'Connell, was named for his newspaper, the *Dublin Pilot*.) O'Connell had called American slavery a hypocrisy and a "stain on your star-spangled banner." He refused to visit the United States and wouldn't shake hands with anyone who supported slavery or, heaven forbid, owned slaves. "Those who countenance the crime of slavery, I regard as the enemies of Ireland," he said.

But O'Connell was long gone, dead since 1847. No other prominent Irish voice had been raised against slavery. In fact, one former Irish leader—John Mitchel, one of the Young Ireland rebels who'd been exiled to Tasmania in 1848 and had escaped to the States—had settled in Tennessee, where he ran a proslavery newspaper. His sons stood ready to fight for the South. Mitchel also stated his belief that Blacks were "innately inferior people," prompting Frederick Douglass to brand him "a traitor to humanity."

The Irish of Boston may not have believed slavery to be a "wholesome institution," as Mitchel did. Unfortunately though, all too many came to view Black people as their inferiors. (Frederick Douglass's son described marching in uniform through Boston, preparing to fight for the Union, when an Irishman had called him a "black nigger," and the *Pilot* was not shy about using racist slurs.) In their wavering and waffling, their rejection of Black neighbors as equals, the once persecuted people whom Douglass had praised for their "spirit of freedom" had chosen not to make slavery their fight.

Worse, they bought into the great lie that Black people were better off remaining as the property of others.

At Jordan Marsh and at Sturtevant House, on the ferry and on East Boston's streets, Bridget had few interactions with Black people, even if she was of the same low working class. Unlike New York, Chicago, and New Orleans, Boston was no model of integration. Of the nearly twenty thousand residents of East Boston at the time, fewer than a hundred were African American; many of them resided at the boardinghouse run by Philip and Coresy Ann Russell and their daughters, freed Blacks from Maryland. And of Bridget's hundred-plus coworkers at Sturtevant House in 1860, all had been white, as were her colleagues and customers at Jordan Marsh.

Free Blacks had first settled in Boston's North End after Massachusetts abolished slavery in the 1780s. When the North End began to fill with Irish, many Black families moved to the north slope of Beacon Hill, creating their own schools, churches, literary societies, and social clubs in the neighborhood called the West End. But the Irish spread there as well, contributing to a decline in Boston's African American population through the mid-1800s. It hovered around two thousand in the years before the Civil War —roughly 1.3 percent of the population, which revealed Boston to be one of America's least integrated big cities.

During the years-long crescendo toward war, the Irish saw hypocrisy in Boston's antislavery zeal. Some complained that Boston abolitionists showed more sympathy for the enslaved people in Southern states than for the Black or Irish people struggling to make a living in their own backyard, professing support for abolition while quashing the rights of local African Americans or Catholics. A decade earlier Harriet Beecher Stowe had published her best-selling antislavery novel, *Uncle Tom's Cabin,* while at the same time her father, Lyman Beecher, continued to stir up anti-Catholic hatred in his sermons. Henry David Thoreau, in his 1854 speech "Slavery in Massachusetts," had called on the state to "dissolve her union with the slaveholder" while elsewhere deriding the Irish as "shiftless," "slow and dull," stupid and drunk and guilty of "filth and folly."

And then there was Abraham Lincoln, who nursed an up-and-down relationship with America's largest immigrant group. Despite past concerns about the ballot-stuffing "Celtic gentlemen" who'd supported Stephen Douglas, the candidate who opposed Lincoln in his 1858 Senate campaign — and despite his wife's complaints about the "wild Irish" who cleaned their home and cared for their children — Lincoln mostly liked and trusted the Irish. They would serve in his army and his administration. He understood their suspicions of false piety among the Know Nothing abolitionists, once asking, "How can anyone who abhors the oppression of Negroes be in favor of degrading classes of white people?" Yet, although Lincoln had carried all of New England in the 1860 presidential election, most of Boston's Irish voted for his Democratic opponent, Douglas.

But when Lincoln's election prompted South Carolina to secede from the Union, followed by six more Southern states, which would together form the Confederate States of America, the Irish and the Catholic Church could no longer straddle. It was time to choose sides.

Bridget and her family and friends likely felt conflicted loyalties right up to the opening shots at Fort Sumter. There, the first victims of the War Between the States turned out to be two Irish immigrants fighting for the Union: one from Tipperary, one from Skibbereen, which had lost nearly half its residents to the Famine and emigration. Both men were killed when a Union cannon accidentally exploded. Among the Confederate musket shots being fired at the fort were those aimed by John Mitchel's son.

The *Pilot* had earlier claimed the Irish would "not move an inch" to support America's "fratricidal war," but now it declared allegiance to Lincoln: "We Catholics have only one course to adopt . . . Stand by the Union; fight for the Union; die by the Union."

Lincoln called up seventy-five thousand soldiers, and among the first to respond were Massachusetts regiments full of Irish soldiers, including the Twenty-Eighth and the Ninth, partly backed by Donahoe's *Pilot,* which played an active role in recruiting and fundraising. Thomas Cass, who had once led an Irish militia (the Columbian Artillery) that had been banned and disbanded by the Know Nothings, paraded his Ninth Regiment through Boston's streets before heading south, and the governor of Massachusetts, John Andrew, raised the Irish flag above Boston Common (a first), praising the patriotism of Boston's "adopted citizens."

When Lincoln approved more regiments from Massachusetts, the governor asked Donahoe to again recruit Irish soldiers, and the *Pilot* enthusiastically solicited volunteers, raised funds, and published stories of heroic Irish troops. "Irish Catholic bravery and patriotism are true to the nation and indispensable to it," wrote Donahoe, hoping the Irish displays of loyalty to the Union would silence the bigotry of the nativists.

Irish soldiers also filled the ranks of New York's Sixty-Ninth Regiment, led by the Irish immigrant Michael Corcoran. He had gained fame earlier for refusing to march his troops before the visiting Prince of Wales. Corcoran called the prince a "representative of my country's oppressors." He was facing court-martial for this action when the war began, but the charges were dropped, and he led his troops south, soon followed by Thomas Meagher, another Young Ireland rebel, exiled in Tasmania, who had escaped to America. Meagher recruited Irish volunteers with speeches and with newspaper ads that read: "Young Irishmen to Arms. To Arms Young Irishmen!" During a recruiting stop in Boston, Meagher told a crowd of two thousand that they now had a chance to prove they truly belonged in America. He would lead the upstart Irish Brigade and, like Corcoran, become a brigadier general.

West Point–trained generals struggled to make soldiers of Irish "street cleaners, bricklayers, and pig farmers," who were quarrelsome and (like the maids) defiantly untrainable. These men played fiddles at night, scorned military decorum, drank too much. Yet when it came time to charge into fusillades of enemy cannonballs, into musket fire and bayonets, they were fierce and fearsome, howling Gaelic battle cries—"Faugh a Ballagh" (clear the way)—and shrieking "For Ireland! For Saint Patrick!"

The *New York Times* saluted "the noble sons of Erin who have so fearlessly thrown their lives into the breach," and Lincoln went so far as to kiss the banner of the Sixty-Ninth Regiment during a visit to a camp south of Richmond, declaring, "God bless the Irish flag." Lincoln would also come to rely on what he called the "replenishing streams" of Irish soldiers.

As the body count grew, Irish troops and the Irish press began using the term "cannon fodder." The war photographer Mathew Brady, also an Irishman, captured the gruesome evidence: battlefields covered by Irish bodies, their arms, legs, and heads blown off. "We did not cause this war," said the *Pilot*. "But vast numbers of our people have perished in it." Bishop Hughes in New York declared that Irish Catholics had shed too much blood for the "clique of abolitionists in the North."

Then Lincoln issued the Emancipation Proclamation, which in early 1863 would make enslaved Black people, the backbone of America's economy up to this point, legally "forever free." Frederick Douglass called it "the greatest event in our nation's history," and the war turned into a moral battle for the freedom of enslaved people.

Some Irish leaders, like Meagher, embraced the moment, pledging "to the national cause" and in time speaking out as full-throated abolitionists. Others—notably Irish priests, bishops, and journalists—*still* resisted the opportunity to fight overtly on behalf of another oppressed caste.

And then the fighting Irish, so lauded for their ferocity and heroism, shot themselves in the foot.

In July 1863, the long-rumored national draft was launched, and heavily Irish crowds protested with a days-long rampage through the streets of New York City.

Many were angry about the terms of the draft, which allowed men of means to pay $300 for an exemption. Irishmen felt they'd already sent their share of bodies into battle and were now expected to send many more. They looted, vandalized, set fires. They attacked newspaper offices and even beat the Irish police superintendent, John Kennedy. Then the protests took a horrific turn as rioters targeted Black men, who could enlist to fight but (as not-quite-legal citizens) were exempt from the draft. Homes and businesses owned by African Americans were ransacked, and many Black people were beaten and killed—as many as a dozen were hanged from trees and lampposts. The mob set fire to the Colored Orphan Asylum as two hundred kids escaped out the back. The initial death toll of 119 was later determined to be far too low; five hundred or more may have died in the riots, most of them Black.

Federal troops arrived to restore order, and dozens of rioters were arrested, but of the sixty-seven eventually convicted, none received long sentences. A federal investigation into the riots petered out. Though funds were raised to help merchants who lost their businesses, the riots led to a steep decline in the city's Black population. At the time of the riots, African American soldiers with the Fifty-Fourth Massachusetts Regiment—the first with Black soldiers, including two of Frederick Douglass's sons—were storming rebel forces at Fort Wagner in South Carolina and, despite heavy losses, earned praise and respect for their valor, opening the door to more Black troops. The Irish, meanwhile, had proved themselves in battle but were now responsible for one of the worst riots in US history. Once again they were branded as violent thugs and "Celtic scum."

Boston worried about similar unrest among its Irish, who felt the draft was a "great injustice done to the poorer classes," said Bishop Fitzpatrick. As conscription notices were delivered, Irish men and even women began rioting in the North End, assaulting police and marshals. Rioters seeking weapons surrounded an armory, whose militia fired into the crowd, killing at least six. Catholic priests circulated letters, begging parishioners to accept the draft with "grace"—and to stay out of trouble. The letters were read at mass, and priests patrolled Irish neighborhoods to keep the peace, soothing angry adults and scolding unruly teenage boys.

Bridget's priests from Most Holy Redeemer walked the streets of East Boston, knocked on doors, pleaded with parishioners to stay inside. The *Boston Journal* reported that East Boston "complied with the order . . . like good citizens," and Boston's mayor thanked the priests "who labored to preserve quiet among their congregations."

Twenty months later, with the Thirteenth Amendment passed by Congress, abolishing slavery, a reelected Lincoln shared his hopes for an end to the war and a "just and lasting peace."

By the time Lee surrendered to Grant, nearly 150,000 Irish-blooded soldiers had fought for the Union (and 25,000 for the South), in some of the bloodiest battles in the history of warfare—Antietam, Fredericksburg, Gettysburg, Chancellorsville. The names of dozens of regiments included the word "Irish," declaring to America that immigrants were capable of fighting bravely and in large numbers. Their service as soldiers helped offset the evidence that the Irish also could be undisciplined and racist. But the nation (up north, at least) was, after four years of war, in a forgiving mood. The Irish emerged from the Civil War bruised and bloody, but smiling victoriously, even a bit cocky. "War-battered dogs are we," an Irish poet would later say of her country's warriors. "Gnawing a naked bone, fighting in every land and clime, for every cause but our own."

Though the Irish had resisted taking on the role of antislavery liberators, the postwar years would bring them progress and advancement, a closure of sorts twenty years after those first rotten potatoes appeared. "This is the only nation where the Irish can reconstruct themselves and become a power," Meagher had said at the start of the war.

Bridget indeed found herself in a remade city, where power would begin to change hands. Any complicated feelings about her people's behavior—the draft riots, the unwillingness to take a stand against slavery—were perhaps offset by the gushing patriotism and pride she'd witnessed at Jordan Marsh, which flew the Stars and Stripes and paid the full salaries of employees who'd enlisted. Eben Jordan had installed a recruiting station on the first floor and helped lead Boston's Sanitary Commission, which supported sick and wounded soldiers.

Like her adopted homeland, Bridget would emerge on the other side of war poised for transformation. Though the conflict hadn't come to her front door, the effects of the war and its aftermath would echo across her life, reshaping her career choices and creating new opportunities for her kids, especially her one surviving son.

Bridget had taken two steps forward—from maid to hotel employee to hairdresser—during the turbulent years since her husband's death. By 1865, the time seemed right for her to embark on a new adventure, another step forward, another risk.

12

Bridget the Grocer

WHILE SOME IRISH women were known to wear black for years after a husband's death — it's one reason Jordan Marsh created its Mourning Goods department, full of black dresses and veils — Bridget had put that grim costume aside long ago. Her black dress had been replaced by a housemaid's uniform at Sturtevant House, then a hairdresser's smock at Jordan Marsh. And now, at war's end, a new uniform altogether. Sporting a white shopkeeper's frock over her housedress, she walked the aisles, tallied her stock, made notes in a ledger book on what was running low, what needed restocking, what was collecting dust.

Over here were the teas, coffees, sugar, and flour, beside the scale used to weigh beans, rice, and spices scooped from barrels and bins. Over there, butter, cheese, eggs, and rashers, perhaps some mackerel, pickled salmon, cod. Standing at attention on shelves: bottles of relish, vinegar, honey, and molasses, beside the sperm and whale oil, the soaps and candles. At the counter, tins of hard candies, baskets of biscuits and bread. Arrayed out front, crates of fruits and vegetables and on a good day maybe the exotic bananas and "pine apples" Bostonians loved. Squeezed in or scattered elsewhere were the assorted dry goods, toiletries, ribbons, buttons, stationery, hosiery, and handkerchiefs that filled so many similar all-purpose neighborhood establishments, giving them their generic names — *variety shop, notions shop.* These immigrant-run mini marts, these mom-and-pop sundry shops, these convenience stores and bodegas: the striving toe-in-the-door outlets and emporiums of every working-class community, before and since.

And behind the counter? The good stuff — cigars and snuff, cider and ale, whiskey and brandy. Like many Irish grocers, Bridget almost certainly sold a bit of liquor or beer, the grocery-groggery combo having proved to be more profitable and customer-friendly than selling produce and staples alone. With sickness lurking in the water, some customers felt that pasteurized beer was a safer alternative, and it was cheaper than milk. As one grocer said of his liquor sales, "A man would hardly have dared to go into business without it." Said another: "Liquor is food."

If Bridget had chosen to apply for a city license, the document would've insisted: "Not to be drunk on the premises." That's if she'd bothered to pay the fifty-dollar fee; many shops and *shebeens* (Gaelic for private or illegal pubs) took their chances and sold liquor without a license.

The shop wasn't much. Just a narrow, street-level room displaying goods in boxes and barrels out front, atop crates and tables throughout the crowded aisles inside. But after nearly twenty years of working for others, she had a place of her own, where she was her own boss — a grocer, an entrepreneur. It had been a dream of hers and Patrick's, one they'd briefly realized before his death. And now she was bringing it back to life.

In Boston proper and in parts of East Boston, a proprietor might specialize in shoes or hats, baked goods or tobacco. In the lower-income neighborhoods, however, a general selection worked best, a bit of everything, sold at razor-thin margins. Assuming that Bridget ran her shop as the hundreds of male grocers did in Boston's immigrant neighborhoods, she would've collected cash and coins in a cigar box, tracked accounts in a handwritten ledger, kept stock in the basement or in her apartment, and allowed regulars to shop on credit, letting them add to their accounts but wary of those known to run up a bill. She'd have charged the going rates—sixteen cents for a dozen eggs, ten cents for a pound of sugar, fifty cents for English tea. She might've offered a money-back guarantee, as other shops did, as Jordan Marsh did. And by choosing to sell some booze (fifty cents for a quart of bourbon), her shop would've become a casual, communal spot for local gossip and grog.

As families settled into an era of peace, Boston's economy revived, putting a few more dollars in people's pockets. No more rationing to support the war effort. Time to get back to normal. It was a propitious time for a scrappy immigrant to become an American business owner.

Bridget's last day at Jordan Marsh marked the start (in 1865, it is believed) of a whole new life, a chance to finally paddle her own canoe. Her final commute across the harbor, perhaps a slow stroll toward the ferry to take it all in, took her north along Washington Street, then right at the Old State House, where the Declaration of Independence had been read from the balcony in 1776 (the building was now being rented out to merchants and small businesses). East to the wharves, then onto the crowded ferry, riding along until it bumped against those familiar wood pilings, heavy with immigrant history, welcoming her home.

Working at Jordan Marsh had offered Bridget a new perspective on how people really lived in the big, historic downtown across from her shaggy island of immigrants. She must've decided East Boston was her true home, the place where she was meant to live *and* work. She had clearly been inspired by her time at Jordan Marsh, by her boss's path from fatherless farm boy to entrepreneur. She'd absorbed motivating life lessons from Eben Jordan, whom the *New York Times* would later describe as a shining example of how "a penniless boy, by integrity, diligence, energy and enterprise, can build up a prosperous business."

Jordan had no doubt been good to her. It's even possible that he took an active role in helping her launch a shop of her own, as other merchants had helped him get his start—encouraging her, coaching her, perhaps even loaning a bit of start-up money. (Jordan was known to invest in other businesses and had a reputation for helping employees. He once paid off the mortgage of a widowed employee struggling to keep her small house and gave her son a job.) At a minimum, Bridget's time working for Jordan had left an impression, filled her head with visions of what was possible. Said the *Boston Globe,* "Jordan imbued every associate and subordinate with his own indomitable energy, constancy of application, and dash."

She'd witnessed the genesis of one-stop shopping at the kind of multilevel store that would threaten to replace neighborhood dry goods shops, tea rooms, and hair salons. She also witnessed women shoppers, socially and economically liberated after the hunkered-down war years, experiencing a new type of freedom. Boston's Edward Filene described these window-shopping destinations as an "Adam-less Eden" before creating Filene's Basement. Some historians credit department-store shopping with giving women a new sense of independence, possibly even accelerating the women's suffrage movement. Untethered from the home, women were becoming consumers and influencers. Like men, they could enjoy a restaurant meal, a social drink with friends. They used public transportation, visited banks and theaters.

Which led to some hand-wringing. The antifeminist writer Eliza Lynn Linton fretted that this trend—women walking the city streets, shopping, getting their hair dyed and styled—"leads to slang, bold talk and general fastness . . . to the desire of money."

In her essay "Wild Women as Social Insurgents," Linton wrote that female entrepreneurs "open shops and set up in business on their own." But she scorned such "shopkeeping and slumming" because it made women "bold and restless, rebellious to authority and tyrannous to those whom they can subdue . . . they are about the most unlovely specimens the sex has yet produced."

Bridget knew that not every woman wanted to shop at a downtown department store, nor could all afford to. There was still a need for the comforting corner store, a place for immigrants to buy directly from someone who spoke with the lilting and familiar brogue of family and friends left behind. The name of her first establishment, if it had one, is lost to history. In Boston business directory listings, it would in time be listed simply as "B. Kennedy" or "Shop by Kennedy," run by the "widow" Kennedy. Her store was located on Maverick Square, two blocks from her apartment and just a few doors away from Sturtevant House, alongside the river of pedestrians and carriage traffic flowing steadily to and from the ferries and the shipping docks.

According to some accounts, Bridget was first hired as an employee, then bought out the owners, who were struggling. Turnover in the grocery business was high, and the local papers, the *East Boston Argus-Advocate* and the *East Boston Ledger,* often advertised shops for sale or rent on Maverick Square or Border Street, some with living quarters situated above the first-floor store. Other accounts say she may have continued working at Jordan Marsh a few days a week after opening her shop and might've had to return to some housekeeping or hairdressing work now and then. She seems to have gotten her start sometime near the war's end — the 1865 state census lists her as "grocer" — though it would take a few years to get firmly established.

But she was largely on her own now, or at least on her way. Like other risk-takers operating a thousand similarly eager little immigrant businesses — saloons, salons, billiard halls, butcher shops, and bowling alleys — she was striving for independence, acceptance, and a slightly better future for her kids. Bridget was hardly one of the wanton "Wild Women" Linton *tsk-tsk*ed about, but her boldness reflected a changing city, in which Irish women and men were on a spirited ascent.

It had been more than a decade since a Galway man (Barney McGinniskin) had walked the beat as Boston's first Irish cop — "the first Irishman that ever carried the stick of a policeman anywhere in this country," the *Pilot* had boasted. McGinniskin would be fired, then reinstated, but fired again, as the Know Nothings rose to power. (He later became a barrel maker.) But McGinniskin's breakthrough into the police force, while brief, heralded the modest beginnings of a period in which the Irish became more fully integrated into city life. For the first twenty years after the Famine, the Irish had been Boston's unwelcome guests. They held the lowliest jobs. They were sick and poor, dirty and desperate, made to feel lucky that the city even allowed them to live there. They huddled together and slowly found their place (at the bottom), and mortified Boston had grudgingly adapted.

The postwar Irish were different. Their ranks now included military veterans, ex-generals, and celebrated heroes. No longer charity cases, they began holding their own as business owners, lawyers, and even landlords. From the late-1860s into the '70s, they found their way into city institutions, making inroads onto the police force and fire department and, in time, the polls. Politically, they had no direct voice: no Irish person had served on the city's eight-man Board of Aldermen, and only one had served on the forty-eight-man Common Council. That would soon change, and dramatically so, but not quite yet. Though the Democratic

Party preferred by the Irish was out of favor, stained by its stance on slavery, and though the party of Lincoln would dominate city elections for years to come, Irish politicians would make their mark on Boston soon enough.

The postwar years also saw Irish women begin to make their mark outside the home. Women had served in empowering new roles during the war, running relief agencies, working in field hospitals, organizing donation drives. They worked at factories and on the assembly lines at arsenals, producing ammunition and other matériel for the war effort. Some continued to work as nurses after the war. Some became teachers, and in time Irish American women would dominate that profession in many US cities. Others would work as labor activists, civil rights advocates, suffragists, and journalists. The *Pilot* would even hire its first female editor, Katharine Conway, a protégée of the paper's new postwar editor, the Irish immigrant rebel and poet-journalist John Boyle O'Reilly.

After the Fourteenth and Fifteenth Amendments expanded citizenship and voting rights for formerly enslaved Black men, leaders of the women's suffrage movement stepped up their efforts. The American Woman Suffrage Association established its headquarters in Boston in 1869, and a year later the *Woman's Journal and Suffrage News* began publishing there. (The National Woman Suffrage Association, more strongly opposed to the Fifteenth Amendment's omission of women, was created in New York, also in 1869.)

Old-school Boston wasn't especially happy about the rise of an Irish middle class, nor the swelling chorus of women agitating for the right to vote. Harvard-trained Protestant elites still dominated the city—the Brahmins, as Oliver Wendell Holmes had dubbed them in 1860, in an article for the three-year-old *Atlantic Monthly* magazine; he named them after a high-ranking class of Hindu priests and teachers in India. These men and their fathers, their names stamped all over Boston—Adams, Appleton, Cabot, Quincy, Lowell, Lodge, Peabody, Winthrop—had overseen one of the nation's most ethnically and culturally homogeneous cities. But as Boston absorbed more immigrants (not just Irish Catholics but newcomers from other parts of Europe and beyond), many founders' families had moved out to the suburbs or their country estates. And with slavery now abolished, more Black families took up residence in Boston, albeit slowly. Despite fighting in the all-Black regiments of Massachusetts, African American veterans would remain largely segregated in their West End community and kept out of certain jobs for years to come. (Boston wouldn't hire its first Black police officer until 1878.)

With other postwar demographic shifts, Boston found itself in the swell of a midlife crisis. The city's status as a leader in American politics, thought, culture, and literature was fading. It was no longer, in Holmes's words, the "hub of the solar system." Once considered the Athens of America, Boston was looking more like America's Dublin. Charles Dickens had found the city "bright and twinkling" on his first visit, in 1842. "Boston is what I would like the whole United States to be," he'd said, but during his return in late 1867, he changed his opinion. After landing at East Boston to start a months-long book tour—to read from *A Christmas Carol* (his tour is credited with easing New England's opposition to Christmas, which would become a national holiday in 1870)—the ailing author found a very different Boston. "The city has increased prodigiously in twenty-five years," he wrote to his daughter Mary. "It has grown more mercantile."

In East Boston, business was indeed recovering from its prewar slump. And in the middle of the action was Bridget's little shop on Maverick Square, close to her husband's former workplace and the docks where he and she had arrived, where immigrant ships continued to land at the Cunard Wharf. His memory surely followed her around like a ghost.

Bridget was busier than ever in those postwar years, tallying and balancing her accounts — more tobacco, rum, and bitters for Henry Barnard, more green peppers and gin for Rhoda Cook, more lamp oil and brandy for Dr. Russell. Her sister Margaret and the Barron cousins dropped in now and then, and her kids — ten-year-old P.J. and his teenage sisters — began to help, afternoons and Saturdays; the shop had become a hustling little family business. Another first-generation Irish boy recalled playing in the storeroom among barrels of sugar and flour at his parents' North End grocery shop, watching customers stream through the door, thrilled at "being right in the middle of everyone, where everything was happening."

At the height of the Famine, the London *Times* had grudgingly conceded this of the Irish: "among the many redeeming virtues of this intractable and unfortunate race is a strength of family affection which no distance, no time, no pressure, no prosperity can destroy." Bridget had for so many years been a victim, mistreated in Ireland and Boston, by the English and the Yankees. But she had emerged on the other side of her American acculturation having protected her family, hoisted them onto her back, and hauled them up to the front row of Boston's postwar economic revival.

Within five years of the war's end, Bridget and her kids seemed headed for a stable and more promising future. Then again, among the ranks of Boston's business proprietors there was that one obvious distinction. She was a *she* — marginalized by gender as well as ethnicity. She was a shop owner but could not easily become an official US citizen. (As a widow, Bridget could have applied to "inherit" her husband's naturalization, but that would entail court fees she couldn't afford.) She was the head of her household and the family breadwinner but not allowed to vote or hold elected office.

Her teenage daughters would confront similar limits. Bridget's son, meanwhile . . . she had high expectations for the young man of the house, despite emerging signs of some hooligan instincts. P.J. *would* be able to vote and *could* run for office, and in time he just might. If she could just keep her youngest out of trouble.

Part IV

BRIDGET AND P.J.

America will not allow her children to love her.

— FREDERICK DOUGLASS

13

P.J. the Rascal

FOR SOMEONE WHO'D later see his son and grandsons attend the best schools in America and who would even have a school named for him, P.J. Kennedy had a seemingly casual relationship with his own education. He was not an especially compliant student — nor, perhaps, a compliant son.

P.J. was seven when the war ended, when his mother opened her first shop. Soon after, he started attending the Lyman School, a crowded East Boston public school that couldn't quite sustain his attention. As was the case for many Boston boys — many left fatherless by heavy losses among Massachusetts troops — the classroom held far less appeal than what was happening outside the schoolhouse door, on the wharves and cobblestones of the postwar cityscape.

The rise of steam-powered, iron- and steel-hulled ships continued to weaken East Boston's boat-building economy, which for decades had thrived in support of sail-rigged clipper ships made of wood. The shipyards and piers became home to coal yards, ship-repair facilities, railroad docks, and freight haulers. Famed builders of three-hundred-foot clippers now settled for constructing thirty-foot tugs and pleasure craft. Other marine businesses converted to mills, shoe factories, lamp and oil factories. Layoffs and closures along the waterfront emptied lots and vacated shipyards, which became unsanctioned playgrounds for roving boys and girls—and, for some, death traps.

One of the jobs Bridget assigned P.J. from a young age, before and after school, was to search the fringes of the shipyards, lumberyards, and his father's former cooperage for scraps of wood for the family stove and fireplace. Broken barrel staves of white oak and fruit boxes for kindling were prized; so were chunks of coal gathered from along the railroad tracks. But danger loomed all around: horses and carriages, older boys and drunks. Seven-year-old James Frell was similarly scouring for bits of wood one day near a ship under construction below Central Square when a heavy plank fell from overhead and "smashed his brains out," said the papers. "His limbs quivered for a moment and he was dead."

Such accidents didn't prevent kids like P.J. from romping along the rough and risky waterfront, barefoot and wearing tattered knickers. He and his friends fished and clammed, swam and paddled in the harbor, skated and scampered across the ice in winter. They learned to sneak onto the ferries and hide in the fire room for a free ride to the city, skipped school to play stickball atop a wooden wharf. "Boston Harbor was a paradise for a boy in those days," one boy would later recall. Another would remember a friend rowing across to Boston to buy milk but, getting lost in a sudden fog, he ended up in South Boston at nightfall.

Kids drowned, slipped through thin ice, flipped over in a rowboat. Three preteen girls once drowned after climbing across a pile of lumber that collapsed into the harbor. Along the tracks, young bodies were ruined by freight trains or died by their own recklessness. One group of boys took turns playing with a pistol they found beside the tracks until the gun discharged into the face of thirteen-year-old William Rathburn; the ball shattered his jaw and dislodged an eye. "His recovery is considered doubtful," said the *Pilot*.

Thoreau once described his shock at seeing a gang of "ill-dressed and ill-mannered" Irish boys, ages ten or twelve, standing around smoking cigars. "A sad sight to behold!" he wrote in his journal, adding that they should be whipped and sent to bed. He also blamed the parents and their environment: the city of Boston. "What right have parents to beget, to bring up, and attempt to *educate* children in a city?"

Busy running her shop, Bridget had her hands full. She had no choice but to rely on others — teachers, priests, neighbors, her niece — to help educate and motivate her children. The *Pilot* would occasionally offer words of wisdom for restive boys, scorning delinquency as the "sins of young men of this extravagant and indolent age" and encouraging them to seek education and/or employment, lest they "turn out to be worthless vagabonds." The *Pilot* was stingier with guidance for girls, mostly advising them to become a "deserving young woman" and a good wife, "without resorting to strong drink." Like the March sisters in Louisa May Alcott's recently published *Little Women,* the Kennedy girls were facing the inevitable transition into young womanhood and the expected life of humble domesticity, and Alcott may have inspired them to believe they could make their own way in the world. But Alcott also knew, as her character Amy March says, "the world is hard on ambitious girls."

While P.J. would never be accused of being a vagabond, Bridget was learning that he wasn't particularly ambitious either. It became apparent that a seat inside schoolhouse walls was not where he'd thrive. No classroom could compete with the call of his island neighborhood, nor could a teacher or priest provide the survival lessons he'd learn on the docks and street corners.

· · ·

Back in 1852, Boston had enacted the nation's first law making school attendance mandatory. It required that children ages eight to fourteen go to class at least three months per year. In East Boston, more than four thousand students were taught at a dozen schools, including the island's first and only Catholic school, one of the first parochial schools in Boston.

Run by nuns from the Sisters of Notre Dame, the all-girls Our Lady of the Isle school had opened a few months after Patrick Kennedy's death, in early 1859, in the old St. Nicholas Church building beside Most Holy Redeemer church. Bridget's daughters may have been among the six hundred early students, although they're not listed as graduates in school records. If they had attended, like most working-class kids they'd have counted down the days until age fourteen, when they could legally leave school to find jobs. Mary, the eldest, would turn eighteen in 1870 and had begun working as a seamstress. Joanna, a year younger, would find work in a thread mill, and Margaret, the youngest, would later join her sisters in the workforce, possibly as a housemaid or a seamstress.

P.J. had fewer educational options than his sisters did, and his schooling began just a few years after a flare-up of protests to Protestant teachings in Boston's public schools. State law required that students memorize and recite Protestant versions of the Ten Commandments and the Lord's Prayer—slightly but meaningfully different from the Catholic versions—and to study the King James Bible, which Catholics despised. Those who declined were often whipped or expelled. Said one Irish boy who experienced the "torture" of public school at the time: "Nothing that was Catholic was right, and nothing that was Protestant could possibly be wrong."

At the Eliot School in the North End, an Irish boy named Thomas Wall repeatedly refused to recite the Protestant commandments

—his father and his priest forbade him to do so—prompting the submaster to whip the boy's hands with a heavy rattan stick until they were cut and bleeding. After thirty minutes of this treatment, Wall fainted. Wall's parents sued the school for assaulting their son, and hundreds of boys at Eliot, Lyman, and other schools joined the protests, refusing to say those "damn Yankee prayers." (The Eliot School's committee chairman was a well-known former Know Nothing.) Many students were expelled, some led away by police escort. Parents who pulled their kids from school risked witnessing their sons placed under arrest, charged with truancy, and sent to the state's reform school.

Bishop Fitzpatrick knew that parishioners' kids like P.J. were exposed to Protestant prayers and English-friendly history lessons that were offensive to Irish parents like Bridget. Ireland's conqueror, Oliver Cromwell, for example, was depicted as a hero in textbooks at the Lyman School, as were British monarchs. Fitzpatrick was disgusted by the "persecuting bigots," but he also made it clear to his flock that it was impossible for the church to build enough private parochial schools to accommodate all their kids. The bishop advised parents to hold their nose and keep sending their kids to the public schools, while he lobbied for change. Which came, but slowly. (East Boston's Father George Haskins would become the first Catholic to serve on Boston's school committee and played a role in convincing state lawmakers to make schools more palatable to Catholics.) When a new state law finally ended the mandatory reading of Protestant prayers, the *Pilot* celebrated the dying embers of Know-Nothingism—"disposed of by the Civil War"—and, Donahoe crowed, "at least we have received good out of evil."

Amid signs of slow-growing tolerance for Irish Catholics, Bridget might've hoped for her son to receive a less-offensive education, one that didn't carry the risk of whipping. But parochial schools were still in their infancy, especially those catering to trouble-seeking boys.

The Eliot School controversy accelerated the Catholic school movement. When Bishop Fitzpatrick died in 1866, his successor, John L. Williams (who'd officiated at Bridget's wedding), pushed even harder. But most of the schools that opened through the postwar years served only girls, leaving P.J. in a void: wrong gender for most Catholic schools, but too young for the new Boston College, which had opened in 1863. There, Jesuit priests taught Latin, Greek, math, and music to young men for thirty dollars a semester, but not to preteen boys like P.J.

So he ended up with other East Boston boys at the Lyman School, built near Maverick Square in the mid-1830s and named for a proslavery former Boston mayor. By the late 1860s, Lyman was crowded with working-class and immigrant kids mixed among Yankees, and P.J. was squeezed into classrooms fit for half as many. (The school would burn to the ground twice, in 1869 and 1871 — taking most attendance records with it — and would later become a branch of the Boston Public Library, considered the first "branch" library in the United States.)

Details of P.J.'s time in school are scant, and it's unclear how long he lasted at Lyman. He was remembered for his "attractive baritone" but showed little interest in sports or extracurricular activities. He was described as "not an earnest participant" but someone who preferred to encourage the efforts of others. A classmate's diary captured the gist of P.J.'s school years: visits to the statehouse or Faneuil Hall on field trips to "the city," library visits and reading assignments, an occasional lecture on temperance, music and choir practice. More interesting were the after-school highlights: racing to see a ship or house fire, watching a new boat launch or a cargo ship depart, sledding down "cow hill," collecting quahogs at the beach, and playing at the wharves until an angry longshoreman gave chase.

In general, P.J.'s prime school years coincided with a low point in education for first-generation Irish kids. Catholic schools were underfunded, crowded, and sometimes staffed by undertrained nuns or priests, who weren't always up to the task. And if parents strongly opposed the Protestant inclinations of the public schools, their kids often just dropped out and found a job.

Or got into trouble.

Ever since masses of Irish began to arrive in the 1840s, Boston had struggled to find the right approach to educating and *domesticating* the immigrants' unruly offspring. In the early post-Famine years, city officers arrested a thousand truant boys a year, many of them Irish, prompting the passage of the state's compulsory school-attendance law. Irish kids haunted Boston street corners for the next twenty years. After the war, the number of castaways and delinquents, orphaned or homeless, swelled further, the casualties of war. Catholic orphanages and public institutions couldn't keep up.

Clusters of boys gathered in public squares, in alleys, near the docks, and outside theaters or their fathers' watering holes. Some boys sought useful work, tending horses, delivering groceries, selling fruit, hawking newspapers, shining shoes. But there were never enough jobs to go around. Other kids formed gangs and sometimes got rounded up, charged with disturbing the peace or with "riotous proceedings" and fined a few dollars—if they were lucky.

The unlucky were sent to Boston's House of Reformation for Juvenile Delinquents, the brainchild of ex-mayor Josiah Quincy III, who'd envisioned a nurturing institution where wayward youth might be rehabilitated. Admirably forward-thinking for its time, this charitable concept drew praise from the occasional famous visitor. Alexis de Tocqueville, after a tour in 1833, called the

House of Reformation a "most original and daring plan of reform." Over time, though, this facility began to fill with not just truants but vagrants and those living "a wanton and lascivious life," as a city report put it. The city also began sending orphaned children there, and by the 1860s the House of Reformation was essentially a crowded prison, and only meager attempts were made at reforming or teaching its juvenile inmates.

Jutting into the harbor just east of East Boston, Deer Island became home to the highest concentration of criminals in all of New England: the House of Correction and House of Industry each held four to five hundred adult inmates, who were not always kept separate from the juveniles at the House of Reformation or the hundreds of unfortunates housed nearby at the Lunatic Hospital, the Almshouse, and the quarantine ward. These facilities were dangerously outdated and overcrowded, with adult prisoners sometimes held in an attic above teen girls and boys. Once, when a boys' dormitory at the House of Reformation burned, the kids were moved into the correctional facility where drunks and prostitutes were held. Annual reports from directors of these institutions reminded city officials that teen truants, orphans, the sick, and the poor too often mingled under the same roof as the criminals, calling the "contiguity of paupers and prisoners irksome and objectionable." One 1864 investigation also found multiple cases of "cruelty and inhumanity" —boys lashed with a leather wagon whip and a seventeen-year-old girl beaten on the back and shoulders with a rattan and held in solitary confinement, where prison inspectors found her bruised and bloody. The unrepentant superintendent boasted, "I struck her with all my might, and sent for a longer stick."

Patrick Donahoe called the island "a pauper and penal colony" and complained for years about Protestants running institutions full of Catholic inmates. After the war, Donahoe joined the Board of Directors for Public Institutions, giving him some say in the city's treatment of Irish "street boys," as he called them.

In 1870, one of those boys was P.J. Kennedy. He joined the hundreds of teen inmates at the House of Reformation, who slept side by side at night in long rows of metal cots, spaced a foot apart, in a facility surrounded by paupers' graves filled with hundreds of Famine victims.

What did P.J. do to earn a visit to Boston's island of miscreants? Was he skipping school, loitering where he shouldn't have been? Was he caught stealing or trespassing, or had the city court designated him a "stubborn child," the catch-all term for a ruffian? Record keeping on Deer Island was notoriously shoddy, and of the few documents that survive, none shed light on the nature of his infraction. If he'd committed a serious crime, he might've appeared in the sheriff's logbook of lawbreakers for 1869 or 1870, but his name isn't among the hundreds of teens charged with assault, malicious mischief, breaking and entering, larceny, or lewdness. Perhaps Bridget asked the city to take P.J. off her hands, to scare him straight for a spell, as Irish widows were known to do. Most likely P.J. was merely a truant, a distracted and indifferent student. At the time, police and truant officers often sent school-skippers directly to the House of Reformation without a court appearance, so their names might never appear in court records. Regardless of what landed P.J. on Deer Island, once there he was treated like all others — that is, like a criminal. One prison inspector wrote: "Some of these boys are taken from good homes and are sent to this Institution to be reformed as well as educated. Instead of receiving schooling, he is worked like a prisoner, fed like a prisoner, and governed like a prisoner." The "reform goals" of the once-progressive House of Reformation had been abandoned, so P.J. would have lived and worked alongside drunks, paupers, and the mentally ill.

Younger boys did attend some classes—math, writing, singing, woodworking—but teens and preteens like P.J. often ended up digging trenches for water pipes, tending to the piggery, working on the farm, maintaining the seawall, mending fences, repairing and painting the superintendent's house. Boys ended up on Deer Island for all sorts of reasons. At the time of P.J.'s detention, most of the 280 boys there—ages twelve to eighteen, a few as young as eight or nine—were truants or vagrants. Some were "common beggars" or orphans awaiting adoption. One boy was charged with playing cards on a Sunday, another with "engaging in a prize fight." Their sentences ranged from a few months to two years. In one infamous case, a twelve-year-old East Boston kid, Michael O'Brien, was arrested for stealing three newspapers and sentenced to *nine* years. He was there at roughly the same time as P.J. until an outpouring of newspaper stories and editorials—including a letter to the *Pilot* accusing the judge of targeting boys who "happen to be called Michael or Patrick"—prompted a judge to pardon O'Brien and release him.

It's not hard to imagine Bridget's fear and frustration when her only son was released and sent back home. (Truants were usually sentenced to thirty days, but P.J.'s precise number of days inside is unknown.) She had tried to keep him out of trouble, away from the temptations of the street, giving him chores and errands around the shop. She might've wished for a more studious and compliant kid, like P.J.'s classmate Aaron Rogers, whose diary chronicles an innocent boyhood spent playing marbles and checkers, having snowball fights with friends, collecting kindling, emptying the ashes, whittling toy tomahawks, and drawing or reading around the fire at night. Rogers also confided to his diary a family life that P.J. might've dreamed of: "Helped father paint house . . . Helped mother make candy . . . Played with my brother."

Back at the Lyman School to conclude his schooling, P.J. returned to the milder routines of class concerts, theater performances, and field trips to the city. He also listened to talks by the governor and one by the longtime US senator Charles Sumner. As the only male in his family, with no brother to play with nor a father to do chores for, P.J.'s visits to the statehouse would have exposed him to the chaotic spectacle of state government, which was entirely dominated by men.

After school, some boys came home to find their mother prepping dinner for a hardworking husband. In the Kennedy household, it was P.J. and his sisters and their hardworking mother, each doing their small part to pitch in after Bridget's day at the shop. Perhaps she was relieved that her children were approaching the end of their school years. The profits from her shop, smaller than others in the neighborhood, couldn't have amounted to a lot. She was ready for her kids to find jobs.

Fortunately, her son would soon find his way into the workforce —slowly at first, then discovering an entrepreneurial talent that he surely inherited from his mother.

14

P.J. the Longshoreman

AFTER HIS ERRATIC early teens — his unimpressive stint at the Lyman School, his time on Deer Island — P.J.'s tentative steps toward adulthood led him down to the East Boston docks.

Years earlier, in a series of motivational articles, the *Pilot* had urged Boston's Irish street kids to "pursue some honest calling" and not be ashamed to be useful.

"Boys," one article read, "banish from your bosom the dangerous desires to live without work. Labor is honorable, dignified; it is the parent of health, wealth, and happiness; look upon it as an invaluable blessing, and never as a burden and a curse."

By his late teens P.J. found the desire to work and a place to be useful. Just like the father he never knew, he joined East Boston's low-rung waterfront working class. He began toiling as a longshoreman, hauling sacks of wheat and sugar, bales of cotton and wool; shouldering fresh beef; and rolling barrels and casks onto and off steamships.

Dockers, wharfies, and longshoremen (abbreviated from "along the shore men" and sometimes printed as *'longshoremen*), and the stevedores who hired them (an anglicizing of the Portuguese *es-*

tivador and Spanish *estibador* — "a man who *stuffs*"), had their own
unique language and social hierarchy, and a well-honed reputation
for drinking, fighting, and dying. Men regularly fell through open
hatches, into ship's holds, and often overboard. Casks and boxes fell
on them (or others), bones were broken, and fingers, toes, and legs
severed. One East Boston longshoreman lost a leg to a fallen box
of bacon; another was crushed by a cask of tobacco. One of P.J.'s
peers got caught between a steamer and the pier and was crushed to
death; another tripped while rolling a barrel of flour up a flight of
stairs — the man and his barrel tumbled right back down the steps
and killed his two-year-old daughter. "The affair was exceedingly
sad," the *Pilot* reported. Other injuries resulted from boozy brawls.
Three men once stumbled out of Glavin's saloon late one morning,
then down to the docks, hoping to get hired to load blocks of ice
onto a steamship. When the stevedore told the drunks he didn't
need their help, they began to argue, and one tossed his drinking
buddy into the harbor. The man hit his head on the way down and
drowned.

P.J. and his fellow dockers faced a gauntlet of risks each day, for
little pay and no guarantee of a stable job. They worked atop rickety wharves that threatened to topple during storms, surrounded
by taut hauling cables that sometimes snapped and severed limbs.
They maneuvered inside aging steamships powered by poorly
maintained boilers that sometimes exploded and sent bodies flying.
Once, when a dock foreman went to fix a pump, the engine's fly-
wheel shattered, "tearing away one side of his head and scattering
his brains in every direction."

At the time, when a ship pulled up to an East Boston pier, a stevedore was hired to oversee the offloading of cargo and was paid by
the ton. The stevedore in turn hired a crew of longshoremen, paying them thirty to fifty cents an hour. Unskilled dockworkers were

at the mercy of the needs and whims of the stevedores, the finances of their bosses at the shipping company, and the unpredictable shipping traffic. If fortunate, a longshoreman might get hired for a month at a time. Most were day laborers hired for just a few hours.

Dozens of men on the stevedore crews for Cunard Steamship Company and National Dock Company in East Boston went on strike in 1872, hoping for a ten-cent increase in their hourly rate of thirty cents. The strike was "an entire failure," the *Boston Globe* reported, as the shipping companies easily found replacement workers, then blackballed the strikers.

After rising briefly to forty cents an hour, longshoremen's pay dropped back to thirty cents during the shipping slump in the late 1870s. That's when P.J. joined this brotherhood — and presumably their union. A longshoremen's union had been created years earlier, but attendance at meetings lagged and the organization was poorly run. When agents from the Leyland Steamship Line and the Warren Company told longshoremen their hourly pay was being cut again, this time to twenty-five cents, the union revived its meetings and tried to rally the public to its cause. The union's president, James Tarone, told a crowd of four hundred longshoremen, "If we wish to be considered men among men, we must stand firm and hold fast to our standard of labor."

P.J. and the others faced a harsh reality: longshoremen were expendable. Like pack mules, these unskilled grunts were needed to shift big loads during peak shipping seasons but were considered just a nuisance during lulls.

One subset of Boston's dockworkers did not join the union. Called "lumpers," they stood near the docks, hoping to get tapped for enough work to afford a few days of drink, like the laborers who'd later stand on corners, waiting to be hired for day gigs. Daniel Skerry, an Irish immigrant lumper in East Boston, described his way of life to a *Globe* reporter: he'd work for three weeks, drink for a few weeks, sometimes get jailed on Deer Island, then find his way back to East Boston's docks.

P.J. wasn't a lumper and wasn't exactly one of the boys—not a day drinker nor a barroom brawler. He did pack on muscle and looked the part: wiry limbs, leathery hands, weathered face. He was just an untrained laborer, not even a tradesman like his father. His only skill was strength; his tools were his arms and his back. The dangerous and sometimes deadly job, which P.J. held through his late teens, into the late 1870s, before briefly ascending a rung to the role of stevedore, exposed him to the politics, corruption, boozing, and violence that would later leave Marlon Brando beaten and bloodied as a whistle-blowing longshoreman in Elia Kazan's *On the Waterfront*. P.J. witnessed the same dockside scuffles between good and evil that Budd Schulberg had mined for his screenplay. As the activist priest played by Karl Malden put it, "You want to know what's wrong with our waterfront? It's the love of a lousy buck. It's making love of a buck more important than the love of man!"

Working among the lowest classes of East Boston workers, P.J. also met the ward leaders and union men who were recruiting grunts to their causes, as well as the saloonkeepers luring them to barstools. He worked beside the Italian immigrants who'd begun to arrive in Boston, taking on the menial jobs as the Irish slowly found work as police officers and firefighters. He observed the simple pageantry of commerce, one bale of cotton, crate of pineapples, and pickle barrel at a time. In later years, he'd rarely mention his time on the docks, though those days clearly resonated deeply and would directly affect his future career choices—and political inclinations.

Also frequently sighted along the waterfront were nuns from the Sisters of Notre Dame de Namur, on the lookout for stray kids and streetwalking women. The nuns would stand by as passenger ships offloaded young immigrant women, scooting them away from the proprietors of houses of ill repute, who tried to recruit prostitutes from among the new arrivals. East Boston's shipbuilding industry may have waned, but one constant remained: the influx of immigrants, still mostly Irish but by the late 1870s joined by new waves of Italians, Jews, Portuguese.

P.J. would see them shuffling down the gangplanks, wide-eyed and wobbly-legged. And Bridget would watch them lug their bags and their children up toward Maverick Square, looking for a meal, a cheap apartment, and a job, just as she had done thirty years earlier. Some of the newcomers would stop at her shop for a loaf of bread or a tin of herring. Among those stepping off the passenger ships onto East Boston soil were Bridget's relatives—sisters, nieces, and nephews, arriving from Liverpool, Dublin, and Queenstown over the two decades that followed the Civil War.

As P.J. continued a jagged path into adulthood, his sisters, aunts, and cousins were making life transitions of their own. His older sisters Mary and Joanna had left school to work in factories—Mary still toiling as a seamstress, now specializing in making shirts, and Joanna working in a jute mill, possibly the Methuen mill in Lawrence, or perhaps the mills in Salem or Lowell. (There's a bit of mystery as to sister Margaret's whereabouts: according to the 1870 census, she wasn't living with Bridget. She would have been fifteen and may have been staying with relatives or possibly working elsewhere.) Bridget's daughters, like anyone then working in a mill, knew the tales of fires and strikes, cruel foremen and child labor, about the injuries and indignities that came with the job of seamstress, weaver, bobbin winder, loom operator, needleworker. Jack London, born around this time, worked in a jute-twine mill at age fourteen, amid the "muffled roar of the loom [and] the pounding, shrieking machines . . . earning no more than when I worked in the cannery several years before." London later wrote about the toll that mill work exacted on young bodies like his: "All his bones ached. He ached everywhere."

The most frightening mill story of all was the 1860 implosion of Pemberton Mill, in Lawrence. This massive sweatshop employed eight hundred workers, many of them women and children, mostly Irish and Scottish. To boost profits, the mill had been overloaded with machinery and the whole building collapsed, trapping hundreds. As rescue efforts began, a kicked-over oil lantern ignited piles of cotton and fire raced through the crumpled building, killing scores of trapped workers. Said the *Boston Journal:* "the black, shapeless mass of debris was wrapped in flames. Before midnight every voice inside the ruins was stilled in death."

At age nineteen, Joanna left home to marry a twenty-five-year-old machinist and "pleasant fellow" from Roxbury named Humphrey Mahoney, also the child of Irish immigrants. Mary and Margaret would find their husbands a decade later, at twenty-seven and thirty-two, consistent with a proclivity among Irish women to work first, marry and procreate later.

Bridget had for years written to her family back in Cloonagh, and to her husband's family in Dunganstown, updating the Murphys and Kennedys on the assorted weddings and births, such as the arrival of her first grandchild, a boy named Daniel, born a year after Joanna and Humphrey had wed. Unfortunately, there was tragic news to share too. Baby Daniel died of diphtheria in late 1875. A month earlier, Joanna had given birth to her second child, Mary, who died at six weeks, also of diphtheria. Daniel and Mary were buried beside their grandfather Patrick.

All three of Bridget's daughters would confront the reality that many first-generation Irish Americans faced: they were hardly guaranteed lives better than those of their immigrant parents. Joanna and Margaret would in time give birth to eight children each, and half of them would die young — five of Joanna's kids and three of Margaret's, gone by age six. Mary would lose two of her six kids. In fact, of P.J.'s twenty-two nieces and nephews, only twelve would live past age six.

In addition to sharing tragic news with her Irish relatives, Bridget continued to suggest in letters to her sisters, Ann and Catherine, that they follow her path—as their sister Margaret and Catherine's daughter, Mary, had done. *Come on over. Now's the time.* And they did.

After raising their families in County Wexford, with more than a dozen kids between them, Catherine and Ann had decided that Ireland, still controlled by the English crown and Catholic Church, held little promise. Like others who'd stayed through the terrible post-Famine years and the country's slow recovery, they were ready to throw in the towel and follow in Bridget's footsteps.

Both had lost a husband: Catherine's had died in East Boston a year before Patrick Kennedy's death, and Ann's husband (also named Patrick Kennedy) died in Ireland in 1870. Bridget's other sister, Margaret, was still living in East Boston but her husband, yet another Patrick, had also died. Three of Bridget's four sisters were now widows, just like her. (Her youngest sister, Johanna, would remain on the family farm in Cloonagh, unmarried.) Catherine came to Boston in 1870 and Ann arrived a year later, each bringing at least two of their children. All of them settled in East Boston, within blocks of Bridget and her shop.

The lives of Bridget, her kids, and her sisters were temporarily disrupted by the series of fires that destroyed parts of East Boston through the early 1870s. One conflagration spread ashore from a waterfront planing mill, destroying acres of homes and businesses along Border and Liverpool Streets. Another fire ravaged a swath of East Boston's wharves, warehouses, and ferry docks, caused by an explosion of combustible hemp bales and sugar sacks, casks of linseed oil and stacks of gunny cloth. The *Boston Globe* lamented "our already sadly burdened city," a reference to the Great Boston Fire of 1872, as it would be known. The worst in city history, its flames visible from a skittish East Boston, the fire left behind blocks of black rubble, bankrupted merchants, left hundreds of families homeless and twenty dead. Among the casualties was Patrick Donahoe's ornate new *Pilot* headquarters and printing press. The loss pushed him to the edge of ruin. Facing bankruptcy, he was forced to sell the *Pilot* to Archbishop John Williams (but would buy it back a decade later).

In East Boston, entire streets were rebuilt, breathing new life into the neighborhoods around Maverick Square, the Kennedys' home turf for decades. Making the most of this renewal, Bridget moved into an apartment in a rebuilt three-story home at 25 Border Street and opened a new street-level shop there, sometime in 1875.

After so many years of moving from place to place—at least a dozen relocations over the years, with five different apartments along Havre Street alone—Bridget had finally settled in the place where she could stay *put*. Border Street would remain Bridget's home for the rest of her days. She had also moved her store a few times before finding this promising new location—a home for the shop, for her family, for herself. Bridget's grocery shop became the hub for her growing family, a constellation of Murphys, Kennedys, Roches, and various in-laws.

At first, P.J. and his sister Mary lived with Bridget above the shop, while Joanna and Humphrey lived next door. Bridget's sisters lived within a few blocks. (They'd later move to Salem.) As always, the memory of Patrick was never far. Her new address was mere steps from their first apartment, just uphill from the spot where they'd arrived thirty years before.

When a chimney fire damaged the house next door, and the

tenant moved out of 23 Border Street, Bridget rented that building too. Bridget now held the lease for the two adjacent properties, 23 and 25 Border Street; she began living at number 23, while her grocery/variety store/bakery occupied the ground floor at number 25. She sublet the upstairs apartments of both houses to her children and other boarders, mostly incoming Irish relatives and other immigrants.

The widowed shop owner was now, improbably, a business owner, a landlady, and, in time, the rare female property owner. She would eventually take out a $1,000 mortgage to buy 25 Border Street outright. (The owner of both Border Street buildings was the wife of a local doctor and druggist who'd died in 1866. She may have sympathized with another widow.)

With her business thriving, Bridget could play other roles: enabler, connector, even matchmaker. She wrote to Ireland, offered relatives a place to stay. Her tenants became friends to her children, and one would become a son-in-law. She helped people, she gave back — to the Irish émigré community, her neighborhood, her church — and taught her children to do the same.

Thus grounded, her shop was able to expand and grow. Family members helped with chores, young ones ran in the aisles and played out back. When he wasn't down on the docks, P.J. would stop by to stock shelves and deliver parcels to neighbors. A nineteenth-century writer described the poetic chaos inside such Irish-run family shops: "piles of cabbages, potatoes, squashes, egg-plants, tomatoes, turnips, eggs, dried apples, chestnuts, and beans rise like miniature mountains round you . . . The cross-beams that support the ceiling are thickly hung with hams, tongues, sausages, strings of onions, and other light and airy articles, and at every step you tumble over a butter-firkin or a meal-bin — while the shelves behind are filled with an uncatalogueable jumble of candles, allspice, crackers, sugar and tea, pickles, ginger, mustard, and other kitchen necessaries." Cigars went for a penny, coffee and a slice of mince pie for a few cents, a tin of ginger snaps for a dime.

As a local businesswoman, Bridget came to be known as a "strong, cheerful woman . . . liked and respected," with "a generous heart" and "a deep native shrewdness . . . a *determined* woman." Other scrappy businesses along Border Street included Ann Brimmer's fancy goods shop, John Foley's boot shop, Charles Milant's cigar and snuff shop, Parker and Grindell's boardinghouse, Mulloy's chocolates, and Keough's grocery. Elsewhere in the bustling community: a coal dealer, a picture framer, shipsmiths, caulkers, saw sharpeners, machinists, coopers, carpenters, blacksmiths, cabinetmakers, boilermakers, and steam fitters. And, as in most Irish tenement neighborhoods, there was plenty of liquor being sold — two dollars for a gallon of port or sherry; California wine for forty cents a quart; "Pure Rye Whiskey" for $2.50 a gallon.

Bridget's shop became a destination for local biddies, cooks, and seamstresses to gather and gossip — and perhaps tipple. One chronicler of urban American life at the time (a roving and sometimes crass reporter from Horace Greeley's *New York Tribune*) said establishments like Bridget's were full of "Irish women and sluttish house-keepers." And along the walls: "upright casks containing lamp-oil, molasses, rum, whisky, brandy, and all sorts of cordials . . . a long, low, black counter, armed at either end with bottles of poisoned fire-water, doled out at three cents a glass to the loafers and bloated women who frequent the place."

No details of Bridget's selling of firewater survive, but her new enterprise on Border Street would clearly have an influence on her son.

At the time, Bostonians were as thirsty as ever for beer and whiskey. Breweries and taverns blossomed, even as the forces of temperance were circling. During the mid to late 1870s, state and local laws governing the sale and consumption of alcohol were in constant flux, a confusing and sometimes contradictory patchwork of statutes. Over some stretches the sale of hard liquor was prohibited entirely, though the laws were often sporadically enforced, leading many Bostonians to risk arrest by selling liquor or beer out of their own homes.

Conflicts over the sale of liquor had escalated in the postwar years. The state legislature had yielded to prohibition lobbyists and proposed banning the sale of all "spiritous" liquor, leaving only lower-alcohol beverages (beer, ale, wine, cider) on the market. The *Boston Post,* in a full-page rant, called this proposal "extreme and unusual" and insisted that "it is the right of every citizen to determine for himself what he will eat and drink." The former governor John Andrews, in heated testimony before lawmakers, blasted the proposal as government overreach and a blow against personal freedom — "fatal to any liberty . . . the cornerstone of despotism." Andrews said banning liquor would kill small businesses (saloons and grocers), punish responsible drinkers, and drive Bostonians to opium. (Andrews died later that year, at his home, while sipping tea.) At one of the many public hearings on liquor laws, even the Catholic Church weighed in, including one of the Kennedys' former priests. Father George Haskins testified that yes, his parishioners drank, and yes, he'd seen liquor sellers multiply in Irish neighborhoods. But prohibiting liquor sales wouldn't eliminate drinking — it would simply "drive it out of sight."

Some legislators complained that such laws punished the seller, not the user. The *Pilot* argued the opposite, decrying the hypocrisy of a system that would send a thirteen-year-old boy to Deer Island for drinking but not "prosecute the parties who sold it to the full extent of the law." The *Pilot* complained: "We have expended our stock of abusive adjectives in writing of the Prohibitory Law; but we wish someone would invent a new dictionary for the express purpose of exposing pharisees and humbug. Under the eyes of our 'stringent prohibitory law' there are 1,768 open bars in the city of Boston!"

By the late 1870s, prohibition efforts had failed and a new (though still evolving) series of laws were enacted. Suffolk County transferred the responsibility of liquor licensing to the city of Boston, which doled out licenses to hotels, grocers, breweries, saloons, restaurants, and pharmacies. The grocers' licenses, as well as most of those for distillers and druggists, gave clear directions about consumption: "Not to be drunk on the premises." And, well . . . good luck with that. Most groceries in Irish neighborhoods could still be counted on to perform double duty as a corner watering hole, whether they opted to get a license or not.

Spots like the whiskey bar at Paul Revere House or the saloon at Hancock House, formerly owned by John Hancock and his brother, willingly paid for their licenses. (It was a new thing, turning Revolutionary War homes into pubs: "ancient temples remodeled to become barrooms and saloons," as one writer described them.) But mom-and-pop shops might prefer not to give fifty dollars to the city, even if they risked penalties if caught. East Boston's District Court regularly heard cases of unlicensed grocers or apothecaries selling liquor, selling to minors, or selling on Sundays, and police regularly raided shops, confiscating any liquor they found. If convicted, violators faced hundreds of dollars in fines or even a stay on Deer Island. The *Boston Globe* detailed the case of a Vermont grocer (also named Bridget Kennedy) charged with 295 counts of illegally selling liquor. Some of her customers, after getting arrested for public intoxication, snitched on her, and Kennedy was sentenced to forty-eight years in jail, which the *Boston Globe* called "oppressive and excessive." She was released on appeal by the state supreme court after two months.

Our Bridget Kennedy does not appear on the lists of grocers

licensed to sell booze at that time. It was rare for a woman to be issued a liquor license, and only a few female names appear among the thousands of licensees during the periods of legal liquor-selling through the 1860s, '70s, and '80s. A female business owner of any kind remained an exception, despite the progress women had made in other areas. In fact, most female entrepreneurs still needed a husband's *permission* before Boston would let her legally open a storefront enterprise. Before launching a sausage shop, boarding-house, bakery, salon, or grocery, most women were expected (based on an 1862 law) to apply for the "Married Women Doing Business" certificate, a rather demeaning document that listed the husband's name and the type of business.

Bridget's "Shop by Kennedy," as it was listed in local records, operated modestly, under the radar. She didn't advertise in the papers, as D & P Morrison did — "Tomatoes 8c per can . . . New Valencia Raisins 5c per pound . . . New Turkey Prunes 5c per pound." She kept her head down, quietly breaking barriers as one of the few female grocers in Boston. In one official tally of business owners, of those declaring themselves "merchants," fewer than a dozen were women; among the grocery stores, none were female-owned. By 1880, having begun selling baked goods at the shop, Bridget told a census worker that her occupation was "baker" — one of just five women counted by the city of Boston in that profession. And yet, in business directories, she and her shop would continue to be listed with that all-important marital status: "Kennedy, Bridget — widow." It was a little degrading.

A city still acclimating to a shift from Brahmin aristocracy to immigrant enterprise was further challenged by the rise of business-savvy and politically inclined women. Although they could not vote, Boston women were increasingly claiming titles other than *mother, wife, housekeeper, widow,* making their way deeper into the workforce as teachers, nurses, and social workers. One *Pilot* story, titled "What Women Are Doing," gushed over the rise of female preachers, doctors, and lawyers. Among journalists in Boston, New York, Chicago, and Philadelphia, "there are hundreds of women who earn a livelihood by their pen," said the *Pilot*. "Within the last few years, women have entered into the writing profession with alacrity, and have pursued it with respectable success." (Though the *Pilot* considered the rise of professional women "wonderful," it would be a few more years before the paper employed its first female reporter.) This period saw the rising careers of the journalist Nellie Bly, the temperance advocate and suffragist Frances Willard, the women's rights activists Susan B. Anthony and Elizabeth Cady Stanton, in a national moment as women found new callings. In 1877, one longtime activist and writer-editor, Sarah Josepha Hale (credited with encouraging Lincoln to declare Thanksgiving a national holiday in 1863), at age eighty-nine wrote her final column for *Lady's Book* magazine (formerly *Godey's*), which she had edited for two decades. Summing up the progress she'd seen among women in the workforce, she wrote: "New avenues for higher culture and for good works are opening before them, which fifty years ago were unknown."

All of which meant that P.J. Kennedy the longshoreman and stevedore came of age during an era of female ambition and advancement. He never knew his father and didn't have a brother. He was raised by the tough-minded women in his life, by sisters, aunts, nieces, and cousins who knew how to make a dollar, and by a strong and resourceful mother who introduced him to the business that would in time make him rich: slaking islanders' thirst for liquor.

15

P.J. the Bartender

WHILE WOMEN LIKE Bridget were finding ways to escape the dead-end maid's life, Irish men were making their own escapes, breaking free from the docks and the trenches into new lines of work.

By his twentieth birthday, having discovered that he wasn't cut out for the back-breaking life of a longshoreman or stevedore, P.J. had found work as a brass finisher at one of the machine shops along Border Street, a short but meaningful distance above the drownings and drunken fistfights of the waterfront. He worked indoors, uphill from the docks and among a slightly higher class of laborer. But if Bridget felt proud to see her son in a safer, steadier, more specialized occupation — and just a few doors from her shop — P.J. would soon veer off that career path too.

Brass finishers in other parts of Boston produced household and retail items: doorknobs, bed frames, plumbing pipes, footrails and bar rails for saloons and restaurants. But at M. Carbee and Company, the oldest machine shop in East Boston, P.J. and his coworkers served the local marine industry, crafting brass propellers, steam fittings, valves, and couplings for ships and yachts. His boss, Milo Carbee, employed a dozen machinists, brass finishers, and pipe fitters. A trade publication described Carbee as "among the best known men in his line," an active member of the East Boston community, and a steady payer of wages. P.J. likely got the job from his brother-in-law, Joanna's husband, Humphrey, who had worked for years as a machinist. Humphrey, Joanna, P.J., and one of P.J.'s co-workers would all soon live at the same Border Street address, two doors up from Carbee's (and upstairs from Bridget's shop).

Brass manufacturing had a deep history in Boston. After the Revolution, Paul Revere made a fortune in brass, supplying bells and other types of metalwork to shipbuilders from his North End foundry. The tedious job of casting, cutting, grinding, sanding, and polishing the copper-zinc alloy into brass sheets, tubes, valves, and other castings meant inhaling metal dust, oils, and solvents all day. Although hardly as dangerous as working on the docks, brass finishers sustained peculiar injuries of their own — burned by solvents or steam, cut or gouged by machinery. Some developed persistent coughs and various lung ailments. P.J.'s brief career in the business coincided with efforts by East Boston brass finishers to create their own union, which would organize in 1882.

A brass finisher's pay was more than a longshoreman could earn, and the job had regular hours. Still, in time P.J. decided factory life wasn't for him, either. It was just a stop along the way. Not until he stood tall behind a brass-railed mahogany bar would he find his true calling.

In mid-1879, the *Boston Globe* advertised the auction of Hayward's saloon on Washington Street in the South End, a rundown place with a sordid history.

It had once been an illegal groggery, and its owner had been arrested a few years earlier. Even as a licensed establishment, Hayward's had been mismanaged and barely stayed afloat. Then came the night when a fifty-eight-year-old man was drinking and playing pool with friends: he excused himself, went down to the cellar, and put a gun in his mouth. His drinking buddies heard the shot and rushed to find "the lifeless body of their friend, who, a few minutes before, had been in the full enjoyment of life," said the *Boston Globe,* beneath the headline "Another Tired Man." The owner decided to sell, throwing in the glassware and fixtures, the marble-topped tables and the billiard table, and his supply of liquor, all for $3,000.

Weeks later, P.J. paid $125 for a Class 4 liquor license and took over. It was his first foray into the risky liquor business. It's unclear whether he renamed the place, whether he had partners or borrowed the money. Many bar owners took loans and rented equipment from breweries in exchange for exclusively selling and advertising their beers, a less-than-ideal arrangement that left the saloonkeeper beholden to his brewery agent. Most family accounts suggest that Bridget and P.J.'s sisters loaned him some start-up money, initiating his life as a liquor man.

On his first day behind the bar at Hayward's, P.J. made sure the front windows were open to the street, as required by the annoying new "screen law," which prohibited the use of any blinds, shutters, curtains, or even stained glass that might prevent beat cops from getting an easy view of P.J.'s patrons. State and city elders had decided that if consuming alcohol in public was to be allowed, the drinkers should be visible to all from the street. P.J. couldn't even display bottles, casks, or barrels in his windows or out front due to the constraints of this "foolish" and "cowardly" law, as the *Globe* described it. Even the city cops questioned its usefulness, as they made clear in an annual report: "While it is claimed that forcing people to drink openly will prevent many from drinking, from a sense of shame, it may also be claimed that public sensitiveness in the matter will become blunted; that any stigma against public drinking will be done away with."

Above: The East Boston waterfront, 1848, where hundreds of coffin ships delivered tens of thousands of Irish Famine refugees. Patrick worked here as a cooper. Boston's North End is across the harbor. *Below:* East Boston waterfront, fifty years later, viewed from the North End.

The East Boston Ferry.

THE STRANGER AT OUR GATE.

EMIGRANT.—Can I come in?   UNCLE SAM.—I 'spose you can; there's no law to keep you out.

Examples of anti-Irish and anti-immigrant cartoons, from *Puck* magazine and Frank Beard, including "The Irish Declaration of Independence That We Are All Familiar With," *Puck,* 1883.

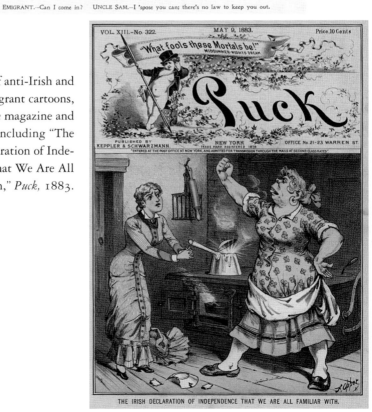

THE IRISH DECLARATION OF INDEPENDENCE THAT WE ARE ALL FAMILIAR WITH.

Courtesy of the Boston Public Library, Leslie Jones Collection

The waterfront was a "paradise" and a playground for East Boston boys like P.J.—and sometimes a death trap.

P.J. at twenty. He'd been working as a longshoreman and stevedore on the docks of East Boston and would soon open his first liquor saloon.

P.J.'s liquor store and tavern, Cotter & Kennedy, at 12 Washington Street, near Haymarket Square at the edge of the North End, about 1890. P.J. owned the place from the mid-1880s.

P.J. in his twenties. At age twenty-eight he would be elected to the Massachusetts House of Representatives — the first of his five consecutive terms there.

Mary Augusta Hickey Kennedy, soon after her marriage to P.J. in 1887.

Members of the Redberry Club, at Old Orchard Beach, Maine. P.J. (lower right) is seated and wearing a bandanna; John F. Fitzgerald (third from left) is standing on shoulders.

P.J. in the mid-1890s, just before leaving the Massachusetts State Senate, having served seven years in the statehouse.

John F. "Honey Fitz" Fitzgerald (left) and P.J. Kennedy (right) in Asheville, North Carolina, where Fitzgerald was recovering from consumption (tuberculosis) and P.J. was keeping him company, 1896.

Mary with Loretta and Joe at Old Orchard Beach, 1896.

P.J. and Mary's children, 1902: Joe, age fourteen, Margaret, age three, and Loretta, age ten.

P.J. (seated at left) playing cards with friends on a Friday night in 1899, at the home of the family doctor.

CORDIAL WELCOME HOME FOR MESSRS KENNEDY AND LALLY

HON PATRICK J. KENNEDY AND HIS DAUGHTERS, MARGARET AND LORETTA.

Among the first cabin passengers on the steamship Ivernia, which arrived yesterday afternoon from Liverpool, were Hon Patrick J. Kennedy, wire commissioner, and Francis Lally of East Boston, who have been abroad for two months. Mr Kennedy said his health, which was far from good when he left here, had been fully restored by the trip. He and Mr Lally had reason to feel gratified at the reception accorded them when the liner entered port. She was met below by the health boat Vigilant and the steam yacht Eleanor, with scores of friends. Upon invitation of Health Commissioner Michael J. Norris a number of friends went down on the Vigilant. Among those on board were William F. McClellan, president of the democratic city committee; James F. Nolan, superintendent of ferries; John J. Quigley, Dr J. Hickey, Alderman Michael J. Leary, City Messenger Edward J. Leary, Dr O'Neill, Edward J. Nelligan of Brighton and others. On the Eleanor were the members of the East Boston Improvement association. Both boats escorted the big ship to her wharf, and Messrs Kennedy and Lally were kept busy shaking hands when they disembarked.

P.J. is reunited with his daughters upon his return from his first trip to Ireland, 1907.

P.J. and Mary with their daughters, Margaret (left) and Loretta (right), around 1917.

Joe Kennedy at Columbia Trust Company, soon after being named bank president, 1914.

John F. Kennedy pretending to smoke grandfather P.J.'s cigar, with sister Rosemary.

P.J., after Mary had died and within a few years of his death in 1929.

It wasn't the smoothest start for P.J. An agent from R.G. Dun & Co. (America's first commercial credit reporting agency) said that the new proprietor was "respectable" and "has paid his bills so far as known," but he was dubious about the saloon's location—and P.J.'s future in the business. "His chances for success are not considered very promising," said one of R.G. Dun's agents, who visited P.J. more than half a dozen times from 1877 to 1880 and, per their credit reports, found him quiet and a bit cagey: "Keeps well covered up."

P.J.'s start as a bartender and saloonkeeper coincided with a sharp shift in how Boston—politically, legislatively, and culturally—viewed and treated the sale and consumption of alcohol, the taxing and licensing of its buyers and sellers. In the late 1870s and early '80s, Bostonians welcomed the full return of saloon life after decades of limited or prohibited liquor sales. By the time P.J. bought Hayward's, Massachusetts ranked tenth (of the then thirty-eight states) in saloons per capita, with one saloon per 245 residents. (Nevada came in first, with a saloon for every 65 residents.) But there was no guarantee the days of happy tippling in America's fifth-largest city would last. Puritanical views on liquor consumption persisted, and anti-alcohol forces worked constantly to make it harder for Bostonians to drink. Smart saloonkeepers learned to diversify. So, with Hayward's up and running and starting to make money, with stevedoring and brass finishing now behind him, P.J. set his sights on a new opportunity in his own backyard.

Turnover was notoriously high in the saloon business, and he didn't need to look far for options. Ads like this one regularly sought investors: "East Boston. For sale, a first-class liquor saloon, good fixtures, two pool tables in fine order, central location, sold cheap, rare chance." Rent for a storefront tavern or a grocery-saloon was roughly $25 a month, and a fully stocked bar, fixtures and all, could be had for less than $2,000. One such ad led P.J. to East

Boston's Elbow Street, a short side lane named for its bent-arm shape. P.J. met with the landlord, a cabinetmaker and prominent landowner named Treadwell, who gave him a tour of the ground-floor saloon, located just doors away from the Lyman School, P.J.'s old elementary school. P.J. signed the papers, which would turn out to be one of the smartest, or luckiest, decisions of his life. He was twenty-three and his timing was perfect, as were his location *and* his choice of beverage: beer.

It seems that P.J. was encouraged by the German immigrant brewer Henry Rueter, who, with the Irish immigrant John Alley, had cofounded the Highland Spring Brewery, one of Boston's largest. An evangelist for suds over spirits, Rueter often lobbied for looser regulations and lower taxes on beer. In testimony before state legislators and a special committee on liquor licensing, he argued that fermented beverages (lagers, ales, porters) were healthier than distilled spirits (gin, whiskey, rum) and less likely to cause drunkenness and other nonsense. In a twenty-eight-page document that he presented with his testimony, Rueter claimed that current laws discriminated against ales and lagers, but that prioritizing "harmless" beer over bourbon could actually lead to a decline in crime and poverty. "Instead of refusing the German lager beer, we should seek to have it introduced into the present grog shops, a comparatively innocuous substitute for those potent liquors that now bring disaster and death into so many families," said Rueter, who eventually became president of the United States Brewers Association. "Cannot total abstinence advocates, as a temperance measure, permit the use of ale and beer, with its lower percentage of alcohol?" (Then again, Rueter also produced the popular high-alcohol Sterling Ale, which was three times stronger than the brews he pitched to legislators.)

Swayed in part by Rueter's lobbying, the committee on licensing recommended to Boston's Board of Aldermen that lunchrooms serving beer, cider, and "edible refreshments" be allowed to operate without a license. "The committee is confident that drunkenness, and consequently pauperism and crime, will be diminished if no restrictions were placed on lager beer."

Rueter and other brewers liked to quote Benjamin Rush, a pioneering physician and signer of the Declaration of Independence, who had scorned "ardent spirits" as a threat to American morality but considered beer a nourishing alternative. In a pamphlet published in 1784, which was still in circulation a century later, Rush wrote that beer, "taken in small quantities, and at meals," resulted in "Serenity of Mind, Reputation, Long Life & Happiness . . . Cheerfulness, Strength, and Nourishment," while cordials and cocktails led to vice, disease and poverty, the poorhouse, prison, or the gallows. P.J. apparently liked that argument and decided that rather than stock a full bar—he'd seen the dark side of whiskey drinking at Hayward's—his new Elbow Street saloon would serve nothing stronger than "good, wholesome" lager beer.

At the time, only three states (New York, Pennsylvania, and Ohio) sold and drank more beer than Massachusetts. Most Boston beer joints were run by German immigrant proprietors—Otto Leutz and Gustav Utz, Fritz Schmid and Leopold Speidel, Carl Wachendorf and Herrmann Saalwaechter. Scores of their saloons and lunchrooms poured cold lagers and lured patrons with free or cheap snacks: sausages, pig's knuckles, herring, and pickles.

Suds were on the ascent. Given the years of off-and-on prohibition laws, P.J. believed selling beer was the safer bet. Maybe the temperance folks would leave him alone and let his Elbow Street saloon operate unmolested. Then again . . . the Women's Christian Temperance Union was growing, and supporters of women's suffrage often worked hand in hand with prohibitionists. And with the launch of the state's new Prohibition Party, saloonkeepers faced a shaky future.

Determining who could sell booze, and what types, at what strength and in what amounts, had been a political point of contention since America's earliest days, a source of debate between the forces of free enterprise and the finger-wagging moralists who favored social regulation. In early postcolonial days, drinking was mostly limited to the home, to inns where travelers were treated to food and grog, and to men's clubs. By the 1680s, only two dozen liquor licenses had been issued in Boston proper: to ten innkeepers, eight retailers, and six wine taverns. When residents complained that that was hardly enough, the General Court agreed to issue more licenses and to allow a wounded soldier, Jeremiah Bumstead, to start selling beer and cider. Thus began the push-pull between thirsty citizens, hand-wringing lawmakers, and anti-alcohol preachers. The Puritan minister Cotton Mather complained that it seemed every other Boston house was becoming a tavern, even though drinking socially and in public wasn't yet Boston's sort of thing.

Over the next century, places like Philadelphia, New York, Chicago, New Orleans, and San Francisco became true drinking towns. In Boston, imbibing was mostly kept out of sight—that is, until the immigrant Irish, followed by Germans and then Italians, nearly overwhelmed stodgy Boston with their beer halls, pubs, grog shops, and wine bars.

At the start of the Irish Famine, there were roughly 850 licensed drinking establishments in Boston. Four years later, in 1849, when the famed abstinence-promoting Irish Catholic priest Theobald Mathew came to town and convinced thousands to "take the pledge," the number of licensed liquor dealers had grown to 1,200. Nearly half were located in the North End, from saloons to billiard halls to bowling alleys; hundreds more operated without a license. The *Pilot* loved Father Mathew, praising him as "the great Apostle of Temperance" and giving him prominent coverage for years as he derided saloons as "a scourge to society" and encouraged Irish immigrants to "turn their backs on the curse of the old country."

"The epidemic has driven many to the bottle and the bottle many to the tomb!"

Mathew's message echoed that of prohibition groups and abstinence clubs, which continued to form—the Massachusetts Temperance Union, the Sons of Temperance, and others—the rare moral cause that Catholic priests and Protestant clergy could agree on. (Frederick Douglass, who had met Father Mathew in Ireland in 1845—and had even taken the pledge—was later "grieved, humbled, and mortified" when Mathew declined to denounce "the sin of slavery as much as the sin of intemperance.")

Through the 1850s and '60s, Massachusetts legislators had played a flip-floppy game with state liquor laws, banning booze, overturning the ban, and then enacting a new ban. For the most part, liquor sales had been stiffly regulated if not outright illegal during P.J.'s life thus far, including the prime years of statewide prohibition, 1852 to 1875. The strict yet shifting rules and the legislative battles they entailed were consistent with the state's habit of trying to regulate all sorts of public behavior, from busking (street musicians needed a license) to praying out loud (not okay) to whistling (ditto) and even playing cards.

After the Civil War, legislators eased up some, and in the late 1860s local jurisdictions were again allowed to issue liquor licenses. Boston and Suffolk County issued thousands during a giddy spree. Records from that era tell the story of a city that very much liked its drink, and the logbooks listing the licensees read like the passenger list of a coffin ship: Quigleys, O'Connors, Finnerties, Foleys, McCartys, and Maguires. Most common was the saloonkeeper "ABC" license—for a fifty-dollar fee, it permitted the sale of ale,

beer, and cider—followed by licenses for grocers, common victual-
ers (restaurants), innkeepers, brewers, distillers, wholesalers, and
druggists.

Then, in 1870, a new prohibition law came into effect, and except
for two years of beer-only sales, Boston went mostly dry (again) for
the next five years. For the most part, Bostonians ignored the laws
and drank privately. Brahmins drank good scotch in their private
clubs, and the poor Irish drank hooch or sometimes their home-
made *poitín* whiskey in tenement basement "jugrooms," back-room
shebeens, or the cellar of their local grocer. One crafty proprietor sold
crackers for five cents apiece, each of which came with a free glass
of beer—until he was arrested and fined $100. Prohibition was
overturned in 1875, and licenses once more began to flow, authorizing legitimate saloons, wholesale dealers, and beer-selling grocers,
whose advertisements flooded the pages of the city's papers.

By the time P.J. got into the business, drinking was finally becoming less private, more public, and generally permissible. Still,
state lawmakers favored establishments that reflected Benjamin
Rush's views: they preferred lunchrooms serving beer to barrooms
serving "spirituous liquors."

More restrictions were coming, but for now P.J. was licensed
and legal as he pulled drafts behind the bar at Elbow Street for his
(mostly Irish) patrons. He'd listen to their hopes and complaints,
offering a sympathetic ear as he wiped down the bar, dried and
shelved the glasses.

P.J.'s unnamed saloon—one friend called it simply P.J.'s "Elbow Street store"—sat just off Maverick Square, a few streets up
from the waterfront and a stone's throw from the herds of pedestrians commuting from Boston by ferry and foot. The narrow, angled
street, more alley than avenue, sat just outside the fray of downtown East Boston, ideally located for a quick nip on the way home.
With an unassuming entrance, like the speakeasies of the future,

the saloon was a dim-lit, quiet place for men (no women allowed) to shuffle across sawdust floors for nickel beers and peanuts after a long day on the docks.

Despite the on-again, off-again rules, such saloons played an increasingly important role in the lives of Boston's immigrant Irish. It was a shared social space — not home nor work nor church — for men from different parts of Ireland, from different backgrounds. A place to learn about news from back home. A place to hold a party, a meeting, even a funeral. A place to get a meal, to talk politics, to find a job. And sometimes, if the owner was willing, a place to sleep.

As a barkeep, P.J. was a known softy, generous and empathetic, willing to offer a free drink to someone with empty pockets, some food to a street kid hanging around outside, a few dollars to someone down on his luck — a practice he'd maintain for the rest of his days. There on Elbow Street, he'd begun a new kind of life. Like his mother, he was an entrepreneur and became a neighborhood fixture. He had a talent for it. Into his early twenties, the restless son of a widow had found his place and his calling — an occupation that connected him, at least spiritually, to his father. His basement storerooms were now filled with handmade wooden kegs and casks.

It's unknown whether Bridget or her daughters drank alcohol (the moderate consumption that her son and grandson practiced suggests not), but it's tempting to imagine her joining P.J. at his saloon for an after-hours glass of beer to celebrate the inauguration of his East Boston business. Perhaps a mother-son toast to health, *Sláinte.* Also tempting, and hardly a stretch: imagining the crowds at P.J.'s place celebrating St. Patrick's Day, the arrival of a new immigrant, the birth of a baby. Or hosting an Irish wake.

Here's P.J. the barman, towel over his arm, apron around his waist, pulling froth-topped drafts behind the counter: medium height (about five foot ten); "well-muscled" and, thanks to his cargo-hauling days, "somewhat larger than the ordinary man"; blue eyes and fair skin ("a rain-washed, rosy complexion"); hair variously described as dark reddish, wavy brown, or glossy black (most photos suggest the latter), atop a "well-shaped head." His most distinctive feature, adopted at about this time and sported the rest of his days, was a dark handlebar mustache, which grew thicker as he aged. It nearly exploded beneath his nose and curled up at both ends, "adding to his air of composure and dignity."

During lulls P.J. would don wire-framed glasses and bury his nose in a book, often something historical, perhaps his way of improving upon his limited formal education. He also devoured the newspapers. He had a soothing voice but was more listener than talker. Rejecting stereotype, he was the rare Irish teetotaler, or at least a modest drinker— "rarely seen lifting a glass containing anything stronger than lemonade," one family historian would claim. Another suggested that P.J. had, as a longshoreman, seen the dangers of drink and "only on the most festive occasions" would allow himself a single glass of beer.

Just as his mother attracted glowing compliments from patrons, P.J. the bartender was universally well-liked and trusted. Foibles, if he had any, went undocumented (leading one chronicler to marvel that a liquor man involved in urban politics could be so "straight"). By all accounts, he was a natural behind the bar, listening to stories and telling a few of his own, remembering names and asking about family members, soaking up and protecting neighborhood secrets. P.J.'s future daughter-in-law, Rose Fitzgerald—her father, John, was also raised by a liquor-selling immigrant grocer—later said that her father-in-law's spot behind the bar positioned him on the front lines of East Boston's "news, gossip, celebrations, hopes and fears, troubles and tragedies . . . He was a good listener, knew how to keep confidences, and had a compassionate spirit. He helped people with loans, gifts, and advice. Often he passed the word on to somebody that so-and-so needed this or that, and P.J. Kennedy would appreciate it, asking nothing in return but goodwill. Everyone knew that he was an honorable man, and everyone respected him."

At P.J.'s bar, off-the-boat Irish immigrants mingled with survivors of the Famine and Civil War veterans. Patrons perked up their ears at the brogue of some new arrivals, maybe stood them for a drink, asked where they'd come from. The proprietor's extended family became regulars — cousins and in-laws, relatives rooming in the apartments above Bridget's shop — but P.J. made everyone feel like family.

Despite the lack of whiskey at Elbow Street, the dark side of saloon life was never far. The bane of a barkeep's night was tending to the hardcore regulars, the drunk and the dangerous. These were men P.J. had encountered on Deer Island in his younger years, witnessing the revolving door of the drunkard's sentence. During P.J.'s time at the House of Reformation, two-thirds of the hundreds of adult inmates housed in nearby buildings were serving thirty days or more for public intoxication, many destined to be back soon. "In this short time, the thirst for intoxicating liquor is not abated," one prison report found. "Many return to their old habits and are returned to the island, sometimes within days." A Deer Island chaplain, paraphrasing the Bible, complained that such inmates "almost invariably fall into their old habits of drunkenness . . . like a dog returns to its own vomit."

And now they were P.J.'s patrons. Men like Daniel Skerry, the longshoreman profiled in a *Boston Globe* story about East Boston dockworkers. He'd get drunk, rough up his wife, get arrested and fined, and, failing to pay his fine, would be sent to Deer Island to dry out for a few months. Many of P.J.'s customers contributed to city coffers by paying court-ordered fines of one to three dollars, over and over again. Others landed in the pages of the *East Boston Argus-Advocate:* "An unusually large number of drunks were gathered in by the police on Saturday night and Sunday," including men who approached the judge "smilingly for a second offense."

Especially in Irish neighborhoods, the barkeep's job was equal parts host, babysitter, referee, therapist, plus banker and, occasionally, enforcer. One Boston bartender at the time handled a rowdy drunk by popping him in the forehead with a hammer but was later arrested and charged with leaving the man in "a dangerous condition and delirious."

Boston's most famous beer joint (until it was dethroned by the sitcom saloon Cheers) was Jacob Wirth's, on Eliot Street in the North End, the first distributor of Anheuser Busch beers. The boxer John L. Sullivan was a regular and once got arrested for assaulting another customer. (Wirth's later moved south of downtown, where it would become a favorite of Babe Ruth and Jack Kerouac. It operated until 2018, one of Boston's longest-running taverns.) Sullivan ran his own saloon on Washington Street, just north of P.J.'s first place, and when he was in town he would stand beside his white-suited bartenders, tossing back drinks and laughing with fans. Born in the South End to Famine immigrants, Sullivan was a barroom brawler turned pro who won hundreds of prize fights across the United States and Europe, becoming America's first sports superstar, a mustachioed god among Boston's Irish. A big drinker and an angry drunk who scuffled with bartenders, patrons, and police, Sullivan later quit the bottle, closed his bars (he had one in New York too), and lectured on abstinence, claiming to have wasted half a million dollars on booze.

Initially, saloon life suited P.J., and he went looking for more investments. His success on Elbow Street and at Hayward's prompted him to invest in a longshoremen's hangout near the East Boston docks and, later, with a partner, a tavern at the famed Maverick House, aka Sturtevant House, where Bridget had worked. A decade after his brief visit to the House of Reformation, it's safe to say P.J. was fully reformed, a model of what could happen when an Irish boy heeded the *Pilot*'s pleadings to shun sloth and pursue an honest calling. True, many Bostonians still considered saloonkeeping less than honest or honorable. But he'd embarked on an enterprise with a seemingly limitless stream of customers, one that would provide income for his family for decades to come.

At some point, though, P.J. seemed to sense that spending *every* night behind a bar wasn't quite his life's work, either. He was ready for something more than serving suds to dockworkers — especially after yet another new state law held tavern owners liable for crimes committed by their patrons. Two years after buying his South End place, P.J. sold Hayward's to a man called Hastings, who took over the license and apparently let it expire: he was soon raided by the city's liquor squad. Maybe the business and social skills P.J. had developed could be used elsewhere? That's what some of his more upscale customers apparently suggested to the young man, who, as a trusted ear, had learned the ins and outs of East Boston, its whims and secrets, its inclinations and alliances. "He hears the best stories," a years-long study of 1880s saloon life said of men like P.J. "He is the first to get information about the latest political deals."

For P.J., there would be much more liquor-selling to come, including a lucrative move into retail, wholesale, and importing. But in the early 1880s, he effectively swapped his barman's apron for a suit. Wisely, he chose to keep the Elbow Street saloon. It became his headquarters as he made a pivot from delivering drinks to delivering votes.

Whether by coincidence or design, P.J.'s Elbow Street shop hap-

pened to share an address with the Democratic Committee Headquarters for East Boston's Ward 2. There, and at the adjacent East
Boston Athletic Club, P.J. Kennedy became a familiar friendly face.
And, as Rose Kennedy would later put it, "Predictably, he became
a political force in East Boston."

16

P.J. the Democrat

EAST BOSTON'S WARD bosses kept hearing the name P.J. Kennedy, seeing it in newsprint for reasons other than the required public listing for a liquor license application.

There were the boat races in which P.J. led East Boston's rowing crews to victory against other wards. There was the work he and his roommate, Nick Flynn, had been doing for the Excelsior Associates social club, assisting with concerts and literary talks and grand balls at Maverick Hall. At one such affair, P.J. served as assistant director and watched proudly as a hundred couples danced at "one of the most agreeable affairs of the season," as the *Boston Globe* described it. There were his efforts as a "guard" for the Hancock and English Club, which was trying to drum up voter support for the Democratic presidential candidate, Winfield Scott Hancock, who in 1880 would lose by a hair to James Garfield.

Some ward leaders got to know P.J. at his beer hall, where he'd still occasionally tend bar, talking politics as he poured them lagers. Or they saw him marching with other Democrats in the St. Patrick's Day parades or working the docks and the streets at election time, reminding people to vote—and for whom. Some had probably gotten to know P.J. at his mother's shop, where she surely talked up her hardworking son.

One Democratic leader in particular took a shine to P.J. Daniel F. Kelly was the low-key but powerful chairman of the Democratic Ward and City Committee for Ward 2 — one of the city's twenty-five electoral wards and, with the adjacent (but more Republican) Ward 1, comprised Boston's so-called island wards. Kelly suggested to his fellow Democrats that they start giving young Kennedy more responsibilities, a chance to prove his worth to the party.

Other Ward 2 operators also took P.J. under their wing: William A. Foss, a blacksmith turned Common Council member who now ran the East Boston ferries; Cornelius Doherty, a coppersmith turned liquor dealer turned Common Council member, who ran Boston's water department; and William J. Burke, a boilermaker turned Common Council member and state representative, now the city's elevator and building inspector. Each represented the ascent of an immigrant — from tradesman to political operative to holder of elected office — a trajectory that P.J. admired. These men opened their doors, welcomed P.J. in. They invited him to speak before local dignitaries at Lyceum Hall, where he stood nervously at the podium and "read some resolutions" before the evening's activities, according to the *Boston Transcript.* He was not the most inspiring of public speakers, he and his mentors would learn. His skills shined brighter behind the scenes, as a community organizer and people manager. He put together a fundraiser for the Irish National Land League, also at Lyceum Hall, where 150 couples dined and danced past midnight. The next day's *Boston Globe* praised P.J.'s "efficient" efforts.

These and other civic and political activities had a few things in common: they occurred within a block of P.J.'s saloon, they aimed to rebuild East Boston's less-than-dominant Democratic Party, and

they were tied, directly or spiritually, to the crusade for Irish independence. News of the latest chapter in that crusade — recent
spikes in evictions, starvation, protests, and imprisonment in Ireland — had reached America. P.J. and his Democratic cohorts took
a deep interest in these affairs, leading newspapers to call them
"sympathizers with Ireland."

This was true, and they did little to hide it. Among the resolutions P.J. recited at one of his Lyceum Hall appearances was a
call for fellow East Boston citizens to "extend our heartiest sympathies to the outraged families of downtrodden Erin in their struggle against tyranny and oppression." P.J. encouraged "every son of
Erin and those of Irish parentage" to lobby for and donate to "the
amelioration and freedom from the serfdom of British rule of their
fellow countrymen." Perhaps it was inevitable that P.J.'s entry into
politics, his introduction to political audiences and newspaper reporters, would be linked to the injustices still grinding down on
his parents' homeland: the troubles faced by his aunts, uncles, and
cousins across the Atlantic.

P.J. hadn't visited Ireland and Bridget had not returned home, but
they'd stayed in touch with family by letter over the years. P.J., who
would become a prolific letter-writer in later years, contributed to
these communications, and from his Irish relatives he learned the
latest news about tenant farmers in County Wexford protesting the
unfair rents charged by absentee English landlords, even as Ireland
faced the harsh blow of another (albeit lesser) famine, in 1879. Poor
rural farmers like the Kennedys and Murphys had been agitating
for decades for more reasonable rents — or, better yet, the right to
own the land they lived on and farmed. But any effort at reform
got slapped down, the reformers arrested, the rents jacked up, the
people's hopes dashed.

In the late 1870s into the '80s, a new movement gained ground, led by an unlikely new Irish hero. Charles Stewart Parnell, son of an Anglo-Irish landowning family (his mother was American), had been elected as an Irish member of the British Parliament. He represented the new Home Rule Party, which championed land reform and an Ireland independent from England. Parnell visited Boston in 1880 to spread the word of the evictions and starving citizens in rural and western Ireland. More than 100,000 people had been removed from their farms over the previous decade, and emigration from Ireland was nearing a post-Famine high; nearly 10,000 arrived in Boston each year, levels not seen since the late 1840s. (This wave led to another spike in the numbers of single Irish women coming to Boston to work as maids—more than 7,000 in 1880.)

Parnell's visit, and visits by his sister Fanny and Irish National Land League cofounder Michael Davitt, lured Americans to the cause. Land League clubs were created across the United States and sent hundreds of thousands of dollars to Ireland. P.J. helped organize East Boston's club, whose fundraisers awakened Boston's Irish to the latest woes of the motherland, where a few thousand English landlords still owned 88 percent of the land. The average size of an estate owned by an absentee landlord was 2,726 acres; meanwhile, five million peasant farmers owned nothing. Said one *Globe* headline: "Boston Shaken to Its Very Centre by the Woes of the Unhappy People of Ireland."

Some farmers refused to work the fields and crops of tyrannical landlords—the term "boycott" was born of protests against the English land agent Charles Boycott, in County Mayo. When Parnell called for a nationwide strike and was arrested, he issued his "No-Rent Manifesto" from inside the notorious Kilmainham Jail, encouraging farmers to stand firm and withhold rent. His words inspired P.J.'s cousins (sons of his father's deceased brothers), who now ran the family farm in Dunganstown. The Kennedys had become disciples of Parnell after hearing him speak to a crowd of twenty thousand in New Ross, urging farmers to "destroy the system of landlordism." Bridget's in-laws became vocal Land League agitators, on the front lines of the Land Wars that would rage over the coming years.

By letter, the Irish Kennedy clan must have implored P.J. and Bridget: *help us!* Their fight for land rights and Ireland's independence would last for decades, with much violence to come. But the transatlantic support from America—from Boston in particular—helped fuel a rebirth of the nationalist movement that would, in P.J.'s lifetime, achieve its goal: a free Ireland. One member of the British cabinet at the time of Parnell's fundraising rallies in America complained: "Now there is an Irish nation in the United States, equally hostile, with plenty of money, absolutely beyond our reach."

P.J. would later acknowledge the symbolic link between his political awakening and the "righteous struggle" for Irish freedom. His efforts on behalf of East Boston's Land League affiliate—speaking at fundraisers, meeting with the ladies' auxiliary branch, distributing Land League circulars to East Boston homes, seeking donations, and inviting neighbors to meetings—effectively launched his political career. He once helped organize a rally at Lyceum Hall that the *Boston Globe* called "the most enthusiastic Land League gathering ever held in East Boston." T. P. O'Connor, an Irish member of Parliament who was visiting Boston, praised the event as "the first important meeting of the Irish in America."

P.J. was twenty-four and gaining more attention from East Boston's political elders, who recognized his emerging leadership skills, his ability to rally others to a cause. They invited him to their meetings and events, asked him to say a few words here and there, and invited him to join their clubs, such as the decade-old Excelsior Associates, full of East Boston businessmen and politicians.

Then, in 1882, P.J. was tapped to run for an elected position on Boston's Democratic Ward and City Committee, where he would serve as captain of his voting precinct (Ward 2, Precinct 3). Ward 2 caucus elections — at least the Democratic primaries, during which party candidates were elected — were notoriously rowdy affairs, drawing hundreds of voters and, often, the police. On the ballot, alongside a slate of Irish rivals, P.J. survived some infighting, and in his first-ever election outran a few splinter candidates called "bolters," who challenged the party slate. He was elected to serve on Ward 2's Democratic Ward and City Committee, a position he'd hold for the next three years. Thus began his decades-long tenure as one of Boston's most trusted and hardest-working Democrats.

P.J. the wunderkind didn't pause long to celebrate victory. As a Ward 2 leader, he oversaw a crew of street-level lieutenants who registered voters and made sure Democrats in his precinct voted. Going door to door, street by street, he checked names off his list. If a street had fifty voters, P.J. was expected to deliver fifty votes. A year later, he was named chair of the Ward 2 caucus, charged with nominating Democratic candidates for Boston's Common Council. (Boston was controlled by a mayor and two elected bodies: the Board of Aldermen and the larger Common Council.) He'd later take on more party responsibilities: joining the caucus that selected Democratic candidates for the US Congress; serving as secretary of the Suffolk County Democratic Convention; getting elected to the Democrats' influential State Central Committee. He attended conventions and caucuses, shared a dinner table with the newly elected member of Congress Patrick A. Collins, met with ward bosses from across the city and Suffolk County, and dined regularly with ward leaders at the Maverick House.

Bit by bit, his old life — fatherless stevedore, Irish bartender, grocer's son — began to mesh and overlap in his upstart political life. Some of the people he had known, from ex-classmates to his mother's customers and tenants, reappeared and took on new roles in his life, as if he'd planned it that way. One friend from his dock-working days was John H. Sullivan, who'd fled Ireland at eighteen, worked at sea for years, landed in Boston in 1867, and worked his way up from longshoreman to head stevedore in charge of the Leland Steamship Line docks. Thanks to P.J.'s support, Sullivan was elected to Boston's Common Council, the start of a long-term political career—and a partnership. Sullivan would become one of P.J.'s closest friends, an adviser and ally.

Sullivan's election, plus the rise of men like Patrick Collins, Patrick Maguire, and Hugh O'Brien—soon to become Boston's first Irish Catholic mayor—would inspire P.J. to step up his own political ambitions. He began considering a run for office. His steady progress from barman to statesman occurred at a transitional time for Boston politics. The party of Lincoln still dominated, and the city was still largely controlled by the Protestant descendants of its founders. But in the immigrant wards—the southern half of East Boston (Ward 2), the North End (Wards 6 and 7), the West End (Ward 8), and the South End (Wards 13, 14, 15)—Irish voters favored the Democrats, even though Democrats were the underdogs, still branded as the party that had countenanced slavery. Republicans held the majority on the Common Council and the Board of Aldermen. This dynamic—old versus new, native versus immigrant—was on full display in East Boston, where wealthier Republicans lived in big houses in the tonier Ward 1 neighborhoods, literally looking down onto the tenements and saloons of the mostly Irish Ward 2.

One lingering point of contention between the parties was P.J.'s business: booze. Republicans tended to favor prohibition, and prohibitionists were a powerful bunch. By the early 1880s, the new Prohibition Party regularly demonized men like P.J. for plying the immigrant classes with liquor and decried the growing political

influence of saloons and "liquor men." Journalists contributed to
the depiction of P.J. and his kind as "a social force in the community" and "a politician in power, with spoils to distribute, work to
give." As the *Nation* had put it in 1875, "the liquor dealer is the
immigrants' guide, philosopher, and creditor. He sees them more
frequently and familiarly than anybody else, and is more trusted
by them than anybody else, and is the person through whom the
news and meaning of what passes in the upper regions of city politics reaches them." William Howard Taft would later highlight the
barkeep's influence, advising other politicians to get to know "the
proprietor of the social club of his neighborhood."

In short, Irish saloonkeepers like P.J. were becoming a powerful force in urban politics. In other Irish-heavy cities—Chicago,
New York, Philadelphia, New Orleans—owning saloons and liquor stores provided not only a route to middle-class respectability
but an on-ramp to elected office. In Boston, though, the jumble of
liquor laws created potholes in that road. Still, P.J. could look to
a small but eminent handful of predecessors for inspiration. Lawrence Logan emigrated from Galway in 1858, worked in his brother's liquor store, started selling whiskey after the war, then became
president of the Boston Beer Company, whose barrels were stacked
in saloons and groceries across Boston. By 1880 he was worth
$100,000; one of his sons was a football star at Harvard, another a
judge, and another a priest. (Logan was also the influential treasurer
for Boston's Democratic City Committee.) The immigrant barman
James William Kenney learned the trade at his brother's North
End liquor store, started making porters and ales on the side, and
in time invested in a brewery that produced 150,000 barrels a year,
earning Kenney a fortune.

Other brewers, distillers, retailers, wholesalers, and saloonkeepers parlayed their business success into politics, making steady inroads as council members or aldermen. A common thread woven

through the published biographies of Boston lawmakers of the 1880s was "born in Ireland" and "engaged in the grocery and liquor business" and "engaged in the saloon business." As the upcoming investigative journalist Lincoln Steffens would quip, the fastest way to empty a city council chamber was to yell, "Your saloon's on fire!"

Much had changed since the anti-Catholic Know Nothing days. Back then, even Irish politicians hesitated to stand up for their own people. D. D. Kelley, a prominent East Boston shipbuilder, had represented Ward 2 on the Common Council for many years. But during meetings in downtown Boston, he'd show off for fellow councilors by mocking Irish *papists* and "half starved Irishmen who come from the bogs of Ireland." He earned chuckles from the Yankee crowd but also the ire of the Irish press — "a most bitter opponent of the countrymen of his fathers," said the *Pilot*. But thirty years later? Kelley was a proud and vocal member of the Land League and a loyal supporter of beer-pouring, Irish-blooded Democrats like P.J. Kennedy.

In 1884, when Grover Cleveland became the nation's first Democratic president in twenty-eight years, it boded well for Boston Democrats. The tide had begun to turn, lifting P.J. with it.

Boston's population had doubled since the Civil War, to nearly 400,000, due partly to immigration but also to Boston's annexation of suburbs such as Dorchester and Roxbury, both full of Irish voters. The number of city wards grew to twenty-five, and the Common Council expanded to seventy-five members (three per ward). Meanwhile, the city's Irish population had passed 70,000 and in a dozen years would reach 200,000. These changes worked to the advantage of Irish Democrats, who were finally learning how to control wards across the city, creating the machinery needed to win votes — machines largely built by two Patricks: Collins and Maguire.

Patrick Collins, a fatherless Irish immigrant, had served as a state representative and senator, as president of the American Land League, and, as head of the state Democratic Committee, led the party's coalition building and fundraising. When he was elected to Congress in 1882, another Paddy took over. Also Irish-born, Patrick Maguire was a printer's apprentice who founded his own Irish-friendly newspaper, the *Republic*. Though he never ran for office, he served for years on the Democratic City Committee. When Patrick Collins went to Washington, Maguire became the primary and influential leader of the city's Democratic Party, even if his name rarely appeared in newsprint — a behind-the-scenes style that P.J. admired.

The Irish had made headway. A quarter of a century after Barney McGinniskin's breakthrough as Boston's first Irish cop, more than a hundred Irishmen now walked a beat. And the Common Council and Board of Aldermen, once almost exclusively Yankee territory, now included their share of Irish-born men and their sons. Maguire and other top Democrats decided the time was right to aim higher: elect Boston's first Irish mayor. Their candidate, Hugh O'Brien, was hardly the typical working-class Mick. Although born in Ireland, he'd come to Boston well before the Famine. He wasn't a saloon-keeper or a liquor man, and instead had worked as a printer before starting his own newspaper, the *Shipping and Commercial List*. By the 1870s he was a rich man, goateed and dressed in tailored suits and known for giving articulate speeches during his seven years on the Board of Aldermen. He was almost Brahmin in demeanor.

Maguire instructed P.J. and other precinct captains and ward bosses to hit the streets and tell voters about O'Brien's promises — lower taxes and improved services. Their efforts paid off with barrier-breaking results. On December 10, 1884, with support from fifteen of the city's twenty-five wards, O'Brien became the first Irish mayor of Boston, and its first Catholic mayor.

O'Brien's election cracked open the door for other Irish candidates, and suddenly men young and old awoke to the idea that they didn't necessarily need a Harvard education or a law degree to run for office. The Irish gift for gab turned out to be a powerful political asset. So did a saloon. By 1885, P.J.'s political patrons decided that their loyal, well-connected soldier was ready.

By now, the route was well-established: an aspiring pol would get involved with his local ward, make a name for himself, and run for the Common Council. In rare cases, he might aim for the more exclusive Board of Aldermen. Showing the same rebellious quality that once drove his mother crazy, P.J. opted for neither. Instead of starting local, he looked past his island wards and set his sights higher: on the gold-domed statehouse on Beacon Hill, the historic home to the Massachusetts General Court that he'd visited as a schoolboy, in the heart of Brahmin Boston.

He was just twenty-seven but decided to run for the Massachusetts House of Representatives. Did he discuss the idea with Bridget? Did she encourage him to take a chance, just as she had? Did she leverage her community connections? Did he get the okay from the ward leaders he'd served well in recent years? Probably all of these. Sometime in mid-1885 he began his run for the office of state representative.

P.J. was an earnest and hardworking candidate, good with names and eager to help "our kind": Ward 2's Irish Catholics. He met with constituents and talked about his support for the labor movement. He favored the new East Boston soup kitchens, which fed the hungry incoming immigrants. As someone raised by a mother, sisters, and aunts, he had a soft spot for ladies' auxiliary clubs and women's groups, and he was always glad to accept their invitations. A steadfast churchgoer, he volunteered for committees and fundraisers at Most Holy Redeemer.

Bridget no doubt played a role in spreading the word that her once rascally son was running for office, gushing about the upcoming election at her shop and after Sunday mass. It had been twenty years since she'd opened her first store. She knew her customers well, and they knew and trusted her. If she suggested to longtime neighborhood shoppers that they consider P.J. Kennedy for the statehouse, her customers (especially the Irish ones) surely listened.

Just four days before election day, however, on Halloween night, P.J. confronted the dirty side of party politics. It nearly cut short his first major run for office.

At the time, many eager candidates were vying for few open seats. Breakaway factions often sought to disrupt ward caucus meetings by nominating their own slates of bolter candidates to compete with those that ward leaders preferred. P.J. should have been a shoo-in for the Democratic Party's nomination for state representative, and the preelection Democratic caucus should have been a perfunctory affair. Instead, hundreds of citizens crammed into the meeting hall near P.J.'s Elbow Street saloon as a group of bolters tried to claim the party's nomination, causing "a perfect uproar," said the *Boston Globe*. Police from Station 7 were called and surrounded the hall as voting continued until 10 p.m. P.J.'s roommate and friend Nick Flynn, secretary of the ballot-counting committee, had to yell to try to restore order.

When the shouts died down and the ballots were counted, the top vote-getter in Ward 2's preelection caucus that night was first-time candidate, P.J. Kennedy. His name would appear on the ballot as one of the two Ward 2 Democrats running for state representative, come election day. His opponents: two Republican nominees and, ironically, two members of the Prohibition Party. The other Democrat was James Fitzgerald, a lawyer and former classmate of P.J.'s at the Lyman School, who had just completed two terms on the Common Council. A popular, upcoming back-slapper of a politician, Fitzgerald had actually led one of the bolter factions, but his hoped-for co-candidate fell short. He and P.J. were now partners on the Democratic ticket, though they remained suspicious of each other.

Four days later, on election day, November 3, 1885, turnout was heavy in Ward 2. Voters crowded the streets and alleys around polling places, most of them within a block of P.J.'s saloon, which was packed with P.J.'s precinct lieutenants and other ward soldiers. Polls closed at 8 p.m. and ballots trickled in until 10. As the count began—with Nick Flynn, as ward secretary, again tallying votes —one ward leader began taking bets, placing hundreds of dollars on P.J. for the win. At 11:15, the results were announced: Kennedy and Fitzgerald had defeated the Republican and Prohibition slates to become the new representatives for Ward 2 on the Massachusetts General Court.

P.J. was the top vote-getter among the East Boston candidates and, citywide, only a dozen of the 127 house candidates received more votes. He'd done it—leapfrogged over all the men his age (and older) with similar political aspirations. Sadly lost to history is his mother's no-doubt proud reaction. Also lost: whether P.J. celebrated by allowing himself one beer.

He was headed to the historic red-brick statehouse—designed by Charles Bulfinch (the architect of the cathedral where his parents had married) and built on land once owned by John Hancock, with a dome sheathed in copper by Paul Revere. On January 6, 1886, a week before his twenty-eighth birthday, P.J. was sworn in as a member of the 107th Massachusetts General Court. At his orientation session he received a copy of the fat *Manual for the Use of the General Court.* He was assigned to the House Printing Committee. He met the longtime house doorkeeper Captain Tucker (a well-known temperance activist) and was assigned his seat, number 85, near the back of the cavernous house chamber, which thirty years earlier had been full of Know Nothing legislators. There, beneath the "Sacred Cod," the five-foot-long wood carving that hung from the ceiling to symbolize the city's humble start as a fishing village and port, he'd serve the people of Boston and Massachusetts.

He began his legislative career under a Republican governor (George D. Robinson), a Republican speaker of the house, and a Republican senate president. He was one of 67 Democrats who'd serve in 1886 alongside 143 Republicans. The *Boston Globe* highlighted the "Democratic Improvement in the Legislature," even though P.J.'s party still lagged far behind, with Republicans holding a two-to-one advantage in both the house and the senate. Still, the Democrats were pleased to make some modest gains and were in a celebratory mood at their annual "Battle of New Orleans" dinner at the Parker House downtown, two days after P.J.'s swearing-in. Boston Democrats had adopted the anniversary of that War of 1812 battle in honor of its hero and their party's founder, an orphaned, British-hating son of Irish immigrants, Andrew Jackson. The defeater of a Boston Brahmin, John Quincy Adams, President Jackson had been nicknamed "Jackass" by his foes. The combative populist had embraced that slur, leading his new party to adopt the donkey as its mascot.

At dinner, Patrick Collins, back briefly from Washington, joined Mayor O'Brien in congratulating the new class of Boston Democrats — the "disciples of the great champion of Democracy, Andrew Jackson."

P.J.'s hard-fought, hard-won victory placed him at the nexus of his city's Democratic engine, which was slowly gaining steam, propelled by urban and saloon politics. But P.J. also knew that the history of state politics was littered with one-term legislators. If he hoped for a second term, or a higher office, he'd need help.

For that, he turned to two immigrants' sons, both liquor men, both named J.J.

Part V

P.J.

In no other country is my story even possible.

— BARACK OBAMA

17

P.J. the Legislator

THE FIRST ELECTION taught P.J. much about the nuances of co-alition building, the intricacies of caucuses, ward factions, bolters, deal making, and horse trading. The next election would teach him the secrets of political longevity: friends, favors, trust, and cash.

After his first six months in office, P.J. kept taking on more roles in Boston's Democratic Party machinery, reelected to ward com-mittees and caucuses. His friend John H. Sullivan, now an alder-man, praised P.J. as the fresh new face of the "young Democracy of the Island Wards." P.J. became more intimately involved in se-lecting candidates for local, state, and federal office, leading the *Boston Globe* to ask in a headline, "Who Will Control the Destinies of the Party in this Town?" The implied answer: the liquor men. In certain Boston wards, voters preferred politicians with a little booze in their background. Candidates who worked as clerks or machinists now claimed to be "in the liquor business" even if, as the *Globe* complained, "the parties have never sold a drop of liquor in their lives."

In November 1886, P.J. the legitimate liquor man was reelected to the General Court. "Genial and popular," said the *East Boston Argus-Advocate,* he won "by an extremely large and flattering vote," far outpacing two Republican challengers and again receiving more votes than all but a dozen of the 140 candidates citywide. Democrats again made some gains, on the Common Council and the Board of Aldermen, in the statehouse and in Congress. The *Globe* called it "altogether a glorious day for Democracy and Reform" and the *Argus-Advocate* said the reelection of Kennedy promised to make Ward 2 a "Democracy stronghold."

Then again, the full General Court was no hub of Irish or Democrats, who now held 75 seats to the 157 held by Republicans. P.J., elected as vice president of the Democrats' city central committee, was tasked with correcting the imbalance. But while many Boston voters supported men like P.J.— Irish, Democrat, liquor seller— other parts of the state were represented by Republican legislators who wanted to make life harder for saloon men.

When Hugh O'Brien became mayor in 1885, the temperance crowd went a little crazy, predicting that an Irish mayor would tolerate a free-for-all of public drunkenness. In response, the state legislature passed a law, just prior to O'Brien's inauguration, that moved control of liquor licensing away from Boston and back to the state. The new Board of Metropolitan Police Commissioners, appointed by the (Republican) governor, was created to oversee licensing, and it started limiting the number of licenses while taking a bigger cut of license fees for the state treasury. Also, the state would soon (in 1888) place its first-ever cap on the number of liquor licenses in Boston.

In short, there would be fewer licenses, they'd be more expensive and harder to come by, leading to fewer saloons and liquor shops and, presumably, less drinking. At least that was the goal. The new licensing board, backed by prohibitionists and Republicans, would see to it that selling beer, wine, and liquor would become less profitable and more strictly controlled. And in a stab at separating drinking from voting, booze from politics, the legislature also enacted a law that forced saloons and liquor stores to close on election days. The beer hall owner Jacob Wirth responded with newspaper ads featuring images of America's founders and the Statue of Liberty, arguing that John Hancock would never infringe upon the "natural rights of man." His point: drinking beer was an expression of American freedom.

All of this led P.J. to rethink his liquor-selling prospects. He'd seen many successful enterprises grow from the partnership of two Irish brothers, their initials linked by an ampersand — D & J Doherty, D & T O'Connor, D & P Morrison. Although P.J. didn't have a blood brother to work with, he looked to his cast of political pals and found two new partners.

John J. "J.J." Cotter was an Irish-born Civil War veteran who'd served aboard the USS *Minnesota,* part of a crew that included African American sailors from Boston who fought in key battles off the coast of the South. After the war Cotter worked at an East Boston livery stable, making harnesses and painting carriages. He became active in Ward 2 politics and Irish affairs, sang in his church choir, marched with the Ancient Order of Hibernians on St. Patrick's Day, and would later represent East Boston on the Common Council. He'd been working as a bartender at P.J.'s Elbow Street saloon, and the two had become friends. As a barman-politician, said the *Boston Globe,* Cotter was "one of the most popular men, both socially and politically, on the island."

P.J. and J.J. found a small first-floor liquor store in Boston at 12 Washington Street, on the southern edge of the North End, near Haymarket Square. It was tucked beneath a carpet warehouse, between a furniture store and a cigar and barbershop (fifteen cents a cut, ten cents a shave). Its double-door entrance was bordered by tall windows, with brass rails running along the storefront. Above, they installed a new sign with their names in two-foot-tall letters in gold relief: COTTER & KENNEDY. Window signs touted IMPORTED LIQUORS, ENGLISH & AMERICAN ALES, and BOTTLED GOODS FOR HOME USE. In addition to selling wine, spirits, and beer, P.J. and his partner obtained a first-class victualer license, allowing them to run a barroom at the back of the shop.

Near Faneuil Hall and Quincy Market, Cotter & Kennedy was in good company, sharing a quaint if slightly shabby quadrant famous for historic taverns, some a century old: the Green Dragon, the Bell in Hand, the Union Oyster House, the White Bull. With brick sidewalks and cobblestone streets etched by streetcar tracks, the neighborhood would one day become a popular tourist destination, but at this time it was a scruffy drinkers' row, a few blocks north of the thirsty newsmen of Newspaper Row and the printshops of Pi Alley.

Meanwhile, the beer saloon on Elbow Street had started to out-live its purpose. The place was cozy and comfortable but "not large enough to hold the numbers of friends anxious to meet for conge-nial intercourse," per one description. The saloon had served P.J. well, helped incubate his political career, but slinging drafts for longshoremen was no longer his passion. Getting elected was. He'd seen other legislators come and go, a term here and there. But to have impact and influence he'd need to string a few together. To do that, he'd need to be more than a barkeep. He'd need money, generated by more respectable businesses. With the new limits on licensing, he'd need each license and each business to yield as much profit as possible. And he knew that wholesale, import, and retail shops could earn more than a cozy beer hall.

As he considered selling his Elbow Street saloon, he decided to open a new business in East Boston, this one in a Border Street building just a block north of his mother's grocery shop. He ini-tially partnered with Charles Quigley, a leather manufacturer and former Ward 2 representative on the Common Council. Then

Charles's younger brother, John J. ("J.J."), stepped in and took over as the day-to-day proprietor at Kennedy & Quigley, a dual-purpose retail liquor store and saloon that would be a Border Street fixture for the next twenty-five years.

The Quigley brothers were born in the Canadian province of Newfoundland, where their Irish parents had immigrated. They moved to East Boston when J.J. was twelve, and he later worked at a Border Street machine shop (where P.J. might have met him, during his stint as a brass finisher). P.J. and J.J. both joined the Excelsior Associates, founded in 1870 and named for Henry Wadsworth Longfellow's poem about a young man who climbs into the mountains and dies clutching a banner that reads EXCELSIOR. Quigley would later own a boat of the same name and would take club members on trips around Boston Harbor and out to their private retreat, Island Club House on Paddock Island, for fish fries. In time, the club would expand its activities into land speculation, with P.J. taking a lead role in buying and selling houses and other properties across East Boston. By the time P.J. was seated in the statehouse, J.J. Quigley had parlayed his own political connections into a job as a city water inspector. He left it to take over management of Kennedy & Quigley and began living above the saloon and liquor store at 81 Border Street, in an apartment beside P.J.'s sister Joanna and other boarders. (One of them was P.J.'s beer supplier, James T. Fitzgerald, older brother of John F. Fitzgerald, who at the time was considering his own run for elected office, in the North End.)

In 1887, as P.J. began his second term, with two profitable businesses to his name—Cotter & Kennedy and Kennedy & Quigley—he found himself surrounded by in-laws, aunts, cousins, nieces and nephews. Somewhat suddenly, he'd become the unmarried patriarch of the Kennedy clan. He still lived on Border Street, less than five hundred feet from his birthplace, in an apartment above his mother's shop. His new saloon farther up on Border Street, plus his duties representing the neighborhood where he was born and raised, kept him anchored to his family and community.

Bridget's extended family had bloomed over the years, with marriages and in-laws and new immigrants. It also had its share of tragic contractions, as she lost grandchildren to illness. By now, all three of her daughters had married, started families—and lost young ones.

Mary had married Lawrence Kane, who had emigrated from County Wexford with his older brother, Martin. The brothers lived beside Bridget, Mary, and P.J. above Bridget's shop until Lawrence and Mary wed. Lawrence worked as a laborer, Martin as a fish inspector. (It's possible the marriage had been arranged, a practice that was still common. The Kane brothers were related to Bridget's side of the family. P.J. had been Lawrence's citizenship sponsor in 1882.)

Bridget's youngest daughter, Margaret, had married the restaurant worker John Caulfield, and the couple had moved to New York City. They'd later return to Massachusetts and settle in Revere, a Boston suburb.

Joanna and her husband, Humphrey Mahoney, were fifteen years into their marriage and living above P.J.'s Border Street saloon with their three children. (They'd lost four others.) Humphrey was now a clothing store clerk and would later become a school janitor.

Bridget's sisters Catherine and Ann had moved from East Boston out to Salem. Her sister Margaret, who'd lived with Bridget and helped care for P.J. and his sisters, had died of cancer in 1880, leaving behind three kids.

Bridget had seen too many loved ones lowered into the ground, leaned on family, the church, and her faith during the hard times. But in the up-down cycle of her immigrant life, good news often followed bad, and finally it was her son's turn to settle down and start a family of his own.

The baby of the Kennedy family was twenty-nine and preparing for his next run for state representative. He'd started to make real money: $650 a year from his legislative salary alone (roughly $18,000 in 2020 dollars), plus expenses, on top of steady profits from liquor sales. He met at 81 Border Street each Monday night with brewery salesmen and liquor importers and made rounds to his businesses, though mostly he let J.J. Cotter and J.J. Quigley run things.

Sometime in 1887 he met his spouse-to-be, a woman who shared his history, his faith, his culture. She was a good Boston-born Irish woman, six weeks older than him, raised by immigrants who'd experienced their own coffin-ship crossing and who'd worked their way up from "shanty Irish" (father a laborer, mother a maid) to respectable. A proper Catholic, she'd been educated at Notre Dame Academy by the same severe nuns who'd taught P.J.'s sisters. She enjoyed music and theater, sang in the church choir, and devotedly attended mass — Catholic "bordering on the puritanical," one chronicler would say.

He called her "Mame." She called him Pat. Among their peers, P.J. Kennedy and Mary Augusta Hickey were far from alone in deciding to marry on the verge of thirty. P.J.'s political contemporary (and sometime rival) Martin Lomasney would not marry at all — "never had a romance, never attended a wedding," he'd crow — and another upcoming Irish politician, James Curley, would roar that he had "no time for girl friends."

Men like P.J. and Lomasney were hyperfocused on *the game:* the caucus meetings amid cigar smoke, the rattle of beer glasses during strategy sessions at the ward office, the obsession with votes, votes, votes. Sensing that the first move would need to be hers,

Mary Hickey chose and pursued P.J. Kennedy—not the other way around, as she would later boast. She'd watched him walk the streets of East Boston, sometimes right past her window, on his way to and from his liquor shops, the ward office, and the ferry, bound for the statehouse downtown. He seemed so determined and self-assured, and Mary decided one day to "set her cap" for the young mustachioed legislator.

Mary was the eldest of six, three boys and three girls, born to James and Margaret, who went by Martha. They'd come from Cork a few years after the Famine, and James Hickey had worked as a laborer in South Boston, then as a steam engineer and machinist. By the 1880s he'd moved the family to a tree-lined street in East Boston, where he ran a construction business and, on the side, a small saloon. Now with an Irish maid of their own, the family lived in Ward 1, comfortably uphill from the smelly tidal marshes and the drone of factories and shipyards.

Mary's brothers epitomized the drive that often propelled first-generation sons. Charles and James, after working together in a shoe store, lit out on their own. Jim was an East Boston police officer who'd eventually become a captain. Charlie worked as a funeral director in Brockton, south of Boston, where he got involved in local politics and eventually became mayor. The youngest brother, John, started attending Harvard Medical School—among the few Irish students there at the time—and would become a popular family doctor in East Boston, known for prescribing strong, effective cough medicine.

And then there was Mary, a force in the Hickey household, "an amazingly quick-witted woman," as her granddaughter would later say, who loved to sing and play the piano. As the eldest, Mary helped her mother run a tight household, which included her younger sisters Catharine (who went by Katie) and Margaret. Devout but ambitious, stern but serious, Mary also had a playful side.

She was kind, hopeful, and upbeat. She walked with purpose, chin up and head high, and always sat with a perfectly straight back. The Hickeys had become the very definition of "cut-glass Irish" —those who'd crawled from their mud hovels to become cleanly, respectably Americanized—and Mary would have made it clear to P.J. that there would be no backsliding. She would be the first to leave the Hickey household; her siblings, all still unmarried, would live with their parents for years to come.

We don't know how or where the two met. Mary was convinced, as her brother once told her, that P.J. was "going to be a marvelous success." Her father gave his blessing, Bridget gave hers, and the couple scheduled their wedding for November 23, 1887, the day before Thanksgiving. On that cool Wednesday morning, with J.J. Quigley as best man and Mary's sister Katie as maid of honor, they were married at the Hickeys' Church of the Sacred Heart, where Mary and her sisters sang in the choir. Father Michael Clarke performed the ceremony.

The wedding was front-page news in the *East Boston Argus-Advocate,* which described pews filled with "friends and prominent people." The guest list included dozens of dignitaries, city councilmen, clerks, police officers, the postmaster, Democratic committee leaders, legislators, including the new senator-elect John H. Sullivan. Mary's brothers were ushers, and P.J.'s cousin Mary played the organ and directed the choir. P.J.'s friend Nick Flynn and his wife were there, alongside J.J. Cotter and J.J. Quigley and their wives. Everyone gathered afterward at the Hickeys' house for a late-breakfast reception, where P.J. gave his bride a pair of diamond earrings to celebrate their union.

Bridget had now married off her fourth and youngest child— twenty-nine years and a day past her husband's death—and she wouldn't have to wait long for another grandchild.

That afternoon, P.J. said goodbye to his mother, sisters, and friends as he and Mary boarded a train for New York, the start of a honeymoon that would take them to Washington, DC, where P.J. met with Democratic leaders to discuss party affairs. A honeymoon to the nation's capital was typical of P.J.'s laserlike focus on politics, and his like-minded bride would not have been surprised by a tour of the US capital instead of a romantic beach resort. In time Mary would become a true partner—in P.J.'s work, his politics, and his liquor businesses. She'd lay out his clothes each morning and in the evening make him eat a bowl of chowder before going to meetings, so he didn't come home hungry and grouchy. A granddaughter would later call Mary "very firm and very severe," and another dubbed her "the power behind the throne."

The newlyweds soon moved into a new home, in a four-story brick apartment building on Meridian Street, East Boston's main thoroughfare, only a few blocks from Bridget's shop but in a part of town with sidewalks and streetcars, nicer shops and loftier homes. Though their union was never described as passionate or especially loving, the newlyweds shared a common goal, the goal of all immigrants' kids: a better life than their parents', and a child that lived past infancy.

Into the late 1880s, the Boston papers regularly reported on the comings and goings of East Boston's handsome young state representative, including P.J.'s journey by train in June 1888 to the Democratic National Convention in St. Louis.

On the crowded platform at the Boston and Albany station, P.J. found Colonel Isaac Rosnosky, a representative from the South End, his travel partner and roommate. Mary came to see P.J. off, waving a handkerchief with the other wives as Boston's top Democrats, in dapper traveling outfits and white hats, waved back. Patrick Maguire and Patrick Collins were there, confident they were headed

off to support the next president of the United States—Grover
Cleveland, the incumbent.

Weeks earlier, Massachusetts Democrats had selected two delegates to represent their congressional district at the convention.
They also chose two alternates: P.J. and his new friend, Rosnosky,
a wholesaler who'd emigrated from Prussia and was president of
Ohabei Shalom temple, near Cotter & Kennedy. P.J. was honored to
be invited to support the national slate, but 1888 was not the Democrats' year. Cleveland would win the national popular vote that
November but lose the electoral vote to the Republican Benjamin
Harrison—only the second time that had happened, and something that would not recur until the elections of 2000 and 2016.

Back home on Meridian Street—"Representative P.J. Kennedy
has returned from St. Louis," the local papers duly reported—P.J.
found his bride eagerly awaiting him. By then, she'd gotten used to
his absences: the late-night meetings, the urgent after-hours knocks
on the door, the occasional overnight trips with other legislators.
Mostly she didn't mind, but in the summer of 1888, she wanted
him home. Mary Augusta Hickey Kennedy was very pregnant.

On September 6, she and P.J. welcomed their first child, a boy.
At Most Holy Redeemer church, in the sanctuary where P.J. had
been christened, the newest Kennedy was baptized. Friends, relatives, and P.J.'s business associates and ward comrades visited the
Meridian Street apartment to bestow congratulations, deliver flow-
ers, and catch a peek at the baby dressed in a lacy oversized christening gown.

Instead of adding yet another Patrick to the Kennedy family tree,
Mary decided to break the chain, shunning the tradition of naming
the first son after his father or grandfather. Instead of Patrick or P.J.
—"no little P.J.'s running around *this* house," she insisted—they
settled on Joseph Patrick. She wanted her son's name to sound more

American. A boy named Joseph, she believed, was less likely to rile up anti-Irish sentiments, which her father, brothers, and husband had all endured.

Bridget was elated by the arrival of her grandson, which was immediately followed by another: P.J.'s sister Mary gave birth to a boy (George) on the day of Joe's christening. For Bridget, the arrival of two more grandchildren was both glorious and daunting. She knew by now to temper her hopes, having lost six grandchildren, taken from her daughters by the illnesses that still haunted the tenement class, lurked in its air and water: diphtheria, meningitis, enterocolitis, cholera infantum. (Of Bridget's eventual twenty-six grandchildren, only fifteen lived past age six.)

Still, with two new baby boys, with her daughter Margaret pregnant again, and with all four of her children now married, Bridget looked forward to the joys of the matriarch, surrounded by grandchildren, babysitting them, celebrating their birthdays, letting them play in the storeroom at her shop the way her own children once had. Maybe one would someday want to take over the shop for "Nana," who was now in her sixties and getting tired of the grocer's life, tired of being on her feet all day.

Though another eleven grandchildren would follow in the decade to come, Bridget would meet none of them. She would not see Joe's first birthday. She would not see another Christmas.

With two births (and no deaths), that fall of 1888 had been mostly happy for the growing tribe of Kennedys. P.J. was reelected, surviving another attempted broadside from rogue candidates. He trounced them at the polls as voters sent P.J. back to the statehouse for a fourth term. "The contest was the most exciting for many years," said the *Boston Globe,* calling it "a Waterloo for the Democratic Association." Weeks later, on a stormy December night, friends threw a large party for Mary and P.J. to celebrate their first anniversary, the arrival of their first child, and P.J.'s victory. They showered the couple with toasts and gifts, including a large reclining chair for P.J. Late into the night, couples sang and friends gave bawdy speeches. The place was filled with state senators, city aldermen, and police officers, with J.J. Cotter and J.J. Quigley there to make sure the liquor flowed.

Bridget wasn't able to make it to her son's party, though. She'd been feeling unwell, tired and struggling to walk, spending more time in bed. (Some accounts claim she was suffering from arteriosclerosis and heart trouble and was confined to her apartment above the store.) Then, on December 18, a week before Christmas, she suffered a cerebral hemorrhage, a stroke. It's unknown whether she was taken to a hospital or spent her final days at home. The end came quickly. Bridget Murphy Kennedy died on December 20, surrounded by her weeping family. Though she never quite knew (or maybe never accurately claimed) her birth date, the doctor and the funeral director would take P.J.'s word that she was born in 1821. She was sixty-seven.

A wake was held at her home, the place busy with Bridget's grandkids and her sisters, her nieces, nephews, and neighbors. Services followed at Most Holy Redeemer. The snow had melted and the temperature reached sixty degrees, downright balmy for Boston in December. In the church, Bridget's casket was mounded by floral wreaths and bouquets. A large crowd gathered, a chorus sang hymns, and Father Lawrence McCarthy, who'd recently baptized P.J. and Mary's boy, praised Bridget as a good mother and a devout Catholic who was loyal to the East Boston community.

Daughter of Richard and Mary, widow of Patrick, mother of P.J., Joanna, Mary, Margaret, and John, Bridget was laid to rest at Holy Cross Cemetery, five miles north in the town of Malden, a resting place that had been developed twenty years earlier for Boston's Irish Catholics. Rather than join her husband and first son at the cemetery in Cambridge, she apparently insisted on being buried in Malden in order to save space at the family plot in Cambridge for her grandchildren.

Days later, Bridget's name appeared in newsprint, possibly for the first and only time. In the thirty years since her husband's death, she'd appeared regularly in the annual Boston City Directory—always as the *widow* Kennedy. Now the weekly *East Boston Argus-Advocate* praised her as "a well-known and charitable lady" while the *Boston Globe* called her "a woman of many noble and charitable traits and her loss will be deeply felt by the community." A historian would later describe her as "determined" and "resourceful," and another as "one of the most successful immigrant women in all of East Boston."

Did she have cut-glass tumblers or a crystal water pitcher? Lace curtains in her windows at 23 Border Street? A parlor room for guests? These benchmarks of success were among the lofty hopes of the immigrant Irish, but Bridget left no evidence as to whether she'd achieved the dreams of so many Famine survivors. She'd at least lived to see her son's success, or the start of it. His name was now preceded by an honorific: the *Honorable* P.J. Kennedy.

She managed to leave behind something for her kids, an actual *estate,* the likes of which might have seemed unimaginable when she first stepped off the coffin ship forty years earlier. After P.J. met with his lawyers to settle Bridget's affairs, his mother's business—the store fixtures and furniture, the mortgage for 25 Border Street—was tallied up and valued at $2,200 (about $60,000 in 2020 dollars). She wasn't rich. But she didn't die poor.

Within a week of her funeral, an ad appeared in the *Boston Globe* that read like a coda to the life of the former biddy Bridget Murphy Kennedy. Perhaps posted by one of Bridget's daughters, it read: "Wanted: strong girl, plain general housework; also small girl to take care baby. 25 Border St., East Boston." The shop would stay open for another year, though it's unclear who ran it during that time. (Seven months after Bridget's death, a squad of East Boston police officers raided 25 Border Street and arrested a couple, Winifred Preston and Thomas Daly, charging them with violating city liquor laws and seizing "a large quantity of malt liquors.") Then P.J. liquidated the place.

Unlike suffragists and other activists, Bridget didn't strive to change the world. She was more the "virtuous old-fashioned Catholic gentlewoman" that Katharine Conway described in the pages of the *Pilot* when she became the newspaper's first female editor. Conway also wrote of women who'd begun to tire of the "tasteless" life of "quiet domestic duties," hungry for more: "something more spicy — something more highly seasoned with novelty and excitement." Bridget had seemed content enough without too much spice, but not content to wither, either.

Bridget's view of life had been fairly simple, reflected in the words of Louisa May Alcott, who died earlier that same year. In *Little Women,* Marmee March coaches her daughters to seek not riches or an unhappy marriage, but to "lead useful, pleasant lives . . . happy, beloved, contented." And in her journal (and in a newspaper column later titled "Happy Women") Alcott had praised "busy, useful, independent spinsters . . . liberty is a better husband than love." All of which aptly described Bridget Kennedy: useful, pleasant, beloved, contented, busy, independent.

In a posthumous discovery, and a poetic epilogue to her death, Bridget's legacy also stretched across the Atlantic, leaving an indelible imprint on the lives of the Irish Kennedys.

Months before her illness, she'd received bad news from relatives back home, where Victoria still reigned as queen, as she had since the Famine. Bridget's nephews were in prison. Through the 1880s, Charles Parnell had continued to urge tenant farmers to withhold rent from their British landlords, which sometimes led to violent clashes when attempts were made to evict those farmers. When Bridget's nephews James and Patrick learned that a neighbor was about to be evicted, they recruited twenty men to blockade the doors and windows and fight off the sheriff and his deputies. But the sheriff was tipped off and came with reinforcements. The Kennedys and others were arrested. James and Patrick Kennedy were released on bail, but at trial in early 1888 they were found guilty of coercion and sentenced to three months of hard labor. They were released on appeal but then ordered to pay two years of unpaid rent to their landlord. When they refused, they were forced to move out of the family farm. Word of their eviction reached America.

Fearing that a land grabber might take over the vacated Kennedy homestead, which could've prevented James and Patrick from ever returning to their ancestral land, someone sent money to the land agent's office to pay the overdue rent, and the Kennedys were allowed back on their farm. Though no record of this transaction survives, the money, about £50 (roughly $250 at the time, or $7,000 in 2021 dollars), apparently came from the American Kennedys —Bridget and perhaps her son and daughters. Which means that just before she died, Bridget had helped save her husband's family farm, which is owned by Kennedys to this day. Later, the Land Purchase Act of 1903 made it possible for English landowners to sell property to Irish tenant farmers, whose families, in many cases, had been living on their farms for generations. The Kennedys agreed to buy their farm, where Patrick Kennedy was born and raised, for £214—$30,000 in current US dollars—paying in twice-yearly installments for the next few decades. They wouldn't fully own the property until the 1960s.

18

P.J. the Senator

AFTER FIVE YEARS in the state legislature, P.J. — the only East Boston man to be elected to the house five times — decided to step back and focus on his businesses.

He'd lost some of his passion for the bedlam of frontline electioneering, the annual circus of caucus battles and campaigning, mobilizing voters, and late-night ballot sessions, which in Ward 2 each fall had reporters describing the "cheers and hisses," the "howling" and "general uproar" of election night. Candidates and their crews worked the sidewalks, handing out campaign flyers and shouting chants that vilified their opponents and touted their own party's slate. As many as a thousand people would pour down Elbow Street and squeeze into Sumner Hall, "packed to suffocation," said the papers. Officers from Squad 7 were always on hand to quell the inevitable fisticuffs. Sample headline: "Stormy Caucus in Ward 2 Closes After Midnight."

"It takes the citizens of Ward 2 to handle politics," said the *Boston Globe* in late 1889, when P.J. won his fifth and final election to the house. In "one of the largest caucuses ever held in Ward 2, it was all the squad of nine policemen could do to handle the crowd."

This type of spectacle rattled P.J., affirming his preference for subtler methods of public service.

Though described as that "popular Democrat of the island district," P.J. came to realize he was more skilled at operating the backroom levers of party politics than the chaotic "contest of opinion," as Thomas Jefferson called election battles waged in newsprint. P.J. decided five years of such contests was enough. He'd descend from the political stage and work behind the scenes again, keeping his influential role as chair of the Ward and City Committee.

If campaigning and making speeches weren't his strengths, neither was getting bills passed. He was no legislative maestro and hadn't been an especially potent lawmaker. Among the few bills he introduced was one to create the Boston Electric Elevated Railway Company, a network of electric-powered trains meant to replace the old steam-powered mass transit system. But his bill got killed in the state senate. Another bill sought to change the name of his East Boston boat club, the Jeffries Club of Boston, to the Jeffries Yacht Club. His statehouse colleagues approved.

Unlike some of his peers — upcoming first-generation Irish pols like Martin "the Mahatma" Lomasney in the West End, John F. "Honey Fitz" Fitzgerald in the North End, James "Smiling Jim" Donovan in the South End — P.J. wasn't brash or flamboyant, neither rogue nor rooster. He didn't give feisty floor speeches or break into song at the pub. He didn't wage internecine battles with fellow Democrats or give headline-making exclusives to reporters — in fact, he rarely spoke to them. They in turn never gave him a catchy nickname. His style was quieter.

During his five years in the house, P.J. did show a passion for two issues that affected constituents on what was still often referred to as Noddle's Island: ferries and liquor.

East Boston's fifty-year-old ferry system operated like an aging mule: it needed coaxing, patience, and sometimes a swift kick. Ferry

boats regularly broke down, piers needed repairs, fees for passage
fluctuated, and all that East Boston residents really wanted was a
fast, *free* ride over to Boston. State and local politicians occasionally
floated the concept of a free state-run or city-run ferry system, but
that idea was haunted by memories of a mid-1870s experiment in
which Boston ran the ferries — badly — before turning the expensive mess back over to private enterprise.

By now, the island's population had grown past thirty thousand,
and ferry ridership had reached thirty-one thousand trips per day.
East Boston residents had lobbied for years for a bridge or tunnel, arguing that other suburbs, such as Chelsea, Cambridge, and
Charlestown, had free access to Boston by bridge. (An East Boston bridge was briefly authorized but then canceled; it would have
blocked the flow of boat traffic.) P.J. and other free-ferry proponents
argued that the tolls prevented island kids from reaching the Boston Public Library, the art museum, Boston Common, and Faneuil
Hall, while preventing poor North End kids from escaping the city
to visit East Boston's parks and beaches.

Yet even while serving on the House Committee for Harbors and
Public Lands, which oversaw waterfront projects, P.J. never managed to build a coalition in support of toll-free ferries, and a tunnel
was deemed too costly and complicated to build. His more successful efforts came at hiring time. When ferry directors needed a new
deckhand or gatekeeper, he'd suggest a local name, hint at prospects for a new toll collector or quartermaster. That was how his
brother-in-law's brother — P.J.'s former roommate, Martin Kane
(whose brother, Lawrence, was now married to P.J.'s sister Mary)
— became a long-serving officer with the South Ferry.

In the legislature P.J. was confronted by waves of petitions seeking to change state liquor laws, changes that could've doomed his
businesses. He voted yea or nay on *scores* of proposed or amended
liquor laws backed by prohibition groups like the Catholic Total

Abstinence Union and the increasingly influential Women's Christian Temperance Union. The proposals included banning the sale of spirits in grocery stores, limiting licenses to those of "good moral character," requiring that liquor be sold only by state employees, banning *underground* establishments, limiting liquor sales to *one room* per business, prohibiting liquor sales at private clubs, and disallowing sales on Christmas, Thanksgiving, and election day. There was even an effort to create a new state holiday, Temperance Day, in late July. This barrage of petitions was designed to make liquor sales as difficult as possible, a constant nuisance for liquor men like P.J.

Some proposals focused on public safety: requiring drunkards to admit where they got their booze, then holding sellers liable if someone got hurt; making it illegal for women and children to work in a business where liquor was sold (Bridget might've taken issue with that); and a three-strikes law that would send recidivists to Deer Island after a third citation for public intoxication.

Other petitions were more aggressive, such as restricting the number of licenses in each jurisdiction to one per one thousand residents and raising license fees to $500 (or more). Then there was the constant push to enact full-scale prohibition. The senate once considered (but rejected) a petition from the Women's Christian Temperance Union to allow women to vote for or against liquor sales in their town. The idea was based on an assumption that women supported prohibition and would make Massachusetts once again a dry state. As he did with most anti-liquor proposals, P.J. voted nay on that bill, even though standing against prohibition meant, in this case, standing against voting rights for women. While he favored other bills that would benefit women—labor protections and shorter workdays, for example—he couldn't bring himself to support suffrage at this point. To do so might have threatened his livelihood.

Another problem for P.J. and other liquor dealers on the General Court was negotiating with lawmakers from elsewhere in the Bay State, including small-town lawyers with no interest in protecting the saloons and liquor men of Boston. Many were also Republicans, and either overt or covert prohibitionists. In time, P.J. would downplay his liquor selling and list his official occupation as simply "trader."

By 1890, Massachusetts was allowing voters to decide annually whether to permit liquor sales in their town. Temperance-minded locales could opt to go dry. East Boston regularly voted "wet" — thanks to Ward 2 voters, who voted yes by large margins. When nearby Chelsea voted to go dry, the enterprising saloon owner Frank Sheridan built his Sheridan House "rum shop" on pilings in Boston Harbor, just across the Chelsea town line. Other entrepreneurs ran floating saloons called "blind pigs."

While P.J. could swat down anti-saloon petitions in the state-house, there wasn't much he could do at the city level. Boston had begun slashing the number of licensed establishments it would allow. In 1889 a new city law set the cap at 780 (one per five hundred citizens), down from at least 2,500 when P.J. first got into the business. This put 1,500 saloons, grocery stores, and wholesalers out of business, or forced them to move forward without selling liquor or go rogue and continue selling without a license. "Famous Old Resorts Among the Unfortunates," said a *Boston Globe* headline. The article listed the iconic Bell in Hand tavern among the victims and predicted mass layoffs: "bartenders will carry hods next year." (Ten years later, Boston would cap the number of licenses at a thousand.) Prior to these dramatic changes, liquor license fees had brought in $336,000 to state coffers, half of it from Boston, making liquor one of the state's biggest revenue generators, after corporate and bank taxes. It was a love-hate relationship: cities loved the tax revenues, hated the drunks. Each year a list of license recipients was pub-

lished, alongside the longer list of rejects. Through the late 1880s
and well into the '90s, as licenses became increasingly precious and
costly, two businesses always made the cut: Cotter & Kennedy in
the North End and Kennedy & Quigley in East Boston.

Saloonkeepers did score one major victory just months after P.J.'s
last term in the house. For years saloons had been required to serve
food: tables and chairs were mandatory, stools and standing forbid-
den. This was part of a years-long effort to turn pubs into cafés,
which one saloon owner called a "relic of the puritanical period."
Prompted partly by the election of a Democrat, William Russell,
as governor (replacing a temperance-minded Republican), the "table law" was overturned in 1891, allowing saloons to operate as
intended, with bars and barstools. Saloon owners owed thanks to
a persuasive young Boston lawyer, Louis D. Brandeis, the future
Supreme Court justice, who took up their cause and argued before
the legislature that the law had done nothing to reduce drinking
or drunkenness. Noting a recent "craze" for silver pocket flasks, he
added that more reasonable laws might do a better job of reducing
illegal liquor sales.

   Even with the return to legal pubs and "perpendicular drinking,"
P.J. had nonetheless decided to let go of the Elbow Street beer hall.
The cost of licenses was rising past $500, on the way to $1,000,
and more proposals for anti-saloon legislation waited in the wings.
Also, vigilante groups and the Citizens' Law and Order League had
begun sending "spotters" to stake out bars, looking for violations
of liquor laws to report to the police. Though he kept his saloon on
Border Street, P.J. decided to focus mainly on his retail and wholesale shops and expand into importing. Such businesses had become
more profitable and less risky, less of a bull's-eye for prohibition-
ist lawmakers, who were slightly more tolerant of places that sold
take-away liquor. Better to have folks drunk at home than in town,

went the thinking. The mass manufacture of bottled beer and spirits was advancing, as was the transportation trade, so P.J. started eyeing another wholesale shop, a downtown import business that would eventually become his most profitable enterprise.

By 1890, P.J. felt ready to pull out of elected office. Until the machine pulled him back in.

He had already seen his friend John H. Sullivan, the immigrant stevedore turned councilman—then alderman, then senator—try to retire from politics. He withdrew his name from the elections of 1888 to "look after business interests" and declared he was "out of the public arena for good." As Sullivan told a reporter, "Public life has lost its charm and novelty." But Sullivan was talked into serving two years on the Governor's Council, and then East Boston's ward leaders decided they wanted more, nominating him as a candidate for alderman without even asking his permission. Sullivan was at home in bed the night of the caucus, in late November 1890, and had to be dragged to the ward hall to grudgingly accept the nomination.

In P.J.'s case, after he declined to run for a sixth house term, his name was put forth in late 1890 as a candidate for state senate —without his consent. The island's ward chiefs had nursed and nurtured his career, and now they wanted their protégé to make the leap from representative to senator. P.J.'s response: *Not so fast.* When a *Boston Globe* reporter asked him why he chose to withdraw from the race, P.J. explained, "It's impossible for me to withdraw from a contest in which I had never announced myself a candidate." Though he declined to run in 1890 (he never publicly said why), he agreed the next year to be his party's state senate candidate. "Patrick J. Kennedy Accepts the Honor Offered Him," said a *Boston Globe* headline, above a story calling him "one of the best-known and most popular men in East Boston." On the same day Charles

Parnell was buried in Dublin (he'd died days earlier, at forty-five, broken and disgraced by scandal), P.J. made a rare public statement, thanking his friends and neighbors for the "prosperous advancement." He promised to devote himself to "the interests of the workingmen who constitute so largely the voters who have honored me in the past."

"I assure you that I shall strive to deserve your confidence," he said. "My hope is that nothing I shall do can be construed as a betrayal of the trusts you have placed in my hands." Congratulating his "warm personal friend of many years standing," John Sullivan told reporters: "There is not another man in the district more deserving of the honor than Mr. Kennedy, valuable to his party in every way, but still more valuable in his friendships." And the *Boston News* predicted that with Sullivan in city hall and P.J. in the state-house, "there should be no doubt of a bridge or anything else that East Boston wants. They are both hustlers from way back."

P.J. won the election handily and in 1892 began a one-year term representing not just his home turf of Ward 2 but also Wards 12 and 16 (comprising the fourth district of Suffolk County). Sullivan predicted that P.J.'s time in the senate would be just a stepping-stone, telling a reporter, "We will make him senator and trust for the future to send him still higher."

P.J. and Mary had welcomed a second son, Francis Benedict, in early 1891, and as P.J. began his senate term in 1892, he and Mary were happily expecting another child, their third.

But a few months past his first birthday, Frank, as they called him, fell ill with a sore throat and fever, which worsened into laryngitis and an infection. After six days in bed at the Kennedys' home on Meridian Street, Frank died. The cause was diphtheria, an aggressive respiratory tract infection. He was buried beside his grandmother, Bridget, at Holy Cross Cemetery in Malden. One of P.J.'s granddaughters later described Frank's death as "unexpected . . . senseless and cruel," and Mary responded by devoting herself completely to her firstborn boy, Joe, who would survive his own frightening bout of diphtheria.

Two months after Frank's death, Mary gave birth to a daughter, Mary Loretta, who'd be known as Loretta. Soon after, P.J. and Mary decided they should move from their apartment building to a less crowded, less sickly part of East Boston—far from the airborne illnesses like those that had killed Frank, had killed P.J.'s nieces and nephews, and before that, his own brother. The family moved to Webster Avenue, in the neighborhood known as Jeffries Point, uphill and east from the ragged streets of P.J.'s youth. Costing $5,275 at an estate sale, their home was smaller than most on the street, but still significantly (and literally) above their station, on a ridge that looked down on the docks where P.J. had once hauled bales of cotton for thirty cents an hour. On Webster Avenue, P.J. and Mary would devote themselves to their only son, as would the two daughters who followed—similar to the family dynamic of P.J.'s childhood, when Bridget and her daughters showered P.J., the lone son, with attention.

P.J. and Mary also decided to spend part of each summer outside the city, whose humid heat brewed a steamy stew of germs. They chose Old Orchard Beach, a resort on the coast of southern Maine, launching a Kennedy family tradition of summering at the beach. Vacationing with Boston's nouveau elite at Old Orchard Beach, where Irish business and political leaders filled the hotels each August, would play an outsized role in the Kennedys' future.

While the family enjoyed fresh-air summers and a home with a yard and apple trees, as Mary planted a garden and P.J. tossed baseballs with Joe, shiploads of immigrants kept spilling onto East Boston's docks—still poor, still sick, still very Irish, but with new nationalities and religions mixed in. Many were fleeing their respective European traumas (disease, famine, religious persecution), including Italians, Russian Jews, Lithuanians, Poles, Greeks, Austro-Hungarians, Serbs, Slovaks, Balkans. Roughly 70 percent of Boston's half million residents could now trace at least one parent back to a foreign land, and soon enough immigrants or their children would account for three out of four Bostonians. These fresh waves of newcomers aroused the nativist anxieties of Boston's Yankees and Brahmins, attitudes that bolstered national anti-immigrant efforts such as the Geary Act of 1892, which required Chinese immigrants to carry residency papers (precursor to the green-card system), capping a decade-long assault on Chinese immigration that had started with the overtly racist Chinese Exclusion Act.

In an 1891 article for the *North American Review* titled "The Restriction of Immigration," the longtime Massachusetts Republican statesman Henry Cabot Lodge called on voters to "guard our civilization against an infusion which seems to threaten deterioration." Lodge preached against "hyphenism"—*Irish-American* or *Italian-American*—and endorsed "100 percent Americanism." A year later, after two terms in the US House of Representatives, Lodge ran for the US Senate against the Irishman Patrick Collins, who'd completed three terms in the House. Lodge was the frontrunner, propelled by his support for strict immigration limits and his proposed federal literacy test for newcomers. (Lodge's ideas, including the literacy test, were later incorporated into the blatantly nativist Immigration Act of 1917.)

At the time, US senators were elected by state legislators, which meant the Massachusetts General Court would determine the outcome of the race. As a state senator, P.J. cast one of the ten votes in favor of Collins, while twenty-nine voted for Lodge, who considered Irishmen like Collins "hard-drinking, idle, quarrelsome, and disorderly." (Counter to the stereotype, P.J. had celebrated his recent reelection with ice cream and salad.)

Lodge had inspired protégés like Prescott Hall, cofounder of the Immigration Restriction League, who asked, in a letter to the *Boston Herald*, "Shall we permit these inferior races to dilute the thrifty, capable Yankee blood?" Another was Thomas Bailey Aldrich, former editor of the *Atlantic Monthly*, whose poem "Unguarded Gates" became an anthem for xenophobes: "a wild and motley throng . . . bringing with them unknown gods and rites . . . Accents of menace alien to our air." The poem was an apparent response to Emma Lazarus's "The New Colossus," an anthem for inclusivity offering "a world-wide welcome" to the tired, poor, homeless, and "tempest-tossed"—words that would later appear beneath the Statue of Liberty.

After losing to Lodge, Collins dropped out of politics. Lodge went on to serve in the Senate for the next thirty years. Collins tended to his law practice and would serve as consul general in London under President Grover Cleveland. Along the way he became friends with P.J., who in turn would assist with Collins's eventual return to public office. But that was still a decade away. P.J., meanwhile, avoided any public commentary on the anti-immigrant sentiments of the day, though he surely saw its effect on Boston's Democrats and the changing complexion of the state senate. During his first term, P.J. was one of sixteen Democrats working alongside twenty-four Republicans. When he was reelected in late 1892, the Democrats were outnumbered, thirty to ten. A year later Republicans would gain three more seats.

Joining P.J. in the Democratic minority in 1893 was a freshman senator from the North End. This orphaned son of Famine immigrants was also the son of a grocer and also vacationed with his family at Old Orchard Beach. He now sat beside P.J. in seat number

7, on the right flank of the chamber. A cocky, chatty fellow named John F. Fitzgerald.

Born in 1863, the fourth son of Thomas and Rosanna Molly "Rose" Cox Fitzgerald, John Francis began his political career at twenty-two, after he lost both his parents. In 1879, his mother was recovering from the birth and death of her twelfth child and was pregnant with number thirteen. (Two other children had died as infants.) Her husband had taken their surviving nine kids (all boys) out to a church picnic, and a rumor reached Rose at home that they had all been killed in a train wreck. She died of a heart attack at age forty-eight. Six years later, Fitzgerald's father died too, and he was forced to give up his studies at Harvard Medical School and forgo his dream of becoming a doctor. Instead, he began working under the guidance of the North End's ward boss, Matthew Keany, toiling by day at Boston's Custom House while studying ward politics at night and helping to raise his orphaned brothers.

A tireless and verbose campaigner, Fitzgerald would parade through his ward with a crew of rowdy supporters, setting off fireworks. He was elected to the city's Common Council in 1891, representing Ward 6. A year later he won a seat in the state senate and served on the influential Liquor Law Committee, while P.J. sat on the less newsworthy Statehouse Committee and Water Supply Committee. Where P.J. was serious and stalwart, Fitzgerald was unpredictable and eloquent, a spirited bloviator, energetic, shrewd, and effective. In time he'd hone a reputation for boozy versions of Irish ballads and his favorite song, "Sweet Adeline," which he'd sing from atop a table or chair at every opportunity. Another politician once complained to a reporter, "Oh, Gawd, here goes that s.o.b. with the drunkard's song again." A reporter who covered Fitzgerald for years called him "his own greatest admirer." P.J. found him "insufferable."

The two men would become sometime collaborators and sometime rivals, then eventually in-laws. For the moment, in 1893, they were two outnumbered Irish Democrats, surrounded by those not fully ready to accept men named Kennedy or Fitzgerald as peers. A young New York legislator echoed the sentiment in a tirade against the Irish representatives in his statehouse: "They are a stupid, sodden vicious lot, most of them being equally deficient in brains and virtue." Theodore Roosevelt considered the typical first-generation Irishman "a low, venal, corrupt, and unintelligent brute who could not string three intelligible sentences together." In the 1890s the popular cartoons drawn by Frank Beard, a devout Methodist and anti-alcohol artist, stoked such sentiments. He regularly targeted saloonkeepers, politicians, and immigrants. Example: a dapper Uncle Sam stands at a gate, the US Capitol behind him, as a barefoot, monkey-faced man carrying bags labeled POVERTY, DISEASE, and ANARCHY asks Sam, "Can I come in?" Beside signs declaring ADMITTANCE FREE and WELCOME, Sam holds his nose and says, "I 'spose you can; there's no law to keep you out." (There were still no consistent or coherent federal laws on immigration—except to specifically suppress Chinese immigrants.)

Men like P.J. were a frequent target of Beard, who railed against collusion between police, politicians, and pub owners. The new Anti-Saloon League, founded in 1893, used Beard's cartoons as propaganda. They sometimes trended dark: one cartoon shows a man waking up from a hangover, his dead wife at his feet beside a bloody ax. Another shows Uncle Sam clutching a copy of the Geary Act and kicking a Chinese man into the water.

P.J. and Fitzgerald would each leave the state senate after back-to-back terms, overlapping in 1893 and mostly voting in sync. Fitzgerald then headed to the US House of Representatives, the only Democrat elected from New England that year (1894, representing the Ninth Congressional District). P.J. was ready to finally, truly head back to the life of a private citizen.

In Congress, Fitzgerald developed a reputation as a hustler and a fighter, described by a fellow Congressman as a "monkey on an organ grinder's rope, always jumping around and chattering." One legislative battle brought Fitzgerald toe-to-toe with Henry Cabot Lodge himself, who felt he had the votes to enact his dream of imposing a literacy test on hopeful immigrants. (Lodge referred to it as an *illiteracy* test.) The bill called for immigrants to be able to read the Constitution, prompting Fitzgerald to give a passionate floor speech against the "insidious" bill.

> It is fashionable today to cry out against the immigration of the Hungarian, the Italian, and the Jew. But I think that the man who comes to this country for the first time — to a strange land without friends and without employment — is born of the stuff that is bound to make good citizens. I had stood on the docks in East Boston and watched the newly arrived immigrant gaze for the first time on this free land of ours. I have seen the little ones huddle around the father and mother and gaze with amazement on their new surroundings.

When the bill passed, Fitzgerald encouraged President Cleveland to veto it, which he did. Lodge later confronted Fitzgerald, calling him "an impudent young man."

"Do you think Jews or Italians have any right in this country?" Lodge asked.

"As much right as your father or mine," Fitzgerald replied.

P.J., on the other hand, left the state senate with a reputation not as an impudent defender of immigrants but as a party loyalist, nonconfrontational, generous, patient, and thoughtful. Colleagues called him "salt of the earth," "a good man," and "a decent man." He never hesitated to reach into his pocket to help someone in need (though anything more than a few dollars he considered a loan, which he tracked in a ledger). Said one East Boston reporter:

"He is genial and popular and, with a heart as large as an elk's, is a friend to all." And if someone asked how they might thank him in return, he'd reply, "In your prayers you may wish to remember my departed mother."

As a legislator, he'd been a reliable friend to the working man, the union man—and the drinking man. He'd introduced legislation to add East Boston firefighters to the pension rolls. Despite opposition from mill owners in the legislature, he favored labor laws that limited a woman's workday to ten hours or less. He voted to create a national holiday, Labor Day, in early September. He supported railroads and public transportation, better hours for rail and streetcar workers, and better pay for state employees. As chairman of the Statehouse Committee, he proposed a costly but overdue remodeling of the aging building. And at the tail end of the 1893 session, during his final months in office, he threw his support behind House Bill 722, "authorizing the city of Boston to borrow the money for the construction of a tunnel to East Boston." P.J.'s recommendation, approved by the senate, was to make the wording more definitive: "Bill to provide for the building of a tunnel to East Boston."

Across his seven years on the General Court, P.J. looked out for his constituents but also voted with an eye to his own interests and his post-legislative career. During his time in office he'd seen a worrisome uptick in voters' support for prohibition, the annual vote to allow liquor sales in Boston becoming closer and the outcome less certain. "The liquor interest of the city received a scare that will last it for some time and will cause them to sleep with one eye open during the next campaign," the *Boston News* said in 1891, when liquor sales barely passed, by a vote of 25,637 to 21,314. "Boston may be a dry city yet!" A similar scare came a year later, when the senate passed a bill requiring liquor sellers to be engaged in some ancillary type of business: selling food or newspapers, or providing amusements such as billiards. The bill's stated purpose was "to promote temperance by the suppression of the liquor saloon and tippling shop." To P.J.'s relief, Governor Russell vetoed the bill, calling it legislative "mischief" more likely to promote evasion than temperance.

P.J. emerged from the senate with his liquor businesses intact, if under constant assault. The threats had prompted him to start planning for a future that didn't rely solely on liquor profits. Thus, a personal capstone to his legislative career was shepherding the passage of House Bill 420. After crossing the governor's desk, it vested a group of sixteen men with the "authority to establish and maintain a safe deposit, loan and trust company in the city of Boston." The directors called it the Columbia Trust Company, and it was headquartered on Meridian Street in East Boston, about fifty yards from P.J.'s old saloon and the Ward 2 headquarters. (The name may have been inspired by the World's Fair Columbian Exposition of 1893, which took place in Chicago. P.J. joined a delegation of legislators there, representing his home state on "Massachusetts Day.")

The bank would become integral to P.J.'s life, a source of income, loans, and prestige, of headaches and investigations, a blessing and a curse. Columbia Trust Company would host some of the highs and lows of the rest of his career—and would later launch his son's career too.

Like politicians across time, P.J. the steadfast and quiet one would capitalize on all he'd seen and learned at the statehouse, deftly navigating and manipulating a system he'd helped shape. Columbia Trust would be just one of many lucrative new private ventures, some of them controversial, all of them requiring a tiptoe around potential legal minefields.

Though some friends and benefactors had envisioned a different future for him—viewing his days in the state legislature as a step toward higher office—P.J. didn't care to move to Washington to serve in Congress, or across the harbor to Boston to take a shot at mayor. He was happy to stay on his island and make some real money. Into the late 1890s, new clusters of first- and second-generation Irish vote-getters kept poking holes in their political ceiling, making strides. But instead of aiming, as Fitzgerald did, for the increased political power that higher office promised, P.J. had other plans; 1894 would mark the first time in a decade that his name did not appear on a ballot—and it wouldn't again for fourteen years.

P.J. harbored "no aspirations to leadership," a colleague later said. He seemed content to play the role of adviser to mayors, governors, congressmen, liquor men, and business owners. He preferred working privately, an influencer and insider, writing letters to friends and colleagues, seeking jobs for their sons, offering suggestions and advice, and swapping favors. Years later, in a profile of his successful son, Joe, *Fortune* magazine would describe P.J. as "a familiar figure in that strange, provincial, pre-War Boston political and financial world . . . in the period when it was possible to be a national figure in Boston and yet remain unknown to the rest of the country." The truth was . . . in a master stroke of misdirection, P.J. had played the role of party loyalist (and continued in that role) while slowly, slyly building a modest empire.

Nearing forty, P.J. ducked out of the limelight, stepped off the stage, and headed for safer waters: back to business. There, he'd find far more political power than he'd held as an elected official. As a private, well-connected citizen, he'd find and exert real influence. And he'd cash in.

19

P.J. the Boss

P.J. STOOD AT the bow of the yacht *Excelsior,* steaming east through Boston's Harbor Islands. Dressed in a light summer suit, his straw hat pulled tight, he puffed on a Havana cigar. Up ahead spread the open waters of Massachusetts Bay, which had welcomed his parents fifty years earlier. To the north he could see the tip of Deer Island, still home to convicts, drunks, and delinquents.

At the helm, similarly dressed and smoking a stogie, stood his friend and business partner J.J. Quigley. Navigating the shoals, currents, and hidden rocks of Boston Harbor wasn't for amateurs, but Quigley (still running Kennedy & Quigley) had been exploring these islands for years, giving friends tours around Peddocks Island, Calf Island, and Green Island. *Excelsior*'s name, like that of P.J. and Quigley's social club, Excelsior Associates, came from a poem by Longfellow; Quigley's other steamer tug, *Resolute,* was inspired by Longfellow's "The Light of Stars."

> *As one by one thy hopes depart,*
> *Be resolute and calm.*
> . . . .

Know how sublime a thing it is
To suffer and be strong.

P.J.'s son, Joe, now six years old, would soon work on Quigley's boats, collecting tickets and selling candy and peanuts during excursions around the harbor, for which Quigley charged twenty-five cents a trip, ten cents for kids. Working for his father's liquor-selling partner would give an early boost to Joe's own entrepreneurial inclinations. But Joe wasn't aboard today, this summer afternoon in mid-1894. The grown-ups had much to discuss: banking and real estate, coal and liquor, ferries and tunnels, and, of course, city politics. A year after leaving the state senate, returning to the life of a liquor seller (and part-time banker), P.J. had also adopted the role of elder statesman, a veteran of the political trenches. Men now traveled across to P.J.'s island, seeking his advice or his blessing. A new phase of life, resolute and strong, had begun.

A group of East Boston's leading businessmen and Democrats had joined P.J. on the *Excelsior,* and now they were headed to Georges Island for a private tour of Fort Warren, formerly a prison for Confederate officers during the Civil War. Also aboard were two of P.J.'s brothers-in-law, Humphrey Mahoney and Lawrence Kane. After the visit to Fort Warren, Quigley sailed the men south to hunt for smelt, which their wives would fry at dinner that night. "Everyone in the party had a glorious time," said the reporter who'd been invited along.

At day's end, as the *Excelsior* returned to East Boston and approached the pier, P.J. looked up at his home, his perch on the hill overlooking the harbor, where Mary and his daughters waited. As a new century approached, P.J. at age forty was enjoying life after the rigors of elected office. He'd soon buy a yacht of his own, a sixty-foot cabin cruiser he'd name *Eleanor.* Harbor outings would become more frequent, on Quigley's boat and his own, but not entirely for pleasure. The need to discuss private business matters outside local saloons or ward headquarters was another motivation. And on days such as this, P.J. might've allowed himself that rare glass of beer.

In the waning years of the nineteenth century, P.J. hit an impressive professional stride, throwing himself into new ventures, both financial and social. Now unconstrained by the limits placed on an elected official, he launched one moneymaking endeavor after another, the likes of which his mother would never have imagined. Stepping onto the age-old carousel of lawmaker turned moneymaker, he began investing in the same concerns that he'd voted for (or against), working with some of the same men he'd met (and helped) at the statehouse.

He and Mary welcomed another child in 1898, a second daughter, named Margaret. After enrolling Joe in East Boston's Catholic schools (Assumption and Xaverian), the couple decided to send him (beginning in 1901) across the harbor to the exclusive, centuries-old Boston Latin School, alma mater of five signers of the Declaration of Independence, plus Paul Revere, Ralph Waldo Emerson, and assorted Lowells, Cabots, and Adamses. Joe, like his father a lackluster student, would later describe the institution as "a shrine." Joe ran to catch the ferry each morning, then hopped a trolley to the school, the first steps in his escape from provincial East Boston.

As a family, they'd entered a new social stratum—undeniably high Irish and fully *lace curtain,* as middle- and upper-class Irish came to be known. And as P.J. got busier (and wealthier), they could afford to hire domestic help, taking on a rotating staff of housemaids and cooks, including an Irish immigrant maid named Bridget Kennedy. A cousin on P.J.'s father's side, "Bridgie" came to

Boston in 1896, at age twenty-four. P.J. paid for her crossing, and she lived with and worked for him and Mary, then later moved to Boston to work as a maid.

P.J.'s elevated status won him more invitations to exclusive clubs and, in turn, more business opportunities. An established member of the typical Irish organizations — the Ancient Order of Hibernians, the Knights of Columbus, the Elks — he was also asked to join the Redberry Club. Founded by vacationing "gentlemen" at Old Orchard Beach, Maine, the club was dominated by Boston's Irish politicians, who fled their steamy city each August for weeks of song and drink, epic baseball games, fireworks, concerts, clambakes, and dances at the coastal village. Favorite events included a parade through town, atop decorated horse-drawn traps and hay wagons, and the annual Redberry Queen contest. The men would meet separately at hotel bars for cigars and whiskey, singing their Redberry Club song: "It has men of every station, of high and low degree, and they gather every summer, at Old Orchard by the Sea." (The fireworks and Roman candles led to the demise of a favorite Redberry haunt, the 350-room Imperial House hotel, which burned to the ground in 1896, after a late-night ball.)

Through his Redberry membership, P.J. became better acquainted with his former senate colleague John F. Fitzgerald, who had been visiting Old Orchard Beach since the early 1890s. Most Redberries traveled by train or carriage, but "Honey Fitz," as he was known — also Fitzie, the Little General, Little Johnnie Fitz (he was five foot two), and other nicknames — often rode the hundred miles on horseback, taking his time and staying with friends along the way. Fitzgerald was still in Congress, still the only Democrat there from New England, and he would serve three terms in the House (1895 to 1901). But he always came home for summers and always made time for his Redberry pals.

Although spending August at Old Orchard was a highlight for

club members, the Redberries also gathered throughout the year, meeting for late-night dinners at the Quincy House in Boston, playing baseball, making day-long boat trips to the Harbor Islands. The Redberries once paraded from downtown Boston to Fitzgerald's house in the North End to celebrate the birth of his son, and when Fitzgerald left town to return to Washington, a party of Redberries would give him a rowdy sendoff at the train station.

But it was mostly at Old Orchard Beach, wearing their matching Redberry swimsuits and singing their Redberry song, that the fates of P.J. Kennedy and John F. Fitzgerald became entwined. To the initial discomfort of both men.

With such similar backgrounds — immigrant parents from County Wexford, sons of a grocer and liquor seller, devout Catholics — they should have been friends, could have been soul mates. Like P.J., Fitzgerald had grown up poor, roving his Irish neighborhood barefoot and looking for trouble. "My playgrounds were the streets and wharves busy with ships from every port of the world," Fitzgerald said. Like P.J., he'd discovered a path to success in politics — "the only field where I could get influence and opportunity."

As two of the city's top Democrats, working together was unavoidable. But they were in many ways opposites, Fitzgerald as voluble and extroverted as P.J. was reserved and introspective. Fitzgerald could talk a blue streak about any topic, while P.J. was more inclined to listen and nod. "I suppose they must have grated on each other's nerves at times," Fitzgerald's daughter, Rose, would write. "But they had many things in common: their immigrant background, the early deaths of their fathers, the personal determination, foresight, and hard work that raised them to their positions, and, of course, their sophisticated understanding of politics. I'm sure they understood each other and each in his way liked and admired the other."

As Irish Catholic politicians, their primary bond was the fight against WASP-y forces still aligned against their kind. In 1895, during Fitzgerald's first term in Congress, riots broke out in East Boston after the secretive anti-Catholic American Protective Association paraded through town on the Fourth of July, ranting about Irish Catholic "aliens" and "enemies of the state." Rioters fired shots at a group of spectators on Border Street, hitting at least four men. A longshoreman named Wills, the father of seven, was shot in the back and killed. A *Boston Globe* artist's rendering of the scene shows P.J.'s liquor store and saloon in the background, beneath a sign advertising LAGER BEER SALE. One of the shooters was arrested next door to Kennedy & Quigley.

Not one for speeches, P.J. asked Fitzgerald to visit and calm things down. At a fundraiser for the murdered longshoreman, Honey Fitz addressed the "intense hatred of everything Irish and Roman Catholic" that still persisted, and he blamed radical, faux-patriotic men's groups for trying to "monopolize all the Americanism in this country."

"We are one people and owe the same duty to our country," Fitzgerald told the crowd. "Why, then, this desire to set one class of people against another?"

Weeks later, the two men joined up at Old Orchard Beach, during the summer that would be remembered as the first time P.J.'s son and Fitzgerald's daughter met. Joe was seven and Rose was five. A group photograph captured them sitting with others on the steps of a hotel. A decade later, as teenagers, they would fall in love, and Rose would always credit their mutual attraction to those festive summers at Old Orchard, "a magical place." (A decade later, a massive fire leveled most of the town, and an exploding soda tank decapitated a man who happened to be standing beside Fitzgerald and other rescuers.)

Those days on the coast of Maine brought their families together, and P.J. and Fitz would one day become in-laws, even if P.J. mostly viewed the jaunty, scrappy, singsongy Honey Fitz as a buffoon. In fact, Fitzgerald had been elected to Congress over P.J.'s opposition. In 1894, P.J. and other ward bosses had supported the incumbent, Joseph O'Neil. But Fitzgerald waged a tireless campaign. He and his brothers had visited every ward, often announcing their arrival with fireworks. It helped that Martin Lomasney, the influential boss of Ward 8, had backed Fitzgerald, bucking the Democratic Party's preference for O'Neil and throwing his weight behind the "pink-cheeked youngster," Honey Fitz.

The Ninth Congressional District comprised nine Boston wards and was, therefore, the rare Democratic district in Massachusetts. Fitzgerald easily beat his Republican opponent. (He would serve with just two other Catholics among 350 members of Congress.) In a testament to his political savvy—and P.J. Kennedy's political heft—Fitzgerald took the ferry over to East Boston the morning after his election and walked uphill to pay his respects at 165 Webster Street. "Now that the fight is over," he said to P.J., "let's shake hands."

A little more than a year later, soon after starting his second year in Congress, an exhausted Fitzgerald was ordered by his doctor to take a medical leave and spend the winter recovering down south. The diagnosis: consumption. Fitzgerald chose Asheville, North Carolina, known for its health spas and tuberculosis hospitals. His brother, James, who sold beer to P.J.'s saloons, arranged for P.J. to make the trip too (likely at Fitzgerald's request). The men stayed at the Battery Park Hotel during the early months of 1896, rode horses, and talked politics, as Fitzgerald recovered from the disease that had killed P.J.'s father.

Soon enough, they'd find themselves on opposite sides of a political battle. Again.

Back in East Boston, P.J. continued to live the quieter life of an ex-politician, though an increasingly wealthy one. The simpler lifestyle did not preclude getting rich. His longtime social club, Excelsior Associates, had years earlier created a real estate arm, Excelsior Investment Company. After leaving the senate, P.J. took over as president and with other Excelsior officers started buying property —a vacant lot here, a shop or tenement house there—based on information gathered at ward meetings and on the streets. Profits went back into Excelsior's coffers or into more East Boston property deals. Through the 1890s and into the early 1900s, P.J. bought and sold dozens of properties and even arranged development contracts for his father-in-law, James Hickey. His partners in the real estate game included Thomas O. McEnaney, who'd been a Ward 2 state representative with P.J. in the 1880s, and Thomas J. "T.J." Lane, a former *Boston Pilot* reporter, shoe salesman, and undertaker who became chairman of Boston's Bath Commission, overseeing public pools, baths, and gymnasiums. (A progressive public steward, Lane was known for hiring women for city jobs and opening public baths to the poor.)

Although one goal of Excelsior's real estate investments was to help young couples get started in a new home, the buying and selling caught the curious eye of a *Boston Globe* reporter, who expressed surprise at how much speculating was being done by an "organization of prominent East Bostonians that was formed purely for social purposes." Said the *Globe:* "Gradually, the organization spread in its scope, began to invest money little by little into real estate transactions, and today the association holds quite a title to property in East Boston."

It wasn't the first time P.J.'s business activities had been called into question. Columbia Trust Company, the bank that P.J. had co-founded at the end of his time in the state senate, had initially been designed to operate small and local, in and around East Boston. But it didn't take long for the press and other legislators to notice that four of the bank's sixteen founding directors were current or former

East Boston legislators, mostly Democrats. Shortly after the bank was incorporated (but before it opened to the public, in 1895), a suspicious state representative from suburban Everett complained that certain "cliques and factions" had conspired to create Columbia Trust, which "reflects dishonor on certain members of the Legislature."

After a front-page story in the *Boston Globe,* followed by a few back-and-forth threats of lawsuits and investigations, the coverage died down and P.J. emerged unscathed; the bank survived. P.J. then tapped his longtime friend John Sullivan to serve as bank president.

The incident revealed a notable P.J. Kennedy trait: restraint. While other bank directors defended themselves in the papers, or questioned their accusers' motives, or threatened legal action, P.J. simply moved on. He could be "ruthless" when necessary, but he was no Irish hothead. As a result, insinuations in news stories or insults from other lawmakers never made much of a dent, leaving him to tend to his carefully braided interests: politics, banking, real estate, liquor, and more. Not only did he emerge unfazed from the Columbia Trust controversy, but within a few years he was co-founding another bank, Sumner Savings Bank, again with fellow East Boston politicians and ex-politicians serving as directors. This neighborhood bank operated right beside Columbia (in a building owned by John Sullivan), and P.J. would serve on the board of directors of both banks for the rest of his days.

Another example of his ability to discreetly profit from his legislative past: coal. Before leaving the senate, P.J. had introduced a bill to enact pollution controls for buildings burning bituminous coal for heat. (This was in tandem with a city effort to retrofit furnaces with pollution-control devices.) He learned a bit about the industry, met a few of the players, and later became director of the Suffolk Coal Company, a processor and dealer with a large factory and warehouse on Border Street, a few blocks north of Kennedy

& Quigley. Suffolk Coal Company delivered coal throughout the city, in bags and in bulk, to tenements and businesses, and in time it would bid on lucrative city contracts to provide coal to public buildings.

Meanwhile, P.J. continued to invest in liquor—and even got his wife involved in the family business. His friend and business partner J.J. Cotter had died years earlier, while on vacation in New Hampshire. He was forty-eight. Afterward, P.J. created a new company, P.J. Kennedy and Company, and began adding Mary's name to his liquor license applications. He changed the name of his Cotter & Kennedy saloon shop to P.J. Kennedy and Company and opened a new importer-wholesaler business under the same name, with offices and a shop on High Street in downtown Boston. He and Mary began handing out wood-handled corkscrews with the inscription COMPLIMENTS OF P.J. KENNEDY & CO., IMPORTERS.

Next, he bought a struggling liquor company, Fisher and Fairbanks, an importer of whiskey, wine, and champagne known for its "celebrated rock cordials," a sweet liqueur with purported medicinal powers that was advertised in newspapers and on trading cards as the "standard remedy for lung troubles and kidney diseases"; it could "mitigate the evils of consumption." P.J. bought the company's stock and the copyright to its rock cordial tonic and recipes for rock candy syrup, then merged it all into P.J. Kennedy and Company. In time, he'd take out his first-ever newspaper ads, promoting "Fairbanks Rock Cordial: The Famous Remedy for Coughs, Colds, Consumption, $1," which was sold by liquor stores and druggists across the country.

Fisher and Fairbanks had come to P.J.'s attention through Thomas Barron, the son of Bridget Kennedy's cousin Patrick Barron. Barron had been a longtime salesman for Fisher and Fairbanks and was possibly a part owner. He was also, according to reader polls taken by newspapers in the early 1890s, one of the city's most popular salesmen, once finishing eighth behind a salesman at Jordan Marsh. P.J. installed Barron as manager at P.J. Kennedy and Company on High Street, where he would work for the rest of his life.

All in all, P.J. had prospered during his post-senate years, making smart investments and good money, keeping his head down and his name mostly out of the papers. That is, until word leaked out about his membership in a small, secretive group of power players that had been dubbed, in mockery, the Board of Strategy. Turns out he hadn't been able to stay far from the running of Boston, one form of intoxication he couldn't resist.

When the Quincy House in downtown Boston expanded and reopened in 1860, the owners had promoted the remodeled hotel and restaurant by using two large oxen to tow a large sign around town. The advertisement said the two beasts would be slaughtered and served for dinner on opening night, launching a new chapter in the story of the legendary institution. On Brattle Street, near the southern edge of the North End, directly behind city hall and just a couple of blocks from Cotter & Kennedy, Quincy House was one of the city's largest hotels, with hundreds of rooms. It hosted weddings, veterans' reunions, and VIP dinners. It had become a haunt favored by lawyers and labor leaders, and by the mid-1890s some leaders of the Democratic Party had adopted it as their unofficial headquarters.

P.J. was a Quincy House regular, and the waiters all knew to usher him up to room 8, where he shared a secret weekly lunch with other city bosses: state senator John A. Keliher, from the South End; James "Smiling Jim" Donovan, also a South Ender, who ran the city's lamp department; and Joseph J. Corbett, from Charlestown, a member of the city's Board of Election Commissioners. Together, these three—soon to be joined by two others of equal renown—decided whose names should appear on which ballots, who was due for a patronage job, or who was ready for a well-paid role as a commissioner.

All were current or former state senators, and they'd all been lieutenants of the city's Democratic boss, Patrick Maguire, who had ruled the party for two decades. Men whose fathers had dug ditches, caulked ship decks, crafted barrels, and stitched together rail lines now gathered in wood-paneled, smoke-filled rooms, sipping whiskey and brandy as they plotted the fate of their city. It was just as Alexis de Tocqueville had predicted: the servant had become the master.

P.J. had known the others for going on twenty years, through their party's many ups and downs. In 1896, he'd traveled to Chicago with Corbett and Maguire to the Democratic National Convention, then suffered a dreary overnight train ride home after former Massachusetts congressman George Fred Williams lost his bid for the vice presidency to Arthur Sewall and former Massachusetts governor William Russell lost the presidential nomination to William Jennings Bryan. (Both men were caught in the battle over replacing the gold standard with silver-backed currency. The Massachusetts candidates and their delegates were gold men, but Bryan's historic Cross of Gold earned him the nomination.) Russell died of a heart attack days later, while on vacation in Canada; he was thirty-nine. Patrick Maguire died later that year, leaving a void atop Boston's Democratic hierarchy. P.J. helped make Maguire's funeral arrangements, served as honorary pallbearer alongside Corbett and Donovan, and began to plot how to replace the boss.

As P.J. and the other ex-senators began meeting at the Quincy House, word reached another party power: Martin Lomasney. They had intentionally excluded him from their lunches. P.J.'s friend John Sullivan once said that Lomasney was like "an owl in a hole. You don't see him, but you feel him." He lurked behind and loomed over all aspects of city politics. It was Lomasney who had derisively dubbed P.J.'s exclusive club the Board of Strategy, a name inspired by the US Navy's "Board of Strategy," whose members sat snugly in Washington while sailors faced the fight in Cuba during the Spanish-American War.

The others knew Lomasney wanted to replace Maguire, but they didn't trust him. No one questioned his power in the West End (Ward 8), his ability to deliver votes, or his commitment to his constituents, of whom he famously said, "The great mass of people are interested in only three things: food, clothing, and shelter. A politician in a district like mine sees to it that his people get these things." Another of Lomasney's famed quotes — "Don't write when you can talk, don't talk when you can nod, don't nod when you can wink," and similar versions of that sentiment — was more applicable to P.J. than Lomasney, a known screamer, unpredictable and vengeful. When giving a speech, Lomasney would whip off his coat and tie, roll up his sleeves, and deliver his message with fist-shaking fury. P.J. and the others began scheming in secret to keep Lomasney in check.

Tensions between P.J. and Lomasney peaked in 1898, during a legendary showdown over that year's Democratic nominee for state senate, the man who'd represent P.J.'s old turf. P.J. and the Board of Strategy had already decided to nominate William Donovan (not related to Smiling Jim), while Lomasney preferred his own man, Daniel Rourke. The nominating convention was to be held at the Maverick House in East Boston, and the candidate's name had to be delivered to the statehouse downtown by 5 p.m.

But Lomasney had concocted a hopeful scheme to trick P.J. and the Board of Strategy by getting his own candidate's name downtown *first*.

Initially, P.J. wasn't too worried about the contest and assumed everything would run smoothly. Lomasney wasn't a delegate and couldn't make the nomination. So when some of P.J.'s men tried to block Lomasney and his men from entering the Maverick House, P.J. backed down—"Never mind, let them go on." But he soon realized his mistake. Lomasney fooled the Democrats into separating into two rooms. When P.J. caught on, he and Lomasney went nose to nose, arguing as the other men cheered and hissed, jostled and booed. The police were called but seemed too befuddled to intervene. Finally, the cops separated the two dueling factions— one group met and nominated P.J.'s man (Donovan), and the other tapped Lomasney's man (Rourke). And then the race was on to see who'd get their nominee's envelope to the statehouse first.

One of Lomasney's crew sprinted out of the Maverick House with his envelope and boarded a Boston-bound ferry. Then, halfway across the harbor, the vessel developed mysterious engine problems and came to a halt. This was P.J.'s doing. He'd been communicating with his friend, the superintendent of ferries, by means of the latest technology, the telephone. There was no way he would let Lomasney's man reach the statehouse by five o'clock.

But the envelope now marooned in the harbor turned out to be a decoy. The real one had been thrown out a Maverick House window into the hands of a college sprinter hired by Lomasney, who raced to the East Boston piers and hopped an awaiting tugboat. When the boat reached the other side, the sprinter handed the envelope to a hired bike-racer, who weaved through traffic, collided with a wagon, but still managed to deliver the prize to the statehouse at 4:48, ten minutes after it'd left East Boston. A second envelope arrived one minute later—delivered via ferry and bicycle, amid the cheers of Ward 2 crowds—containing paperwork with the name Donovan, the party's official candidate. It was signed by P.J. Kennedy. But would that one-minute advantage be decisive for Rourke?

For days, the papers were filled with stories about the bizarre infighting among the Democrats. The *Boston Globe* offered a front-page depiction of the "opera bouffe," complete with sketches of the sprinters and bikers. Once the confusion settled down, and Lomasney's gambit was revealed, the city's Ballot Law Commission determined that Donovan was in fact the legitimate candidate, and he'd go on to win the election.

In the aftermath, Lomasney went on a rampage, accusing the men of Ward 6 (led by Fitzgerald) of colluding with the men of Ward 2 (led by P.J.) to marginalize the men of Ward 8 (led by Lomasney).

But despite the public displays of sibling rivalry, the Democrats were on a steady rise. They'd finally gained control on Boston's Common Council and the Board of Aldermen and had held the mayor's office for all but two of the past fourteen years, ever since Hugh O'Brien's breakthrough in 1885. Save for a loss here and there, the twentieth century would see Irish Catholics completely dominating that office and others, as a remarkable era of political power (and corruption) began.

If they could just survive the family squabbles and their own incivility, that is. But like brothers scrapping for the top spot in the family, they were often at each other's throats. P.J. the quiet one often found himself caught in the middle. And sometimes in the crosshairs.

Until that Maverick House incident, the Board of Strategy had been familiar to Democratic Party insiders but not the general public. That changed a year later when the *Boston Globe* published a full exposé, citing unnamed sources — "gentlemen conversant with affairs at city hall" and "those who are assumed to know the workings of the board." The *Globe* said the board was composed of "alert politicians, each credited with the ability to 'carry his district,'" and each had "proved his political strength." Now there were two newer members. One was the mayor, Josiah Quincy VI, a Democrat finishing his second two-year term. (Quincy's grandfather, as mayor, had created the House of Reformation, P.J.'s onetime residence.) The other was Congressman John F. Fitzgerald, who had become a viable successor to Maguire—and Lomasney's chief nemesis.

That made P.J. and Honey Fitz, at least for a while, comrades.

When Fitzgerald was reelected to Congress in 1899—with the Board of Strategy's support and over Lomasney's opposition—the newspapers predicted that Lomasney was "done: his days are numbered." Yet he continued to run for office, serving as alderman, state representative, and state senator through the 1890s (with many more successful elections to come). He often played the role of gleeful obstructionist, sometimes working with Republicans against his own party. Said a journalist for New York's *Evening Sun,* after a visit to profile the man who had been dubbed "the Mahatma," "No man can surpass Lomasney in the vindictiveness of his pursuits."

In this period of personality-driven politics, featuring onstage theatrics and backstage trickery, P.J. found himself better suited to the wings. The strategy board and the press seemed to agree. Whereas most board members were known for their speaking skills, "Mr. Kennedy is said to be the silent man," the *Boston Globe* once wrote. He may have lacked the eloquence, the performative tics, or the vindictiveness of some of his peers, and no longer had the imprimatur of being elected to office, but P.J. was nonetheless recognized as a major power in politics.

"He is classed among politicians as a man of extremely good sense and judgement, an unselfish man, whose work is almost always directed to serving some friend rather than himself," said the *Globe,* which deemed him the "undisputed leader of the democracy of East Boston." P.J.'s ascent to this role was partly due to the shocking death of his close friend John Sullivan.

They'd been dockworkers, poll watchers, Ward 2 upstarts, and business partners, their friendship lasting decades, ever since their youthful days as longshoremen and stevedores. They lived a few doors apart (on Webster Street), having moved up together in business and politics. But Sullivan had been suffering from diabetes and other ailments, and one Sunday morning in early 1899 he shot himself with a small pistol—whether this was intentional, accidental, or due to a delusional pique was never determined. He left behind a wife and seven kids.

Mourners gathered at Sullivan's home and stood by the big man's body as it lay in the parlor, telling stories before moving to the Maverick House for late-night drinks and toasts. As he often did for friends, P.J. personally managed the funeral, where he welcomed numerous dignitaries, including the Board of Strategy crew, who served as honorary pallbearers. Hundreds turned out for the event. Sullivan was fifty-one.

Putting aside party squabbles, Fitzgerald praised Sullivan as "an ideal citizen" and an ally to the "poor and unfortunate," while Lomasney deemed him "an honest man—What better can be said of any man?" (At the time of his death, Sullivan was still head of Columbia Trust. He was being investigated for thousands of dollars in liabilities he owed the bank. Examiners later deemed the debt too small to "seriously embarrass the condition of the company," and P.J.'s friend Frank Wood became the new president.)

After Sullivan's death, the Board of Strategy sought to avoid further turmoil and guide Boston into the new century—ideally under Democratic leadership. Over the course of a few Quincy House lunches, the next steps were decided with brisk efficiency:

- Patrick Collins, recently returned from serving as President Cleveland's consul general in London, should replace the outgoing Josiah Quincy as mayor.
- Joseph Corbett should resign as election commissioner to manage Collins's campaign.

• P.J. should replace Corbett on the influential Board of Election Commissioners.

Quincy had to act quickly to appoint P.J. before his term expired at year's end. To maintain a public display of humility, P.J. initially declined — "for business reasons." Weeks later, encouraged by fellow Democrats, he relented and agreed to join the four-man board — two Democrats, two Republicans — which managed the elaborate machinery of the city's elections.

Describing him as "one of the older generation of politicians," a front-page *Boston Globe* story featured a sketch of P.J.'s spectacled, mustachioed face and said his appointment "means that his name and influence will continue to be felt in Boston's political arena." It didn't hurt that the job came with a $3,500 salary (more than $100,000 in 2020 dollars). P.J. promised to deliver "promptness, honesty, and accuracy." The job required little effort for much of the year but was a heavy load in the final quarter. Election commissioners oversaw more than a thousand employees (wardens, clerks, inspectors); a budget of $130,000; scores of portable voting booths (many of them newly heated) and hundreds of ballot boxes across 191 precincts; the counting of votes, of course; the swearing-in of newly elected officials; and the investigation of disputes or fraud.

Collins lost the mayor's race in 1899, but he ran again in 1901 and won by one of the largest votes in city history. Fitzgerald had considered running, but the Board of Strategy chose to back Collins. And Collins, in turn, would reward the board. P.J. would be tapped for another new job and an even larger salary. But he and the strategy board would also pay a price for this devotion to Collins — and to their own zeal for power.

Some voters began to resist having their city controlled by a handful of Irish ward bosses.

20

P.J. the American

A HALF CENTURY past the Great Irish Potato Famine, Boston had become a city thoroughly shaped by the decades-long fallout from that tragic event, a city dominated — politically, culturally, economically — by the children and grandchildren of the Patricks and Bridgets who'd invaded the stolid, learned hub of Brahminism. Boston was now run by, and often for, its Irish, even as newer immigrants continued to arrive from various oppressed corners of Europe and elsewhere. The city's ethnic makeup continued to evolve, as did its size, now pushing 600,000, nearly four times what it had been at the time of P.J.'s birth.

In East Boston and the North End, Italian groceries and Jewish bakeries and kosher markets operated alongside Irish taverns. On the docks, the brogue once dominant among longshoremen now harmonized with new accents and languages, as newcomers took the working-class jobs the Irish were happily casting aside in their ascent to the middle class and, for some, to political power. As P.J. wrote to a cousin in Ireland, "The Irish immigration here has fallen off of late years very much, and the Italians and other nationalities are coming in very strong."

There were new foods, new fashions, new churches and synagogues. By 1905 East Boston boasted one of the largest Jewish communities in New England. The island's Italian community had swelled, their families cramming into tenement apartments around Maverick Square as the Irish had before them. By now the Democrats were printing election posters and postcards in Italian and Hebrew. There were still few Black families in East Boston, and no Black lawmakers. (The first African American legislators in Massachusetts, Edward Walker and Charles Mitchell, were elected to the General Court right after the Civil War, in 1866, but served only a year.)

Now holding most of the city's elected and appointed positions, the Irish had created a formidable new style of politics: emotional, colorful, familial, and increasingly fraught with patronage and graft. They got things done, to be sure. East Boston was finally getting its harbor tunnel, being dug by Italian and Irish laborers and set to be completed in 1904. It would connect the island to downtown Boston's subway system (the nation's first, opened in 1897).

But the city leaders also largely helped their own kind, and sometimes they crossed a line. This was happening in other Irish and Democratic cities too — Boss Tweed and his successors running Tammany Hall, in New York; corrupt bosses like "Hinky Dink" Kenna and "Bathhouse John" Coughlin ruling Chicago's Loop. These alleged protectors of the working class practically invented the cynical big-city corruption that pioneering investigative journalists like Lincoln Steffens and Ida Tarbell were uncovering in the pages of *McClure's Magazine.*

P.J. was no Boss Tweed, who as a state senator and head of New York's Democratic machine had also owned real estate and a hotel, served as director for a bank and a railroad — until he was brought down by corruption charges, arrested, and convicted; he escaped, was captured, and died in jail, owing millions. P.J. had become both participant and beneficiary in his party's self-serving tilt toward what some were calling the Tammanyization of Boston. That tilt would lead P.J. and his peers into increasingly brutal political battles, and a chorus of accusers would claim that the Board of Strategy was fleecing the public.

For P.J., a once thrilling and empowering game was getting rougher. Party alliances were fracturing. The public was getting testy and more demanding. The press was a pain.

P.J. had advised and supported Patrick Collins for years, dating back to Collins's time in Congress; he preferred the Harvard-trained lawyer's restrained approach and modest style to the volatile ambitions of men like Lomasney and Fitzgerald. When Collins became mayor in 1901, he began handing out jobs, including high-paying city appointments, to the men who'd helped get him elected: the members of the Board of Strategy. His first official act after his inauguration was to appoint James Donovan as superintendent of streets. Next, Joseph Corbett was offered the powerful role of corporation counsel, overseeing the city's law department, at $7,500 per year. (Corbett declined and returned to his private law practice; he was later named a schoolhouse commissioner.)

When it was P.J.'s turn, he was initially offered the role of water commissioner, but he'd been doing business with a heating and plumbing company that sold supplies to the city, so he declined the offer to avoid any conflict of interest. He later accepted a different cabinet-level position, commissioner of wires, which he deemed a more aboveboard move.

In his new job (accepting it required resigning from the election board), P.J. oversaw the power grid of an increasingly electrified city, managing crews that were steadily removing tangles of overhead electrical wires and moving the messy grid, one street at a time, underground. It wasn't the most exciting position, but he was paid handsomely — $5,000 a year (more than $150,000 in

2020 dollars). Not only was he one of the best-paid city employees, but the pace and character of the job suited him: a low-key mission with tangible results. (Look, no more wires!)

As commissioner, he had official duties and an office downtown, and he commuted by ferry a few days a week. He continued to meet for lunch with the Board of Strategy, but ever since the *Boston Globe* had dragged the board into the news, there had been a backlash against its considerable power—word was out about who really ran the city.

One benefit of P.J.'s new job: for the first time in many years his schedule required fewer late nights, and he could spend a bit more time at home. P.J. had never been one to stay out late, tossing back whiskeys. Instead, he preferred to play baseball with Joe—the two had become "inseparable," Joe's sisters had noticed—or to toss sticks for the family's Saint Bernard, Rex, who loved to chase the girls as they sledded down the backyard hill. P.J. had paid his dues during his peak political years, attending weddings, christenings, funerals, dinners, and speeches. He had served on so many committees for parades, carnivals, galas, and church fundraisers, and now it was a joy to have meals at home with Mary and the kids. If he had business in the city, he'd do his duty, then catch the first available ferry home, where he was tended to by not only his wife and daughters but a growing staff of maids and cooks.

Elsewhere in Boston, Irish politicians continued to run their wards from private clubs, their home-away-from-home gentlemen's joints, where pre-caucus candidates were selected, where aspiring politicians were made or broken, where eager constituents made their case for a job or a loan. Martin Lomasney lorded over his Hendricks Club in the West End, while Honey Fitz held office hours at his Jefferson Club in the North End. But P.J., long past his beer-pouring and bartending days, was now more distant from the political club scene. He preferred taking Joe to a ballgame or

listening to a game on the radio or meeting with friends for Friday
night card games, playing rounds of "45" at the home of Dr. William Grainger, who had delivered his and Mary's children. (P.J. became a devotee of baseball when the American League was created
in 1901 and Boston got a second team, called the Boston Americans, to distinguish it from the city's National League team, the
Braves. P.J.'s team — soon to officially adopt its nickname, the Red
Sox — won the first official World Series, in 1903, and did the same
again in 1904, on the way to three more pennants through 1918.)

Thanks to his years as the loyal Ward 2 soldier and Democrat,
as representative and senator, as barkeep, real estate man, banker,
and coal dealer, P.J. knew his island neighbors well. Even without
a club or office hours, he was attuned to East Boston's needs. He
knew when an out-of-work longshoreman needed a city job, when
a widow and her kids needed food or a few dollars for rent or some
coal. Some names went into his ledger of debts, some didn't. He
wrote dozens of letters seeking the "personal favor" of a job or a
business permit or acceptance to a school for young men he described as good Catholic boys, or "a personal friend of mine" or
"one of our kind" or "highly recommended" (although, in one letter
he admitted that the nephew for whom he sought a position was
"not the brightest boy, but I know you will find him honest and
modest"). Like many savvy politicians, he distributed food baskets
at holiday time. And unlike Fitzgerald, who was more showy about
his do-goodery, P.J. didn't invite photographers along as witness.

"We never sat down to dinner but what the doorbell would ring,
and it would be someone down on their luck, coming to Papa for
help," P.J.'s daughter Margaret later told a newsman. Joe too would
later recall such incidents — his father's empty chair at dinner, his
mother's wince and a plea to "tell them we're eating" — though
with a bit of disdain. "All I could see was their predatory stare,"

Joe told a friend, and he worried about the "incessant demands" on his father.

P.J. and Mary once took a neighbor's son into their home when the boy's parents hit a rough patch. They raised the boy, Johnny Ryan, alongside Joe for a time, as if they were brothers. They never adopted him, and the agreement was understood to be temporary. Joe and Johnny became lifelong friends. (The arrangement was clearly inspired by Bridget, who had taken in two boys, Michael O'Brien and Nick Flynn, and raised them as P.J.'s brothers.)

Though opponents would claim otherwise, P.J. hadn't served in politics or in the Collins administration or on the Board of Strategy just for the buck. He truly believed the words on the plaque he kept at his desk: "I shall pass through this world but once. Any kindness I can do, let me do it now, for I shall not pass this way again." As one Ward 2 friend put it, "Everyone knew that P.J. Kennedy's word once given was always good and never broken."

And if he made a few dollars along the way? Well, what was the harm in that?

Collins was generally an honest man and a popular mayor and was reelected by a wide margin in 1903. He was also accused of being a pawn for the Board of Strategy, disinclined to enact reforms that could be helpful to Bostonians but which might upset the board's powerful members. "Who has controlled Boston for two years? Has it been Mayor Collins?" asked the *Boston Globe*. "No! Has it been the board of strategy? Decidedly, yes!" The *Globe* complained that when the board told Collins what to do, "he has meekly done it."

P.J. tried to maintain his loyalty to Collins and his commitment to the board, but it was becoming harder to play the middle. He had begun to tell Joe, "Don't make mistakes," which was how he'd tried to conduct himself in politics. A writer later described

P.J. as "remarkably unsullied." He didn't curse and he told boozy candidates to "quit drinking" or he wouldn't support them. One writer marveled that "not even his bitterest enemies ever placed Pat Kennedy in a company of thieves. He was, they said, 'straight,' and it would have been futile for any of his foes to maintain that Pat was open to a little under-the-table graft. No one would have believed it."

But now he was caught inside an increasingly patronage-driven administration. That is, until Patrick Collins died suddenly while vacationing at Hot Springs, Virginia, in 1905, throwing Boston politics, and P.J., into a new cycle of mayhem.

For P.J., Collins's unexpected death (caused by a bowel hemorrhage) capped more than a decade of losses, of both friends and family. He had already lost his liquor business partner, J.J. Cotter, and his friend John Sullivan, and had served as pallbearer for too many others, from Excelsior Associates club mates to political mentors to statehouse alums to fellow directors of the Columbia Trust. His brother-in-law Lawrence Kane had died that summer of 1905, two months before Collins. The pickle dealer, who'd married P.J.'s sister Mary and helped with Ward 2 campaigns, had launched his own contracting firm and was working outside during a heat wave. He came home and collapsed. He was forty-five. Months later, P.J.'s close friend T.J. Lane, the former *Pilot* reporter who'd become chairman of the Boston Bath Commission, died of cancer at fifty-three.

For more than a dozen years, starting with the death of his own son in 1892, P.J. was donning his dark suit all too often, making the rounds from Holy Redeemer to East Boston's two newer churches, Assumption and Sacred Heart, sending bouquets, and joining processions of carriages to Holy Cross Cemetery at Malden, now the go-to burial ground for Boston's Catholics. Among P.J.'s extended family, three more of his sister's children had died, as had two aunts — Bridget's sisters Catherine and Ann, both in nearby Salem. P.J.'s father-in-law, James Hickey, died of Bright's disease at his East Boston home on November 22, 1900 (the date on which P.J.'s father had died in 1858). Mary's sister Margaret had been caring for their father and after his death moved in with the Kennedys, but she died two years later, of a sudden asthma attack. And Patrick Barron, P.J.'s mother's cousin and one of his dearest family members, widowed and still living in East Boston, had died in 1901 at age eighty-one.

Honey Fitz viewed funerals as a political opportunity — he'd search the morning papers for deaths in his ward, then drop in to pay his respects, looking for a chance to sing "Sweet Adeline" or display his skill for producing tears on demand. By contrast, P.J. served as the somber pallbearer and behind-the-scenes organizer. (He did, however, get involved in the death business as director and eventually vice president of the New England Seamless Casket Company, whose factory in nearby Chelsea produced an "imperishable casket.")

Within days of marching shoulder to shoulder in Collins's funeral procession, P.J. and Fitzgerald found themselves on opposite sides of the late-1905 battle to replace Collins as mayor. The Board of Strategy had decided to back city clerk Edward J. "Ned" Donovan, a protégé of none other than Martin Lomasney. Then Fitzgerald announced his preferred candidate: himself. The papers noted that Fitzgerald's campaign was risky, since he was "not on terms of intimacy with the members of the democratic board of strategy."

The convoluted backstory went something like this: years earlier, during an election fight, P.J. had asked Fitzgerald to endorse his candidate, but Honey Fitz ignored P.J.'s plea and backed another one. Now P.J. refused to support Fitzgerald's run for mayor, as did other members of the strategy board, as did Fitzgerald's onetime fan, Lomasney. During a visit to East Boston, Lomasney let loose with a tirade against Fitz, mocked his "crying and weeping."

"With one hand in front of him and the other behind his back, Fitz is going around telling how he will take care of you," shouted the bald, bare-armed, barrel-chested Lomasney. "Whenever he appears before you, think what East Boston has done for him and then ask yourselves what he has done for East Boston." When reporters asked P.J. why he'd declined to support Fitzgerald, he told them he had "no statement to give out" — as was his way.

Despite the opposition of the city's kingmakers, Fitzgerald ran an impassioned campaign, touring by automobile to visit all twenty-five wards, giving ten speeches a night, and declaring his stand against the city's "bosses." He won the Democratic primary and went on to beat his Republican opponent, becoming the thirty-eighth mayor of Boston. Before election day, P.J. had come around and donated $500 to Fitzgerald's campaign. (Fitzgerald and the Democrats spent $30,000 on that year's election, a new record.)

When Fitzgerald took office, rather than punish P.J. for not fully supporting him, he agreed to keep him on as wire commissioner. Just as Fitzgerald had visited P.J. years earlier to shake hands after a bruising election, the two men found a way to make amends. Yet the experience — Collins's death, the brutal election fight — rattled P.J. He'd put on weight lately, was feeling tired, and seemed to be in poor health, a condition that worsened a year into Fitzgerald's volatile term.

Fitz had promised to guide Boston into a new era of honesty and prosperity — a "bigger, better, and busier Boston" was his campaign pledge. He vowed to control public spending and eliminate "wasteful and unnecessary purchases." Instead, the new mayor found himself under scrutiny for rewarding his supporters with city jobs. Fitzgerald appointed a pub keeper (who'd been booted from the state legislature for election fraud) as street commissioner; gave an East Boston liquor dealer the job of superintendent of public buildings; placed another saloonkeeper on the Board of Health (replacing an actual doctor); and appointed as weights and measures deputy a man who had recently been acquitted of trying to shoot Martin Lomasney's brother.

A new Finance Commission, tasked with cleaning up the flourishing system of patronage and corruption, began investigating Fitz's administration. While looking into city contracts for coal purchases the commission found that officials appointed by Fitzgerald had taken bribes, overpaid for coal, and given contracts to companies that promised to deliver votes. Suffolk Coal Company, P.J.'s enterprise, was selling coal to the city at the time, though his was among the smaller contracts, and neither he nor Suffolk Coal would be accused of wrongdoing. Even so, the headlines decrying "Alleged Fraud in the City Coal Deals" and the proceedings of the so-called Coal Graft Hearings, run by the Finance Commission, spooked P.J.

He and Mary had continued to escape Boston for vacations at Old Orchard Beach, and in the summer of 1906 they'd witnessed the blooming romance between P.J.'s son and Fitzgerald's daughter, now teenagers. While Joe and Rose played lawn tennis or went for walks on the beach, P.J. would visit Fitz on the porch of his summer cottage—called Bleak House—discussing wire commission work and, presumably, the expanding investigations into Fitzgerald's now-tarnished administration. By early 1907, as Fitzgerald began his second year as mayor and the Finance Commission began issuing a series of damning investigative reports, P.J. was feeling increasingly sick and *spent*. It was time to take a break. His wife made the decision for him.

Mary always seemed to know when he needed a vacation and would scheme with others to plan one without his permission. She'd make the arrangements, enlist a friend to travel along, ask one of her maids to drag out the travel trunks and air them. Whenever P.J.

saw those trunks gaping outside the house, or his travel clothes stacked on the bed, he knew Mary had something planned—a train ride to Florida or a westward trek to California.

Often, his traveling companion was Frank Lally, an East Boston businessman, member of the Excelsior Associates, a former Land League leader, and one of P.J.'s Friday night card-playing mates. (P.J. and Mary's first son, Francis, had been named after Lally, who never married.) Lally's sisters would conspire with Mary to plan the men's itinerary, and when P.J. asked Lally if he knew where they were going, Lally would say, "I don't know, Pat—Jenny and Lottie have me packed too. I know we'll have a wonderful time, though."

In early 1907, Mary's plan was to send her husband on his first-ever grand tour of Europe, the highlight of which would be a week in Ireland, where P.J. could finally meet the Irish Kennedys and Murphys. With clusters of Democratic leaders seeing them off at the pier, along with a reporter from the *Boston Globe* chronicling the departure of "one of East Boston's best known citizens and public-spirited men," P.J. and Lally boarded a Cunard steamer, the SS *Ivernia,* bound for Queenstown, Ireland, and then Liverpool, where P.J. would start his journey.

After weeks of touring through Europe, with stops in London, Paris, and Rome, P.J. sailed into Dublin, finally setting foot on Irish soil. He took a southbound train through the beautiful countryside that sixty years earlier had been the setting for scenes of horror.

He visited what was left of his mother's aging farm, now run by a cousin named Roach, and spent a day with his father's family at the farm in Dunganstown. He visited Vinegar Hill, where his ancestors had fought British soldiers. At a fair in Enniscorthy he met a priest who had been a Land League agitator. He rode the country lanes in an open-air, two-wheel, horse-drawn jaunting car that terrified him, but he found the Irish horses to be the finest he'd ever seen. His only regret was not planning for more time in Ireland. As a parting gift his cousins gave him a tattered copybook that his father had used during his brief time in school. It was a highlight of the trip, to hold an item that had belonged to the man he never knew.

He and Lally traveled west to Queenstown to meet the SS *Ivernia,* which had begun its westward journey in Liverpool. (Queenstown had been renamed during Queen Victoria's 1849 visit at the tail end of the Famine but would later revert to its original Irish name, Cobh.) P.J. and Lally were among the fifty-five VIPs in the first-class cabins, while another two thousand traveled below, in steerage or second class. The *Ivernia* was a six-hundred-foot workhorse, one of the largest cargo ships in the world. It had made scores of trips between Liverpool and East Boston, sometimes ten per year, bringing tens of thousands more immigrants to America. Unlike ships in the days of the Famine, the *Ivernia* carried a multinational mix: Norwegians, Croatians, Italians, Greeks, English and Irish, plus hundreds of Jewish refugees "fleeing to this country to escape persecution," reported the *Boston Globe,* adding that more than twenty nationalities "mingled together into one great family." Unlike the weeks-long journey his parents suffered, P.J.'s sail home took one week. After his eight weeks abroad, P.J. looked forward to showing his wife and kids photos of Ireland and all the places he'd visited, but he discovered that his photographs had been destroyed—by cordial. The bottle of liqueur that he'd bought in Rome had broken.

As the ship neared Boston, the captain radioed shore. P.J.'s friends received word and sailed into the harbor to greet the incoming ship, including J.J. Quigley at the helm of P.J.'s yacht, the *Eleanor.* The pier was crowded with hundreds of East Bostonians, waiting to welcome him home. His mother had arrived at the same spot fifty-nine years earlier, among the unwashed and unknown, and now her son was receiving a "royal welcome," greeted by friends and powerful politicians and journalists who reported the return of "Commissioner Kennedy" and his sidekick.

"Both looked to be in the best of health," said the papers.

Which wasn't quite true. P.J. had gained even more weight, and in a *Boston Globe* photograph showing him being greeted by his daughters he looked heftier than ever. He'd soon admit to himself and his wife that his health was "far from good."

As P.J. and Mary returned to their home on Webster Street, the pier stayed busy. Jack "Dock Parson" Burns, the longtime stevedore turned justice of the peace, conducted his usual ceremonies, marrying incoming Irish women to the men who'd been waiting for them.

Later that year, P.J. wrote to his cousin Jim Kennedy, belatedly thanking him for the hospitality in Ireland and expressing regret that he couldn't stay longer. He explained that he'd been unusually busy with work and politics, the latter not going well . . . "You remember me speaking of Mayor Fitzgerald," he wrote. "He and the party went down in defeat in a very exciting campaign." Although he proudly noted that the Democrats held the majority on the Board of Aldermen and the Common Council, he concluded that "our party, as far as the city is concerned, is out of power."

After two years in office, Fitzgerald had lost the mayor's office that fall of 1907. His opponent had been the city postmaster, George Hibbard, a Republican backed by the still-angry Lomasney. A rogue Democrat had joined the race and pulled votes away from Fitzgerald, who lost to Hibbard by two thousand votes. (Hibbard would die two years later of consumption, at age forty-five.)

Something about the trip to Ireland, the stories of his cousins' Land League feuds, plus Fitzgerald's loss amid the ever-shifting political landscape apparently invigorated P.J. and prompted him to get back in the game. He decided to run for office once again. In early 1908, he resigned as wire commissioner (possibly anticipating that the new Republican mayor was about to replace him) and announced his decision to vie for one of the few city cabinet positions elected by voters, the powerful and well-paid role of street commissioner.

He was considered a shoo-in and garnered support from every name that mattered — Fitzgerald, Lomasney, Donovan, and others. But in a shocking upset, he didn't even win the primary, losing by three hundred votes to an upstart Democrat, a police captain named Dunn. P.J. received an outpouring of supportive letters from stunned friends, and the papers claimed his loss was a sign that Boston voters had grown tired of "bossism." Said the *Boston Globe:* "The great surprise of the voting was the defeat of Hon. Patrick J. Kennedy by Capt. James H. Dunn . . . Mr. Kennedy, who is a good party man, was defeated because he was favored by bosses." Another reporter said voters made the "poorer choice" by not electing P.J., with his experience and his "fairly clean record of public service." Never one to burn a bridge, P.J. wrote a gracious letter of congratulations, wishing his opponent success in the election (Dunn would go on to win) and "hope for a long continuance of our pleasant personal relations."

That brief letter could also have been read as a broader concession.

P.J. would not run for elected office again, nor would he hold an appointed city job, not even after Fitzgerald was elected mayor once more in 1910. Instead, he and Mary would soon leave East Boston altogether and move north to the beach community of Winthrop.

Some chroniclers would suggest P.J. was miffed at losing the election, frustrated to lose a well-paying city job, and had moved out of vexation. This seems unlikely, given his wealth and civic-minded graciousness, although Joe would later say his father grieved his

1908 defeat. It's also possible that P.J.'s move was partly prompted by the massive fire that destroyed the Suffolk Coal Company and other businesses along Border Street in 1908. Among the worst fires in East Boston history, it destroyed Suffolk Coal's warehouses, its wharf, and ten thousand tons of coal.

Whatever factors led to P.J.'s retirement from Boston politics, the decision to leave East Boston — to leave the city of Boston entirely — was a remarkable one. As someone known for constancy and routine, for his commitment to East Boston citizens and his devotion to Ward 2 politics, the move caught some by surprise. He'd been a ward leader for half of his fifty years, a Democratic soldier for even longer. Friends urged him to regroup and run for mayor. Wrote one prominent businessman: "I believe you can get the mayoralty nomination and know you are one man that the Democrats can elect mayor of Boston."

But he was done with politics. There was plenty of business ahead — more banking, more liquor sales — and he would continue to play an elder statesman's role on the somewhat diminished Board of Strategy. But another new phase had begun, farther from the spotlight and out of Ward 2 entirely, for the first time in his life. He seemed okay with that. His heart wasn't in it. He'd made enough money for himself, his wife, enough to help their daughters, enough to keep helping friends and neighbors. He had plans. He'd sail his yacht and swim in the ocean. He and Mary would take the train to Boston to see plays and musical shows. In time their kids would marry, and he'd take his grandchildren to the beach, teach them to sail, shower them with toys and gifts.

But as a ward boss and Democratic leader — and as patriarch of the Kennedys of Boston — it was time to yield the floor. As his son Joe would later observe, after years of tagging along with P.J. to ward meetings and caucuses and fundraisers, "Never was there a single moment when someone didn't want something from him;

never was there a single stretch of peaceful time when he could thoroughly relax and totally enjoy a good meal or a good book."

The next years of city politics would be up to Fitzgerald and others to win or lose, P.J. had decided.

And leading the Kennedy clan into the twentieth century? Twenty years past Bridget's death and fifty years past his father's, P.J. was counting on the next generation. It would be his son's family now — the son of a barkeep, as Joe sometimes called himself. Joe would do things his way, on his terms, in time taking the Kennedys to stunning new heights.

EPILOGUE: JOE AND JOHN

The wisest Americans have always understood the significance of the immigrant.

— JOHN F. KENNEDY, *A Nation of Immigrants*

Joe

BY THE TIME Joe Kennedy set out for Harvard College in the fall of 1908, his parents were wealthy and Joe was a young man of great privilege. He'd been given a life of comfort and access that any respectable Brahmin would recognize if not envy. At Harvard, he was captain of the baseball team and class president, popular and competitive and social, though a mediocre student who earned C's and D's. (Joe tried to influence a few professors with bottles of Scotch from his father's liquor shop.) When Joe graduated in 1912, America's oldest, most prestigious, and most Yankee of all educational institutions was still mostly full of proper Boston Protestants, with sprinklings of Irish and Jews. But the school gave its graduates more than an impressive diploma. It provided connections and legitimacy to last a lifetime.

Opting not to follow his father into politics — he'd later say that for politicians like his father, no matter how devoted and successful, "ultimate defeat is inevitable" — Joe decided to pursue banking. He moved back home with his parents, and P.J. helped him find a job, setting Joe up with a mentor and a position at his bank, Columbia Trust. Next, possibly with P.J.'s help, Joe scored a job as a state bank examiner and spent a year traveling across Massachusetts and learning the ropes of the banking business. After a summer in Europe with Harvard chums, he went back to work at Columbia Trust, which was then threatened with a buyout by a larger bank — a move that would downgrade P.J. and other founding directors to minority shareholders.

P.J. needed to raise enough capital to fend off the buyout, and he turned to his son for help, tasking Joe with finding investors among his Harvard pals and others he'd met while traveling to banks across the states. Joe raised the funds, some from his mother's brothers, and helped save his father's bank. In early 1914, he was rewarded with the role of bank president and was soon celebrated as the youngest bank president in the state, if not the country, though the papers often failed to mention it was the bank of his father and friends. P.J. would take the reins three years later and serve as Columbia Trust's president from then on, while Joe moved on to new ventures. (During World War I, he'd work as an assistant manager at the Fore River Shipyard in Quincy, which built destroyers.)

Joe finally managed to impress John Fitzgerald, who had been elected mayor in 1910 and in the fall of 1913 was running for re-election. Joe, who'd started dating Rose, helped with her father's campaign until Fitz's opponent, James Michael Curley, threatened to expose the mayor's affair with a young hostess and cigarette girl nicknamed Toodles. Fitz bowed out and announced his retirement, citing health concerns. In a rare public statement, P.J., who'd helped Fitzgerald as he recovered from a bout of consumption years earlier, told the papers he felt Fitzgerald needed a good rest and he was "glad to learn of his retirement."

The apparent end of Fitzgerald's political career (which was hardly the end) didn't affect Joe's pursuit of Fitz's daughter. In late 1914, in a small ceremony at the home of Cardinal William O'Connell, P.J. and Mary watched as their son married Rose Fitzgerald, linking two of Boston's most prominent and influential Irish American political families. The wedding was front-page news in the *Boston Globe.* A three-column-wide photo of the bride and groom —a union of "intense interest," the *Globe* called it—was framed by stories about the escalating war in Europe.

Joe and Rose left Boston and settled in the upscale suburb of Brookline, where they started their family. Rose gave birth to Joseph Jr. in 1915, then John in 1917 (Joe's sister Loretta was his godmother), and Rosemary in 1918, with six more to come. P.J. and Mary loved being grandparents, visited Joe and Rose often, and spent summers with the kids at the beach. Mary joked that Joe and Rose would soon need their own bus. As he had with Joe, P.J. played baseball with his grandsons, taught them to swim and sail and row, took them fishing on his yacht or for a birthday cruise into Boston Harbor. He and Mary eased into a comfortable retirement, growing stout and gray. Daughters Loretta and Margaret still lived at home—"my two Kennedy heiresses," P.J. called them. Loretta worked as a teacher, and Margaret had volunteered for the war effort, creating care packages for soldiers overseas.

Then, in the late 1910s, after forty years of battling puritanical anti-alcohol forces, P.J.'s remaining liquor businesses faced their demise. The prohibitionists had finally found the political support they'd sought for decades and the country would soon enter its strange thirteen-year experiment in temperance, starting on January 16, 1920, two days after P.J.'s sixty-second birthday. He and

Mary kept their liquor businesses running until the last possible moment, applying for renewed licenses into late 1919. P.J. then gathered up all his unsold liquor stock and, with Joe's help, moved boxes of wine, champagne, and spirits into the cellar of his house in Winthrop. He'd not live to see the day when a man might again legally drink a cold lager.

In these later years, Mary spoke often of how fortunate she felt, how blessed she'd been. She remained a steadfast churchgoer and befriended the local Catholic priests. She and P.J. created a small altar in their home and would invite a priest over to say a private mass. But Mary did not live to see her family reach full bloom. Diagnosed with stomach cancer, she died in 1923 at age sixty-five. A throng of hundreds attended her funeral. She and P.J. had been married thirty-five years, with Mary running a tight ship at home while P.J. tended to the whirl of business and politics. They'd been a good team. A year later, to distract themselves from Mary's death, P.J. and his daughters traveled to Europe with Mary's sister, Katie. They toured Ireland, England, France, and Italy, where P.J.'s connections gained them an audience with Pope Pius XI. Back home, Margaret married in 1924 (to Charles Burke, the son of P.J.'s next-door neighbor, who worked as a tailor), and Loretta married in 1927 (to George Connelly, a Harvard grad who worked for his father's marine-supply company).

With his wife gone and his daughters moved out, P.J. found himself alone in his big house overlooking Massachusetts Bay. Two of his sisters, Mary and Joanna, had died in 1926; sister Margaret would die three years later. Nick Flynn, P.J.'s not-quite-brother, had lost his wife and moved in with P.J. In 1928, P.J. saw three more grandchildren enter the world, as each of his kids welcomed a new child—Joe's eighth, and a first child each for Loretta and Margaret. He had lived to meet ten (of an eventual thirteen) grandchildren. Unlike Bridget, he did not have to bear the tragic loss of a young grandchild, and all of them would survive into adulthood.

John Kennedy would later describe his Grandpa Kennedy as more stern and austere than Grandpa Fitzgerald, and Sunday afternoon visits to P.J. in Winthrop were remembered as serious affairs: "He wouldn't let us cut up or even wink in his presence."

Joe and Rose moved to Bronxville, New York, but Joe was often in Hollywood, living in a rented cottage with two Irish maids and producing movies (while cheating on his wife). He borrowed from Columbia Trust to start his own production company, then bought another, and by the late 1920s was making piles of money from his pictures and other investments. A family friend would later note: "Joe Kennedy inherited his father's business acumen, but not his soul."

Over the next year, P.J.'s health declined—he was diagnosed with heart troubles and a degenerative liver disease. He visited Rose and her brood at their new summer vacation spot in Hyannis Port, brought along bags of toys, and loved watching the kids swim and romp at the beach. Joe was back in L.A. when he received the news that his seventy-one-year-old father had suffered a heart attack and died, on May 18, 1929.

More than a thousand people attended the funeral of Patrick Joseph Kennedy, praised in the headlines—"Esteemed by All Men" and "Kind and Generous" and "Noted Banker and Politician Was 71 Years Old"—and carried to the grave by Honey Fitz and two members of the Board of Strategy, with former governors, mayors, and congressmen as ushers and honorary pallbearers. Like a swarming family reunion, lawyers, doctors, police officers, firefighters, newsmen, longshoremen, and politicians all came, rich and poor, including many whom P.J. had helped over the years. They expressed not just admiration but real love for the man. Priests who led the funeral mass included one from Most Holy Redeemer and the chaplain from Deer Island. P.J.'s body was paraded by police escort through East Boston, where the shops closed and the flags flew at half-staff. They went straight down Meridian Street past his old home, his old saloon, past the bank where he was still listed as president, within two blocks of his mother's old shop. P.J. was buried at Holy Cross Cemetery in Malden, near his mother's resting place.

"Mr. Kennedy was a remarkable man. He went about his life doing good for his fellow man," Honey Fitz said in his eulogy. "His charity had no bounds; he freely gave to the poor. 'P.J.,' as this lovable man was known, was a tremendous power in East Boston. He was great because he had the human touch, tempered by kindness and charity."

Not including a few unsold East Boston properties, his shares in Columbia Trust, Sumner Savings Bank, and Suffolk Coal Company, P.J.'s estate was determined to be worth $55,000 — respectable, for sure, but not nearly what it might've been, if not for his perpetual generosity. "Pat gave away two fortunes in his day," a nephew would later say. (A number of outstanding loans remained at the time of his death, and family members would later say P.J. was worth far more than the papers reported.) It was hardly the $5 million his moviemaking son was then estimated to be worth. Joe, who'd later claim that P.J. had been too free with loans and donations, was unable to make it home for his father's funeral and stayed in Hollywood.

Joseph P. Kennedy thus ascended to become the patriarch, father of impressive and good-looking kids, a stock-playing genius, a moviemaking millionaire, a bedder of starlets. He'd soon enter the liquor business as a post-Prohibition importer of scotch and gin. He'd become chairman of the SEC, ambassador to England, and the driving force behind his sons' political ascent. Many millions of words would be devoted to Joe's meteoric rise to wealth and power, his vast influence on the American political landscape of the twentieth century. With a drive bordering on the maniacal, he wanted more and more and more. He'd at times be portrayed as a Horatio Alger type whose pluck and smarts, whose competitive drive and salesmanship, had helped him escape the slums of East Boston. "Saloon Keeper's Son to Multimillionaire," read one head-line. Joe would perpetuate this story, playing up his humble youth, the barkeep's son.

At the same time, Joe remained wary of his backstory and rarely acknowledged his *immigrant* roots. He couldn't get far enough away from tales of the auld sod and the Famine echoes. He never knew his grandmother Bridget, barely knew his other Irish grandparents, the Hickeys, and felt little connection to his ancestors, the land they'd fled, or the hopes and fears that drove them. In public life he rarely credited his refugee grandparents or his up-by-their-boot-straps parents. His mother had intentionally bestowed on him a not-obviously-Irish name, and though a few of his kids were given Irish-ish names, he strove to be fully *Americanized.* Joe often seemed to view the Irish and Ireland as inferior, not among the winners, and he expected his sons to be winners. He even turned down an offer (from President Roosevelt) to serve as ambassador to Ireland —not prestigious enough.

Then, in a remarkable full-circle achievement for the grandson of Famine Irish, in late 1937 Joe was named by Roosevelt to serve as ambassador to the Court of St. James's, the first Irishman to hold the ambassadorship to England. His grandparents would have spat at an English queen if given the chance, and now Joe and his children were kneeling before one.

While living in London, Joe and Rose were able to visit Ireland with their kids.

John became especially interested in the land of his ancestors.

John

His older sister Kathleen, known as Kick, had married into British royalty and became an Irish landowner. Her husband, William "Billy" Cavendish, the Marquess of Hartington, was killed in
World War II (just weeks after Joe Kennedy Jr. was killed, in August 1944), but Kick still had access to her husband's castles, one
of them in County Waterford. In 1947, John visited his widowed
sister at Lismore Castle (a year before her own death) and, with
another visitor — William Churchill's daughter-in-law, Pamela —
borrowed a car and drove south to New Ross.

Exactly a century after his great-grandparents had left County
Wexford, John toured the area, met with aunts, uncles, and cousins,
and seethed over Churchill's complaints that his still-poor relatives
reminded her of Tobacco Road hillbillies. Seeing his great-grandfather's cottage, still standing, was "magical," and that night back
at the castle John was struck by the contrast. He began to explore
and embrace his Irish heritage, studying the country's history and
the battles of Irish Civil War regiments. John had just been elected
to Congress, having campaigned in P.J.'s old haunts, meeting with
longshoremen at the bars and wharves of East Boston's waterfront.
He now represented the congressional district once led by his other
grandfather, Honey Fitz, who at eighty-three had helped John celebrate victory with a rendition of "Sweet Adeline."

At the time, Ireland was a twenty-five-year-old nation, having
defeated the British in the War of Independence that led, in 1922,
to the creation (finally) of the Irish Free State. Unlike his father,
John revered the Irish and would return to Ireland. "This is not
the land of my birth but it is the land for which I hold the greatest
affection," he'd later say. And this: "No country in the world, in the

history of the world, has endured the hemorrhage which this island endured."

Yet, except for occasional nods to his eight Irish immigrant great-grandparents, John is not known to have publicly mentioned Bridget (or P.J.). Even so, over the course of his career, as he found his voice politically, he discovered a sensitivity that drew on his ancestors' hardships.

"I want a better life for every American. I want to see every American walk with his head up," John said, in a speech during his 1952 Senate campaign (he went on to defeat the grandson of the nativist Senator Henry Cabot Lodge). "Confident that he can provide his children with opportunities for a fuller and more useful life. This is my political creed."

John's visits to Ireland would inspire him (as a US senator) to write *A Nation of Immigrants,* his homage to America's secret strength, its mix of peoples who chose to "sail across dark seas to a strange land." The book was first published in 1958 (two years after John's Pulitzer Prize–winning bestseller, *Profiles in Courage*), as a pamphlet commissioned by the Anti-Defamation League. Kennedy later revised and expanded it. It was published posthumously in 1964.

Though this sensitivity to the immigrant seemed to skip Joe, Rose was known to show her children and grandchildren old "No Irish Need Apply" newspaper clippings saved in a scrapbook, and one legacy of the grandchildren of P.J. and Mary Kennedy was to be an ingrained compassion for the poor, the unemployed, the disenfranchised, and the immigrant. As Honey Fitz once said of P.J., the Kennedy kids had "the human touch, tempered by kindness and charity."

As president, in June 1963, John made his last visit to Ireland and to the Dunganstown homestead. At the quay in New Ross, John famously gave a shoutout to Patrick, the barrel maker: "When my great-grandfather left here to become a cooper in East Boston, he carried nothing with him except two things: a strong religious faith and a strong desire for liberty. I am glad to say that all of his great-grandchildren have valued that inheritance."

John's inheritance and his success became a culmination of sorts for the Irish in America, and for the century-long saga of the Kennedys in America.

Weeks after Kennedy was killed — on the same date (November 22) that two of his great-grandfathers had died — the *Boston Record American* published a series of stories about the exceptional family. In a story about P.J., the "Uncrowned King of Celtic Enclave," a reporter expressed wonder that P.J. had survived and thrived in the brutal era of Boston politics that burned most of his peers (including Fitzgerald). P.J. was "cut from a different cloth," he wrote. "Curley, Lomasney, and their kind were accused of every offense, political and criminal, that could be laid against them. Sometimes their accusers were the Brahmins, but just as frequently the charges were made within the family, as one ward boss warred against another."

Incredibly, P.J. had remained untarnished and admired to the end — the silent one, the decent one. He was gracious, compassionate, devout. Unlike many first-generation children of Famine refugees, he wasn't a drunk or a Deer Island recidivist, nor a disgraced politician. He didn't flame out. His legacy wasn't one of gaining power at all costs, but power for the good of others.

Something of that legacy passed to P.J.'s grandchildren, many of whom tried to do good with their inheritance — Bobby fighting for civil rights, Eunice creating the Special Olympics, Teddy as a longtime Democratic senator and legislative maestro. As John had put it, paraphrasing the words of Jesus, "for of those to whom much is given, much is required."

America would sustain a lasting fascination with the flawed and fabulous Kennedys, the style and the glamour, the shortcomings and tragedies, the promise of John and Bobby and other lives cut short — including John's son, John Jr., who died in a plane crash less than thirty miles south of the family's summer compound at Hyannis Port, less than seventy miles south of the waters that welcomed his great-great-grandparents to America 150 years before.

Yet none of the Kennedys' accomplishments, nor the fantasia of Camelot, would have occurred without P.J. — and certainly not without the brave ambition of his mother, a resilient immigrant maid making her way in a less-than-tolerant America, paving the way. What's largely forgotten about the Kennedy saga is that it started with nothing. Just a poor, hardworking widowed grocer named Bridget and her four fatherless children in an East Boston tenement.

THE KENNEDY FAMILY

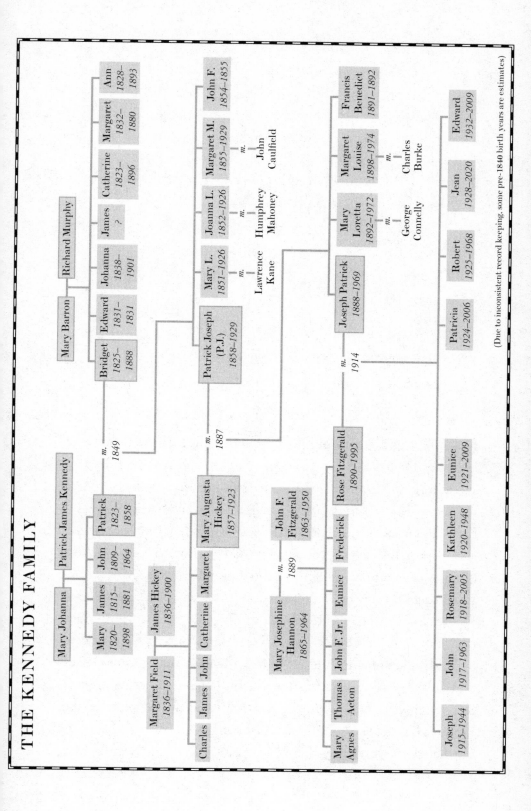

(Due to inconsistent record keeping, some pre-1840 birth years are estimates)

ACKNOWLEDGMENTS AND
AUTHOR'S NOTE

All of us are immigrants / Every daughter, every son

— STEVE EARLE, "CITY OF IMMIGRANTS"

Finishing this book during the COVID lockdown posed some challenges as I reached the final leg of research, keeping me from late-stage digging through library stacks and archive folders — one of my favorite parts of this job. So I'm grateful to those who helped virtually and from afar, including freelance researchers Mariya Manzhos and, especially, Kylie Nelson; the staff at Boston City Archives (John McColgan, Kayla Skillin, and especially Marta Crilly); Katie Devine at Boston Public Library; Sarah Patton and Diana Sykes at Hoover Institution's Center for the Study of Popular Culture collection, at Stanford University; staff at the Massachusetts Historical Society, especially Hannah Elder and Heather Wilson; Thomas P. Lester at the Archdiocese of Boston; Caitlin Jones at the Massachusetts State Archives; Melissa Murphy at Harvard Business School's Baker Library; Giordana Mecagni at Northeastern University; Nancy C. Barthelemy, archivist at the Sisters of Notre Dame de Namur; Matt

Knutzen and Paul Friedman at NYPL; staffers at the New England Historic Genealogical Society and the Burns Library at Boston College. Also, Janis Duffy, Tom Putnam, and Jerry Manion.

A special shoutout to the staff at the John F. Kennedy Presidential Library, who went above and beyond (before and during COVID), including Christina Fitzpatrick for facilitating the release of the P.J. Kennedy Papers, Maryrose Grossman for help with photos, and especially Karen Abramson, archives director, for graciously addressing my years of questions and requests.

A hat tip to the remarkable digital treasures at Ancestry.com, FamilySearch.org, MyHeritage.com, Archive.org, Archives.gov, Jstor.org, and especially Newspapers.com, where I spent many online hours reading news from the nineteenth century (usually with music suggestions from FlowState.fm in the background).

In Ireland, I'm grateful to those I'd met during an earlier (2006) research trip, including Patrick Grennan at the Kennedy homestead; Phyl and Michael Conway and their son Patrick (near Bridget's family home); Sean Pierce; Jenny Nuthall; and Sean Reidy at the Irish Immigration History Centre and Dunbrody Famine Ship. More recently, big thanks to Michael Demsey and Eileen Morrissey at County Wexford's library and to genealogist whiz John Grenham. And I'm especially indebted to the independent researcher Celestine Murphy, who cracked open a few key mysteries.

Among members of the Kennedy family, Rory Kennedy, Amanda Smith, Stephen Kennedy Smith, and Kerry McCarthy were all generous with their time. My gratitude to other Kennedy, Irish, Catholic, and Boston historians who shared time and advice: Larry Tye, Thomas Maier, David Nasaw, Laurence Leamer, David Horowitz, Eddie Laxton, Kerby Miller, James O'Toole, and Anthony Sammarco. And thanks to Andrew Pierce and Ed Galvin for sharing some of their own excavations into Kennedy family history.

I'm grateful once again for the productive time spent at the University of Washington's amazing Whiteley Center at Friday Harbor Labs. Thanks (and a happy retirement) to Kathy Cowell, and to Stephanie Zamora and others.

Assorted readers, cheerleaders, and enablers who helped along the way: Tim Egan, who gave me a deadline (and threatened to write this story if I didn't hit it); Mitch Zuckoff, for inspiring me to revisit this; Colum McCann, for introductions and encouragement; Brendan Kiely; Andrew Chapman; Neal Bascomb; David Shields; Darcey Steinke; Mia Funk; Beth Macy; Martha Bebinger; Melissa Ludtke; Walter Kirn; Megan Abbott; Michael Chabon; Adrienne Brodeur; David and Katherine Reed; Joe D'Agnese and Denise Kiernan. (And he may not be aware of it, but a casual comment by Peter Heller—"You're a writer. That's your natural state. Go for it"—prompted me to quit a stable job and plunge into a project that I'd tiptoed around for too many years. Thanks, Pete.)

A large thank-you to Bruce Nichols for bringing this book to Houghton Mifflin Harcourt, and to my sharp-eyed and patient editor, Rakia Clark, and her wonderful assistant, Ivy Givens, for carrying it (and me) through the twists and churn of the publishing business. (Hello, HarperCollins!) Additional thanks to production editor Lisa Glover, designer Brian Moore, and a special shoutout to copyeditor Susanna Brougham for her meticulous work.

To my tireless, nurturing, fervent, clear-sighted agent, Rob Weisbach, thanks for believing in this one and shepherding it (and me) along. You're a gem of a guy.

My uncle Bob and aunt Patty were early and enthusiastic champions of this book, and I'm heartsick that Patty left us too soon to hold this in her hands.

Like many families, ours was rattled by the pandemic. My eldest son, Sean Marco, moved home with my wife and me, and it was a joy to spend time with a young man who I rarely saw in high school (or middle school, actually). My youngest, Leo Patrick, had been at school in Victoria, BC, when COVID hit, and we've been separated ever since. Canada (wisely) shut its border to Americans and has not reopened as of this writing — ten times longer than I've ever been separated from my boy. A very small taste of the power of borders to separate families.

Most of all, to Mary — my first, last, and best reader, my travel buddy, my counselor and consoler, my quarantine companion, my partner in all things . . . None of this could've happened without you, and all of it is for you.

Finally, a few closing words about my grandparents, Bridget and Patrick, who left Ireland fifty years after the Kennedys. Bridget Agnes "Della" Fox, the oldest of ten, raised on a muddy farm west of Roscommon, left home at age twenty, choosing New York instead of Boston. She worked as a maid and later a seamstress, and met and married Patrick Burke, who drove a streamroller and later Texaco trucks. They lived at 125th and Amsterdam on the west edge of Harlem and loved to visit jazz clubs. When Bridget later became a naturalized citizen, she changed her name to Della (after a favorite jazz singer) — "She hated the name Bridget," an uncle would tell me.

At thirty-eight, Patrick got sick and died of cancer. My grandmother carried on, a poor immigrant widow raising my mother, age twelve, and two sons, one four years old and the other eight months. Ignoring the welfare workers' suggestion that she put the two boys up for adoption, my grandmother moved out of an airy apartment above a New Jersey candy store into a small public-housing apartment, in a complex of subsidized two-story brick apartments where she'd spend the rest of her days.

Here's what I remember about childhood visits: You kept the percolator plugged in all day, drinking strong black coffee until switching to eight-ounce cans of Bud in the late afternoon. You wore house dresses and clunky shoes. You cursed like a dockworker, with the staccato brogue of your County Galway. You didn't open your own shop or become an entrepreneur, but you did raise a daughter who, after helping raise her two younger brothers, became the first in the extended family to attend college, then became a nurse. You always encouraged my writing and nudged me toward journalism, suggesting that I become a television newsman, like your favorite, Dan Rather. I chose print instead, and you died just months after I started my first newspaper job.

Like Bridget Kennedy, you created the opportunities that allowed your children and grandchildren to become what they dreamed of becoming. Yours is the story of the promise of the immigrant, and this book aspires to serve as the story of all Bridgets like you.

N.T.
Seattle, Washington
June 2021

NOTES AND SOURCES

As astute readers may have noticed, Bridget and Patrick Kennedy left behind no known letters, diaries, or other personal effects, and there are no known pictures of them. In an attempt to bring them to life, I relied on accounts of the day, including diaries, letters, and books from contemporaries, as well as news accounts (mainly from the *Boston Pilot* and *Boston Globe*). Any dialogue or anything enclosed in quotation marks comes from a written source such as a letter, newspaper article, memoir, or diary. While details about Bridget's life are scarce, the P.J. Kennedy Papers and other related documents at the JFKL proved invaluable.

Abbreviations

ARCH — *History of the Archdiocese of Boston in the Various Stages of its Development, 1604 to 1943,* by Robert H. Lord, John E. Sexton, and Edward T. Harrington. New York: Sheed and Ward, 1944.

BG — The *Boston Globe.*

BP — The *Boston Pilot* / The *Pilot.*

ELG — Edward L. Galvin, "The Kennedys of Massachusetts," in *The*

Irish in New England. Boston: New England Historic Genealogical
Society, 1985.

JFKL—John F. Kennedy Presidential Library, Kennedy Family
Collection and Joseph P. Kennedy Papers.

KMMS—Kerry McCarthy, "The First Senator Kennedy,"
unpublished manuscript.

MHS—Massachusetts Historical Society.

NYT—The *New York Times.*

PJKB—P.J. Kennedy "biographical sketch," 1933, JFKL.

PJKP—P.J. Kennedy Papers, JFKL.

INTRODUCTION

page

xii   *cover the story:* Details on JFK Jr.'s crash from author's reporting for the *Baltimore
Sun* (some co-written with Todd Richissin): "Media, Bystanders Gather Outside in
Impromptu Vigil," July 18; "On Cape, They Wait and Pray," July 19; "Weather
Suspected as Cause of Crash," July 20; "Plane Nose-Dived into the Sea," July 20.
Also John Murphy, "Saratoga Aircraft Called Reliable by Aviators," *Baltimore Sun,*
July 18, 1999; Mitchell Zuckoff and Matthew Brelis, "Plane Fell Fast, Probe Finds,"
BG, July 20, 1999; Rinker Buck, "Experts: JFK Jr.'s Flight May Have Been Illegal,"
Hartford Courant, July 21, 1999; "Ted Kennedy Pays Tribute to His Nephew," CNN,
July 23, 1999.

PROLOGUE

1   *thirty-five years old:* Details on Bridget and Patrick, their family, and Patrick's burial:
US Census records; Patrick's death certificate; John Kennedy's burial records; ELG;
Archdiocese of Boston records and cemetery receipts; Boston City Directories;
Leamer, *The Kennedy Women,* p. 24.

3   *a train will plow through:* BP, February 2, 1859.
City officials have passed: O'Connor, *The Boston Irish,* p. 80.
"Our country is literally": William Whieldon, *Bunker Hill Aurora,* in Ed Callahan
and Dan Casey, "A Celtic Cross at Bunker Hill," December/January 2010, https://
irishamerica.com/2010/01/a-celtic-cross-at-bunker-hill/.

4   *"a woman of many noble":* BG, December 24, 1888.

1. BRIDGET'S ESCAPE

7   *she walked on up:* Sources that were helpful in re-creating Bridget's journey to America: Whyte, *Robert Whyte's 1847 Famine Ship Diary;* Kelly, *The Graves Are Walk-*

ing; Laxton, *The Famine Ships;* Kinealy, *This Great Calamity;* Coogan, *The Famine Plot;* Tóibín, *Irish Famine: A Documentary;* also numerous newspaper articles in *BG* and *BP.*

8   *"a leap into the unknown":* Kennedy, *A Nation of Immigrants,* pp. 3, 5.
   "half naked and starving": Tóibín, *Irish Famine,* p. 25.
   One little girl escaped: BP, January 6, 1849.

9   *"The pigs are looked":* Woodham-Smith, *The Great Hunger,* p. 277.

10 *forced into prostitution:* Mary Luddy, *Prostitution and Irish Society, 1800–1940.* Cambridge, UK: Cambridge University Press, 2008, p. 261.
   "young girls, incurably sick": Melville, *Redburn,* chapter 38, Gutenberg.org.
   "as numerous as maggots": Tóibín, *Irish Famine,* p. 25.
   "human swinery": Thomas Carlyle, "Reminiscences of My Irish Journey," IrishHistorian.com, and Coogan, *The Famine Plot,* p. 219.
   "the scum of Ireland": Kelly, *The Graves Are Walking,* p. 264.

11 *"No one who has any":* James Joyce, "Ireland, Island of Saints and Sages," *The Critical Writings of James Joyce.* Ithaca, NY: Cornell University Press, 1989, p. 171.

12 *"our murderers, the spoilers":* Lady Wilde, "Sign of the Times," in *Poems by Speranza.* Dublin: M. H. Gill and Son, date unknown, p. 22, Gutenberg.org.

2. BRIDGET AT SEA

13 *built for half as many:* Additional details of Bridget's crossing come from various accounts of coffin-ship journeys during the late 1840s, including Laxton, *The Famine Ships;* Gallagher, *Paddy's Lament,* p. 214; Whyte, *Robert Whyte's 1847 Famine Ship Diary;* Woodham-Smith, *The Great Hunger;* Charles Dickens, "American Notes," *The Works of Charles Dickens, in Thirty-Four Volumes.* New York: Charles Scribner's Sons, 1868.

14 *"ghastly yellow looking":* Laxton, *The Famine Ships,* p. 45.
   "We thought we couldn't": Gallagher, *Paddy's Lament,* p. 214.

15 *Biddy Beaman, Bridget: Tarolinta* passenger list (and other manifests from 1840s); Laxton, *The Famine Ships.*
   Washington Irving in 1849: KMMS, p. 4; Davis, *The Kennedys.*
   is the Tarolinta: Details on the *Tarolinta* and the *St. Petersburg* from passenger lists of both ships and numerous newspaper articles, including *Waterford News,* December 8, 1848, p. 5, and *BP,* June 12, 1847, and January 15, 1848.

16 *"A singularly unfortunate": BP,* May 1, 1847.
   "remarkable for size, strength": Waterford News, December 8, 1848.

17 *"No Fever or Sickness":* Laxton, *The Famine Ships,* p. 23.
   thirty-five pounds of potatoes: Waterford News, December 8, 1848.
   "A piercing shriek": Liverpool Mercury, August 25, 1848.

18 *Ghostly faces bobbed:* Laxton, *The Famine Ships,* pp. 45–47; Gallagher, *Paddy's Lament,* pp. 210–11; Whyte, *Robert Whyte's 1847 Famine Ship Diary,* p. 113.
   "Hundreds of poor": Laxton, *The Famine Ships,* p. 59; P. J. Meghen, "Stephen de Vere's Voyage to Canada, 1847," *The Old Limerick Journal,* vol. 32, Winter 1995.

19 *"a calamity without":* House of Lords Select Committee on Emigrant Ships, in Gallagher, *Paddy's Lament,* p. 209.

thousands of pregnant women: Mark Holan, "Ireland's Famine Children 'Born at Sea,'" Genealogy Notes, *Prologue,* vol. 49, no. 4, Winter 2017–18.

"flung into the sea": Gallagher, *Paddy's Lament,* p. 214.

"One got used to it": Gallagher, *Paddy's Lament,* p. 231.

"swollen and mangled body": Henry David Thoreau, "The Shipwreck," *Cape Cod.* Princeton, NJ, and Oxford, UK: Princeton University Press, 1993, p. xiii. Originally published in 1865.

"Bridget such-a-one": Thoreau, "The Shipwreck," p. 6.

20   *"like the smell of":* John Winthrop, *The Journal of John Winthrop, 1630–1649.* Cambridge, MA: Harvard University Press, 2009, p. 32.

"every person who has": *Waterford News,* March 4, 1855.

21   *Deer Island Quarantine:* BP, June 12, 1847.

"torn away forcibly": Whyte, *The Ocean Plague,* p. 83.

22   *"The wharf of East Boston":* Miller, *Emigrants and Exiles,* p. 507; Sammarco and Price, *Boston's Immigrants, 1840–1925.* Both works quote Timothy Cashman's journal.

23   *"lamentable to see":* Coogan, *The Famine Plot,* p. 198.

At the time of Bridget's: O'Connor, *Bibles, Brahmins, and Bosses,* p. 147; Laxton, *The Famine Ships,* p. 33.

"huddled together like": Dolan, *The Irish Americans,* pp. 86–88.

"These wretched people": Whyte, *The Ocean Plague,* p. 105.

the 1820s and '30s: Passenger manifests and US Census records; author's interviews with Andrew Pierce and Celestine Murphy; Boston City Directory (multiple years).

24   *led the way west:* "Raising a Glass to Irish American Women," National Women's History Museum, March 14, 2017, www.womenshistory.org.

3. BRIDGET ON THE FARM

25   *life on the farm:* Details on the Murphy family and farm, meals and potatoes, life in Cloonagh: The Irish Folklore Commission Collection, The Schools' Collection, County Wexford, found at www.duchas.ie; Kinsella, *County Wexford in the Famine Years;* Ó Tuathaigh, *Ireland Before the Famine;* author's interviews with Andrew Pierce, Celestine Murphy, and Michael Demsey (County Wexford Library); US and Irish census records; Ancestry.com; ELG; Richard Griffith, "General Valuation of Rateable Property in Ireland," County of Wexford, multiple years (commonly known as Griffith's Valuation Books); Maria Pepper, "Celestine Shines New Light on JFK Ancestor," *New Ross Standard,* September 15, 2018; Richard Andrew Pierce, "Murphys and Barrons of Cloonagh, Parish of Owenduff, Co. Wexford: Further Ancestors of President John F. Kennedy," New England Historic Genealogical Society, AmericanAncestors.org.

a one-room farmhouse: Griffith's "General Valuation of Rateable Property," 1845.

Bridget's parents had met: Author's interview with Phyl and Michael Conway; Laxton, *The Famine Ships,* p. 148.

27   *"a fatal malady has":* Kinsella, *County Wexford in the Famine Years,* p. 14.

28   *a "total failure":* Kinsella, *County Wexford in the Famine Years,* pp. 78–93.

"the one weak place": Siobhan O'Neill, "Remembering the Irish Famine Orphans Shipped to Australia," *Irish Times,* October 25, 2018.

"Ireland is our disgrace": Siobhan O'Neill, "The Story of the Irish Famine Orphan Girls Shipped to Australia," *Irish Times,* November 7, 2019.

Publications like Punch: Coogan, *The Famine Plot,* p. 218; Peter Gray, "Punch and the Great Famine," History Ireland, Summer 1993; Jenni Snåre, "From Hopeless Apes to the Hopeful Erin," master's thesis, University of Oulu, Finland, Spring 2018.

29   *"indolence, improvidence, disorder":* Tóibín, *Irish Famine,* p. 13.

"God sent the calamity": Gallagher, *Paddy's Lament,* p. 86.

"The Almighty, indeed": Mitchel, *The Last Conquest of Ireland (Perhaps),* https://www.libraryireland.com/Last-Conquest-Ireland/Contents.php.

peasant "cottier" farmers: Caoimhín Ó Danachair, "Cottier and Landlord in Pre-Famine Ireland," *Béaloideas,* Folklore Society of Ireland, no. 48/49, 1980/1981, pp. 154–65.

30   *"humbly requesting" food:* Kinealy, *Women and the Great Hunger,* p. 53.

"It is a terrible time": John McConville to Bridget Hughes, Hughes-McConville family letters, 1846, Boston College library collections.

31   *killed dogs to make soup:* Poirteir, *Famine Echoes,* pp. 61, 74, 113.

exiled to Tasmania: Egan, *The Immortal Irishman.*

32   *"Mary Connell, found dead":* Tóibín, *Irish Famine,* p. 14.

more than five hundred: Kayla Hartz, "500 Children Found in Great Hunger Workhouse Mass Grave," IrishCentral.com, October 11, 2019.

"All day long carts rumbled": Tóibín, *Irish Famine,* p. 22.

Jane Colclough Boyse: Details on Jane and Thomas Boyse and their estates: Tom MacDonald, "Jane Kirwan Colclough Gauthier," *Bannow History;* J. C. Tuomey, "The Bay and Town of Bannow," *Transactions of the Kilkenny Archaeological Society,* vol. 1, no. 2 (1850), pp. 194–210; Tom MacDonald, "Tom Boyse Makes Great First Marriage," *Bannow History;* Griffith's "General Valuation of Rateable Property," County of Wexford, multiple years; Main Manuscript Collection, Irish Folklore Commission Collection, www.duchas.ie.

"climate disagreed with me": Saunders Newsletter and Daily Advertiser, March 6, 1857.

33   *"a person of very unamiable":* Saunders Newsletter and Daily Advertiser, March 6, 1857.

Magdalene asylums and laundries: Asmae Ourkiya, "How the Great Famine Affected Irish Women," RTE.ie, July 30, 2019.

"insane mothers": Kinealy, *Women and the Great Hunger,* p. 72.

34   *"a Celtic Irishman":* Kelly, *The Graves Are Walking,* p. 255.

"natural vivacity": Gallagher, *Paddy's Lament,* pp. 14, 27.

"bosom of America": Gilliam Brockwell, "Would George Washington Embrace the Migrant Caravan?" *Washington Post,* November 8, 2018.

4. BRIDGET IN THE CITY

36   *"at work on the Railroad":* This notice and those following were compiled by Northeastern University and the New England Historic Genealogical Society in a three-volume set, *Searching for Missing Friends,* with introductions by Ruth-Ann M. Harris, ed. The set is searchable online at www.ancestry.com/search/collections/5060.

"left me and spent": Information Wanted, *BP,* July 6, 1850.

"come you all together": Ruth-Ann M. Harris, introduction to *Searching for Missing Friends,* vol. 2, p. i.

37   *"But I can assure you"*: "Moving Letter Home to Mom and Dad from an Irish Famine Emigrant in 1850," Irishcentral.com, July 22, 2017.

"wretched, dirty, and unhealthy": Lemuel Shattuck, "Report of the Committee of Internal Health on the Asiatic Cholera," 1849, available at GlobalBoston.bc.edu/index .php/cholera-report. Hereafter referred to as "Shattuck Report."

"herd together in poverty": BP, September 8, 1849.

"To linger here is": BP, September 8, 1849.

38   *"but in every instance"*: BP, January 13, 1849.

"dear, delightful, bigoted": O'Connor, *Fitzpatrick's Boston,* p. 47.

"We really do not know": BP, May 4, 1849.

39   *"The majority of those"*: BP, August 11, 1849.

despondent nineteen-year-old: BP, September 8, 1849.

"literally born to die": Shattuck Report; Coogan, *The Famine Plot,* p. 205.

"women who have been": BP, August 18, 1849.

dozens were buried: Mike McCormack, "Deer Island," Ancient Order of Hibernians, June 4, 2019, https://aoh.com/2019/06/04/deer-island.

40   *"Unless immigrants wish"*: BP, May 4, 1849.

Irish Emigrant Society: BP, September 8, 1849; BP, June 29, 1850; BP, December 10, 1870.

41   *"human wretchedness, pauperism"*: BP, September 8, 1849.

"where the prairies, towns": BP, June 29, 1850.

"intelligence offices": Dudden, *Serving Women,* p. 79; Lis Adams, "Louisa May Alcott and Working Women," Concord Historical Collaborative, March 10, 2016.

42   *"coarse, ignorant, unintelligent"*: Dudden, *Serving Women,* p. 81.

"good breeding": Goodwin, *The Fitzgeralds and the Kennedys,* p. 48.

43   *"the hub of the solar"*: Oliver Wendell Holmes, "The Autocrat of the Breakfast-Table," *Atlantic,* vol. 1, no. 6, 1858.

"harmless, inoffensive, untitled": Okrent, *The Guarded Gate,* p. 33.

5. BRIDGET GOES TO WORK

47   *Brigid of Kildare*: Hugh de Blacam, "About the Name Brigid," in *The Saints of Ireland.* Milwaukee: Bruce Publishing, 1942.

Ireland's first abortions: Maureen Dowd, "Scarlet Letter in the Emerald Isle," *NYT,* May 19, 2018; Maeve Callen, "Of Vanishing Fetuses and Maidens Made-Again: Abortion, Restored Virginity, and Similar Scenarios in Medieval Irish Hagiography and Penitentials," *Journal of the History of Sexuality,* vol. 21, no. 2, May 2012; "Irish Saints Once Carried Out Abortions," *Irish Central,* February 3, 2021.

48   *"As we can not dispense"*: Robert Tomes, "Your Humble Servant," *Harper's,* June 1864.

One post-Famine survey: Diner, *Erin's Daughters,* pp. 46–47.

priests discouraged early marriage: Andrew Urban, "Irish Domestic Servants," *Gender and History,* 2009, p. 264.

49   *"Nothing but a closet"*: Lynch-Brennan, *The Irish Bridget,* p. 93.

"Six o'clock is none too": Lynch-Brennan, *The Irish Bridget,* p. 103.

50   *"I am so tired and almost"*: Lynch-Brennan, *The Irish Bridget,* pp. 110, 112.

"premeditated ugliness": Lynch-Brennan, *The Irish Bridget,* p. 114.

"malicious" and "contemptible": "A Letter from 'Bridget' in reply to 'Veritas' in the *Transcript,*" *BP,* February 14, 1852.

Bridget would have earned: Miller, *Emigrants and Exiles,* p. 407; Lynch-Brennan, *The Irish Bridget,* p. 91.

"It is not so very easey": Miller, *Emigrants and Exiles,* p. 319.

"We secretly acknowledged": Land, *Maid,* p. 142.

51   *born in Ireland*: Handlin, *Boston's Immigrants,* p. 243.

city's maids were Irish: Dezell, *Irish America,* p. 92; Lynch-Brennan, *The Irish Bridget,* p. 84.

"I'd see them, even if": Land, *Maid,* chapter 6.

Boston's intolerance: *BP* editorials, "No Irish Need Apply," September 30, 1854, and November 27, 1858.

52   *"Trouble in Families"*: "A Letter from 'Bridget' in Reply to 'Veritas,'" *BP.*

"narrow-minded bigots": *BP,* September 30, 1854.

uneasy relationship: Dudden, *Serving Women,* pp. 63–65; Danielle Phillips, "Searching for Sisterhood," *U.S. Women's History: Untangling the Threads of Sisterhood.* New Brunswick: Rutgers University Press, 2017; Patrick McKenna, "When the Irish Became White: Immigrants in Mid-19th Century US," *Irish Times,* February 12, 2013.

"ignorance and awkwardness": Lynch-Brennan, *The Irish Bridget,* p. 94.

53   *"both the necessity and"*: Tomes, "Your Humble Servant."

"I didn't want to do": Lynch-Brennan, *The Irish Bridget,* p. 98.

In an ambitious act: The "Bridget" letters appeared in the *Pilot* in February and March 1852. "Troubles in Families" was published on February 21 and 28.

54   *"If we do not do"*: Tomes, "Your Humble Servant."

55   *Thursday nights off*: Margaret Lynch-Brennan, "Ubiquitous Bridget," *Making the Irish.* New York: NYU Press, 2006, p. 343.

6. BRIDGET GETS MARRIED

56   *modest two-acre farm*: Author's visit to Dunganstown and interviews (with Sean Pierce, Patrick Grennan, Andrew Pierce, Celestine Murphy, and Kerry McCarthy); Richard Andrew Pierce, "Patrick Kennedy of Dunganstown, co. Wexford, Great-Grandfather of the President," New England Historic Genealogical Society, Summer 1990; Sean Pierce, "The Kennedys Who Left and the Kennedys Who Stayed," *New Ross Standard,* 1963, included in a self-published manuscript; local history page of the school, Scoil Mhuire, at Horeswood, http://homepage.eircom.net/~horeswoodns/local_history.htm.

57   *Patrick likely played*: Scoil Mhuire, at Horeswood.

illegal "hedge schools": Scoil Mhuire, at Horeswood.

58   *Kennedys grew wheat, barley*: Author's interview with Sean Pierce, 2006.

"the money scarcely warm": Whalen, *The Founding Father,* p. 5.

the O'Cinneide clan: Maier, *The Kennedys,* pp. 11–12.

59   *brief period of eviction*: Sean Pierce, "The Kennedys Who Left and the Kennedys Who Stayed."

Cherry Brothers Brewery: "Cherry Brothers Ltd.," BreweryHistory.com; "Creywell Brewery, New Ross," Wexford Guide and Directory, 1885, via LibraryIreland.com.

A helpful thread can be found at forum.irishwhiskeysociety.com/viewtopic.php-f=40
&t=2674.html.

"evil effects of drunkenness": James Birmingham, *A Memoir of the Very Rev. Theobald Mathew.* Dublin: Miliken and Son, 1840.

60   *the poorhouse in New Ross:* Author's interview with Jenny Nuthall, Wexford library, 2006.

It is believed that: Author's interview with Sean Pierce; Maier, *The Kennedys;* Klein, *The Kennedy Curse,* p. 34; Davis, *The Kennedys; Waterford News,* December 8, 1848; Boston Passenger Lists, 1820–1891, FamilySearch.com; Andrew Pierce, "Patrick Kennedy of Dunganstown."

61   *His son would later say:* P.J. Kennedy's passport application, 1923 (via NARA).

"gone with a vengeance": Maier, *The Kennedys,* p. 28.

only a single fatality: Washington Irving passenger manifest, 1848–49.

62   *during the passage:* KMMS; Davis, *The Kennedys,* p. 11.

stolen by a visitor: Lisa Wangsness, "Relic of Cross Stolen from Cathedral," *BG,* July 13, 2010.

63   *"a tall, spare, tight-lipped":* O'Connor, *Fitzpatrick's Boston,* pp. 156–57.

distant relatives: Author's interviews with Andrew Pierce and Celestine Murphy.

Bridget had been living: US Census, Ward 12; Davis, *The Kennedys,* p. 13.

Patrick had resided: US Census, Ward 12; Davis, *The Kennedys,* p. 13.

64   *larger island of East Boston:* Sumner, *A History of East Boston;* "Noddle's Island (now East Boston)," Friends of the Boston Harbor Islands, http://www.fbhi.org/noodle-island.html; Sammarco, *East Boston Through Time;* Sammarco, *East Boston.*

65   *taverns and "groggery":* O'Connor, *Fitzpatrick's Boston,* p. 83.

unskilled laborers: Handlin, *Boston's Immigrants,* p. 250; Davis, *The Kennedys,* p. 14.

cooperage factories: Harry Schenawolf, "Coopers Had the Colonists over a Barrel," *Revolutionary War Journal,* January 21, 2019; Kenneth Kilby, *The Cooper and His Trade.* London: John Baker Publishers, 1971.

66   *"we have lost much by":* Vowell, *The Wordy Shipmates,* p. 94.

Kennedys' annual income: Boston, Ward 2, tax assessor report; Maier, *The Kennedys,* p. 33.

"driven like horses": Miller, *Emigrants and Exiles,* p. 318.

"often so tired that": Miller, *Emigrants and Exiles,* p. 318.

67   *only the luckiest:* Shattuck Report.

"the lamp of life": Shattuck Report.

68   *"As might be expected":* Shattuck Report.

"mass of pollution": Shattuck Report.

one in seventeen: Handlin, *Boston's Immigrants,* pp. 114–15.

69   *"hives of human beings":* Shattuck Report.

7 . BRIDGET THE MOTHER

70   *as long as she could:* Women often waited, per Dudden, *Serving Women,* p. 205.

71   *at least five times:* ELG; Boston City Directories, multiple years; US Census, multiple years; Massachusetts State Census, 1855.

72   *"prompt payment under":* Shattuck Report.

flooded with effluent: Davis, *The Kennedys,* pp. 20–21; Shattuck Report, p. 12; Petersen, *The City-State of Boston,* p. 570; *BP,* June 28, 1856.

"ignorance, carelessness": Shattuck Report.

"in a state of intoxication": New England Farmer, October 9, 1852.

"once orderly and peaceful city": O'Connor, *Fitzpatrick's Boston,* p. 85.

73   *marched on the convent:* ARCH, vol. 2, p. 206; Ursuline Convent Collection at the Catholic University of America, University Libraries, Digital Collections.

vandalizing and looting: ARCH, vol. 2, pp. 243–50.

paid professional force: Brief History of the B.P.D., www.cityofboston.gov/police/about/history.asp.

sympathy for the Irish: Puleo, *Voyage of Mercy,* pp. 144–45.

Robert Bennet Forbes: Puleo, *Voyage of Mercy;* Robert Bennet Forbes, *The Voyage of the Jamestown on Her Errand of Mercy.* Boston: Eastburn Press, 1847, p. 52.

74   *"tremendous tide":* Lee, *America for Americans,* p. 49.

"It is notorious": Lyman Beecher, *A Plea for the West.* New York: Truman and Smith, 1835, archive.org.

"were open to anyone": David Frum, "Is America Still the 'Shining City on a Hill'?," *Atlantic,* January 1, 2021.

75   *just a few state laws:* Lepore, *These Truths,* pp. 314–15; Hidetaka Hirota, *Expelling the Poor.* Oxford, UK: Oxford University Press, 2017; Noah Lanard, "An Old Anti-Irish Law Is at the Heart of Trump's Plan to Reshape Legal Immigration," *Mother Jones,* September 6, 2018; Peter F. Stevens, "You Walked Right In," *Boston Irish,* March 1, 2018.

"All the news is famine": Eavan Boland, "A Woman Without a Country," *A Woman Without a Country.* New York: Norton, 2014.

76   *"we are sadly off for":* BP, June 7, 1845.

renamed it St. Nicholas: O'Connor, *Fitzpatrick's Boston,* pp. 69, 146.

77   *"loved and venerated":* Obituary, *BP,* May 26, 1855.

78   *"The United States will":* Maier, *The Kennedys,* p. 29.

"This is our country now": BP, January 5, 1850.

79   *"a race that will never":* Maier, *The Kennedys,* p. 38.

"idolatrous Roman Catholick": Cullen and Taylor, *The Story of the Irish in Boston,* pp. 25–29; "The Last 'Witch' Executed in Boston Was an Irish Speaker," *Irish Times,* October 24, 2016.

"ridiculous and childish": O'Connor, *The Boston Irish,* p. 16.

open on Christmas: Stevens, *Hidden History of the Boston Irish,* p. 132.

80   *sometimes burned alive:* Vowell, *Wordy Shipmates,* p. 57.

sold them into slavery: Vowell, *Wordy Shipmates,* p. 196; "Pequot Massacres Begin," This Day in History, History.com.

America's original sin: Frum, "Is America Still the 'Shining City on a Hill'?"; Andrew Martinez, "Old South Church Observes the Legacy of Slavery," *Boston Herald,* August 25, 2019; "History of East Boston," http://samuelmaverick.blogspot.com/2012/03/history-of-east-boston.html.

"swarthy" Germans: Lee, *America for Americans,* chapter 2; Okrent, *The Guarded Gate,* p. 41.

81   *"one neighborhood of":* Loughery, *Dagger John,* p. 72.

as a secret code: Lepore, *These Truths,* pp. 208–9.

"whore of Rome, and all": Okrent, *The Guarded Gate,* p. 42; Paul Leicester Ford, ed., *New-England Primer: A Reprint of the Earliest Known Edition.* New York: Dodd, Mead, 1899.

"effeminate, licentious": Loughery, *Dagger John,* p. 122.

"ignorant . . . idle, thriftless": Lee, *America for Americans,* p. 57. (Lincoln borrowed from an 1850 speech: "democracy — of all the people, by all the people, for all the people." And King would paraphrase a speech, "The arc of the moral universe is long, but it bends toward justice.")

"explain, diffuse, and defend": O'Connor, *Fitzpatrick's Boston,* p. 16.

82   *"completely uncontrollable":* O'Connor, *Fitzpatrick's Boston,* p. 86.

8. BRIDGET THE ENEMY

83   *flock of Irish-haters:* John Bach McMaster, *A History of the People of the United States.* New York: D. Appleton and Company, 1913; ARCH; BP, May 13 and 20, 1854; NYT, August 30, 1854; Thomas O'Connor, *Boston Catholics: A History of the Church and Its People.* Boston: Northeastern University Press, 1998.

the "Wide Awakes": McMaster, *A History of the People of the United States,* p. 86.

84   *"Keep cool, keep away":* BP, March 20, 1854.

"abstain from whiskey": BP, March 20, 1854.

85   *"Orr is not insane":* BP, May 13, 1854.

"and Catholicism forever": Loughery, *Dagger John,* p. 75.

their "foreign influence": Know Nothing Constitution, MHS.

86   *could never be true patriots:* Stevens, *Hidden History,* p. 24.

a Catholic takeover: Lee, *America for Americans,* p. 54.

secret handshakes, passwords: Stevens, *Hidden History,* p. 23.

87   *"Why are you poor?":* Lee, *America for Americans,* p. 54.

"eccentric museum": O'Connor, *Fitzpatrick's Boston,* p. 47.

"that atrocious and impious": ARCH, vol. 2, p. 336.

"He may be poor, weak": Lepore, *These Truths,* p. 313; *Charles Sumner: His Complete Works,* vol. 3 (of 20). Boston: Lee and Shepard, 1900, Gutenberg.org.

88   *"the liberties of a people":* BP, September 30, 1854.

"imminent peril of Freedom": Know Nothing Constitution, MHS.

"shall not be permitted": Minutes of the East Boston chapter of the Know Nothings, MHS, www.masshist.org/object-of-the-month/objects/the-know-nothing-party-2005 -01-01.

candidates swept elections: Okrent, *The Guarded Gate,* p. 42. The number includes five senators and forty-three representatives.

89   *"procure and pay for":* ARCH, vol. 2, p. 686; Know Nothing Constitution, MHS.

"guerilla warfare" tactics: Jelani Cobb, "Our Long, Forgotten History of Election-Related Violence," *The New Yorker,* September 14, 2020.

"barbarism which could": Lee, *America for Americans,* pp. 39–41.

"followed by a hard-hearted": Peter Smith, "Recalling Bloody Monday," *Louisville Courier-Journal,* August 6, 2005.

"roasted to death": BP, September 1, 1855.

"appetite for blood": BP, August 7, 1855.

"*As the know-nothings*": BP, October 14, 1854.

90   *anti-immigrant legislation:* Records of EB chapter of American Party, MHS; Know Nothing Constitution, MHS.

deported to Ireland or Liverpool: Boston Daily Advertiser, May 16, 1855.

"*across the seas for*": Hidetaka Hirota and Natalia Molina, "It's Time to Fulfill the Promise of Citizenship," *Washington Post,* July 29, 2018.

91   "*As a nation, we*": Letter to Joshua Speed, August 24, 1855, http://www.abrahamlincolnonline.org.

"*tilting against foreigners*": O'Connor, *The Boston Irish,* p. 80.

"*Know-Nothingism Is in*": BP, September 29, 1855.

an "*American tradition*": Lee, *America for Americans,* p. 44.

92   "*gruel*" *that could quickly:* D. W. Young, M.D., "Cholera Infantum: Its Cause, Pathology, and Treatment," Read Before the Illinois Medical Society, March 18, 1871, US National Library of Medicine, Digital Collections; Shattuck Report.

"*thrives and fattens on filth*": Young, "Cholera Infantum."

"*we ought to insist upon*": Young, "Cholera Infantum."

93   *outlawed or destroyed:* Egan, *The Immortal Irishman,* p. 11.

statutes to prevent Catholics: O'Connor, *The Boston Irish,* p. 80.

authorities had closed it: BP, October 13, 1855.

94   "*dropped on the floor*": BP, September 29, 1855.

"*A cloud upon my spirit*": BP, September 29, 1855.

9. BRIDGET THE WIDOW

99   *stuffed into window cracks:* Dineen, *Ward Eight,* p. 7.

likely a midwife: Meridith Anness, "Irish Births with Midwives from 1865 to 1875," The Irish in Cincinnati website, University of Cincinnati Archives and Rare Books Library.

brusque no-fuss affair: Details from author's interviews with James O'Toole.

102   *striving for $10 a week:* Nasaw, *The Patriarch,* p. 7.

an assessor's report: Meier, *The Kennedys,* p. 33.

managed to save $400: Boston, MA.: Provident Institution for Savings, 1817–1882 (online database: AmericanAncestors.org, New England Historic Genealogical Society, 2020).

brother-in-law Nicholas Roche: Massachusetts Deaths, 1841–1915; Massachusetts Vital and Town Records.

"*vile destroyer of the parent's*": BP, May 1, 1858.

103   *Patrick Donahoe, whose wife:* BP, December 17, 1853.

"*mitigate the evils of consumption*": Ad, *Boston Globe,* June 18, 1881; ad, *Boston Post,* April 3, 1880; *Boston and Bostonians.* New York: American Publishing and Engraving Company, 1894, p. 163.

"*lull the feelings of*": BP, May 28, 1859.

104   "*a cacophony of hacking*": Frank McCourt, *Angela's Ashes.* New York: Scribner, 1999, p. 10 (describing Limerick).

"*the spoiling meat*": Caoilinn Hughes, *The Wild Laughter.* Tullamarine, Australia: Bolinda Audio, 2020.

fourteen years: Shattuck Report.

105   *Scant details survive:* Davis, *The Kennedys,* p. 22; *BP,* December 11, 1858. Patrick's
      death certificate lists the cause of death as consumption, but some sources and histo-
      rians instead blame cholera.
      "public nuisance": O'Connor, *The Boston Irish,* p. 80; *BP,* November 17, 1849.
      "If the wishes of some": BP, November 17, 1849.
107   *"like a dark epic poem":* Leamer, *The Kennedy Women,* p. 16.
      "A dreadful darkness": Anne Brontë, "A dreadful darkness closes in," 1849, Poetry-
      Foundation.org.
      Exhume the corpse: Crystal Ponti, "When New Englanders Blamed Vampires for Tu-
      berculosis Deaths," (October 25, 2019), History.com.
      "I have just read": The Journal of Henry David Thoreau, vol. 12, chapter 7, September
      26, 1859, p. 356, Walden.org.
108   *"The savage in man is never":* Journal of Henry David Thoreau, September 26, 1859.
      "his life gradually wasted": BP, November 27, 1858.
      titillating stories: O'Connor, *The Boston Irish,* p. 100; Puleo, *A City So Grand,* pp. 71,
      80; assorted *BP* articles.
      "angry about something": Puleo, *A City So Grand,* p. 80.

10. BRIDGET THE SERVANT

110   *worth nearly nothing:* Suffolk County Probate Court records, 1858, #42040, p. 300.
      Digitized records at FamilySearch.org.
111   *survive past age five:* Whalen, *The Founding Father,* p. 13; Puleo, *A City So Grand,* p. 73.
      women were still fleeing: "Raising a Glass to Irish American Women," National Wom-
      en's History Museum.
112   *"The city is dangerously":* Holloran, *Boston's Wayward Children,* p. 45.
      "grave fears are entertained": BP, October 11, 1879.
113   *"A good healthy orphan":* BP, December 4, 1858.
      "vagabond, ignorant, ungoverned": Charles Loring Brace, *The Dangerous Classes of New
      York, and Twenty Years' Work Among Them.* New York: Wynkoop and Hallenbeck,
      1880, p. 321.
      "Evangelical child-savers": Holloran, *Boston's Wayward Children,* p. 63.
      "a Protestant plot": O'Connor, *Orphan Trains,* p. 168.
      Father George Haskins: ARCH, vol. 2, p. 632.
114   *"stubborn and wayward boys":* BP, July 20, 1861.
      "in praise of Liberty": Charles Dickens, "American Notes," *Collected Works,* p. 34.
115   *on lockdown for weeks:* BP, September 3, 1859.
      "treated worse than brutes": BP, January 9, 1864.
      "organized scheme for stealing": BP, January 10, 1852.
      "fated to remain a massive": Handlin, *Boston's Immigrants,* p. 55.
116   *"Positively no Irish":* Dudden, *Serving Girls,* p. 70.
      "It seems to us that": BP, September 30, 1854.
      "learn common sense": BP, November 27, 1858.
      "totally ignorant of": Tomes, "Your Humble Servant"; Dudden, *Serving Women,* p. 65.
      "sick of the Irish . . .": Dudden, *Serving Women,* p. 59.
      "I hope someday will": Letter compliments of Kerby Miller.
117   *Maverick Square:* Sumner, *A History of East Boston,* pp. 505–20; Sammarco, *East Bos-*

ton; BP, January 25, 1857; *Boston Transcript,* January 26, 1857; *Boston Journal,* January 26 and 28, 1857.

"attentive to all their wants": Sumner, *A History of East Boston,* p. 507.

118 *"tasty and convenient":* Sumner, *A History of East Boston,* p. 514.

the Underground Railroad: "George S. and Susan Hillard House," National Park Service, NPS.gov.

119 *one of Boston's wealthiest:* Sumner, *A History of East Boston;* Sammarco, *East Boston,* p. 12; *Boston Traveler,* February 24, 1859; *Boston City Directory,* 1860; *Boston Traveler,* February 24, 1858.

scores of employees: US Census, 1860. The census lists a Bridget *Murphy;* like others working at Sturtevant House, she may have been counted twice — once at home, once at work.

Bridget's personal effects: US Census, 1860.

seventy-two thousand Irish: Holloran, *Boston's Wayward Children,* p. 64.

120 *"Eager to be independent":* Louisa May Alcott, "How I Went out to Service," *The Independent,* June 4, 1874; Louisa May Alcott, *Work: A Story of Experience.* Boston: Roberts Brothers, 1875.

121 *"permanent inequality . . .":* Alexis de Tocqueville, *Democracy in America,* vol. 2. New York: The Colonial Press, 1900, 189–91. Originally published in French in 1840.

122 *"the most elegant and splendid":* Boston Traveler, February 24, 1858.

11. BRIDGET THE HAIRDRESSER

123 *killed while traveling:* BP, December 14, 1861; *NYT,* December 5, 1861. In *Yankee Destinies: The Lives of Ordinary Nineteenth-Century Bostonians* (Chapel Hill: University of North Carolina Press, 1991), Peter R. Knights suggests that the death might've been a suicide.

"one of the oldest and most": NYT, December 5, 1861.

124 *"wealthy and well-known":* BP, December 5, 1861.

"discriminatory and oppressive": Bunting, *Portrait of a Port,* p. 154.

"the busiest corner": Sammarco, *Jordan Marsh,* p. 26.

125 *"enterprising, progressive":* Julia Houston Railey, *Retail and Romance.* Boston: Walker Lithograph and Publishing Company, 1926, p. 9.

three of them Irish: US Census, multiple years.

nervous or impatient: Richard H. Edwards, *Tales of the Observer.* Boston: Jordan Marsh Company, 1950, p. 14.

126 *"this energetic firm":* BP, November 15, 1873.

"Satisfy her at any cost": Railey, *Retail and Romance,* p. 20.

127 *"The better you serve":* Sammarco, *Jordan Marsh,* p. 27.

"warm-hearted, generous": O'Dowd, *Lincoln and the Irish,* p. 38.

128 *"hate and despise the colored":* O'Dowd, *Lincoln and the Irish,* p. 38.

"the cruel lie . . .": O'Dowd, *Lincoln and the Irish,* p. 11.

was a "calamity": Loughery, *Dagger John,* p. 308.

"one of the most perfect": Loughery, *Dagger John,* p. 39.

slavery "in the abstract": O'Connor, *Fitzpatrick's Boston,* p. 168.

"a curse and blight": ARCH, vol. 2, p. 705.

"shocking" and "regrettable": ARCH, vol. 2, p. 706.

"This is a simple truth": BP, July 20, 1861.

129 *"escape from the chains":* Garrison's response to Daniel O'Connell's 1841 "Irish Address," digital scans at TheLiberatorFiles.com.

"treat the colored people": Egan, *The Immortal Irishman,* p. 161.

the Dublin Pilot: ARCH, vol. 2, pp. 335–36.

"stain on your star-spangled": Gilbert Osofsky, "Abolitionists, Irish Immigrants, and the Dilemmas of Romantic Nationalism," *American Historical Review,* vol. 80, October 1975, p. 890.

"Those who countenance": The American Anti-Slavery Society, "Daniel O'Connell upon American Slavery: With Other Irish Testimonials," 1860, African American Pamphlet Collection, Library of Congress.

"innately inferior people": O'Dowd, *Lincoln and the Irish,* p. 75.

"a traitor to humanity": Egan, *The Immortal Irishman,* p. 316.

a "black nigger": Blight, *Frederick Douglass,* p. 396.

"spirit of freedom": "When Frederick Douglass Came to Ireland — in His Own Words," review of book edited by Christine Kinealy (*Frederick Douglass and Ireland*), RTE.ie.

130 *bought into the great:* Jay Caspian Kang, "Noel Ignatiev's Long Fight Against Whiteness," *The New Yorker,* November 15, 2019.

fewer than a hundred: US Census, Ward 2, 1860.

Philip and Coresy Ann Russell: Massachusetts State Census, 1855.

all had been white: US Census, 1860.

least integrated big cities: Peterson, *The City-State of Boston,* p. 583; US Census, 1860; "Imagine Boston," Boston Planning and Development Agency, PowerPoint presentation, October 26, 2016.

131 *"shiftless," "slow and dull":* Frank Buckley, "Thoreau and the Irish," *New England Quarterly,* vol. 13, no. 3, September 1940, p. 389.

"Celtic gentlemen": O'Dowd, *Lincoln and the Irish,* p. 32.

the "wild Irish" who: O'Dowd, *Lincoln and the Irish,* p. 11.

"How can anyone who": Egan, *The Immortal Irishman,* p. 162.

by John Mitchel's son: Egan, *The Immortal Irishman,* p. 174.

132 *would "not move an inch":* Egan, *The Immortal Irishman,* p. 171.

"We Catholics have only": BP, January 12, 1861.

Boston's "adopted citizens": O'Connor, *Fitzpatrick's Boston,* p. 195.

"Irish Catholic bravery": Loughery, *Dagger John,* p. 301.

"representative of my country's": Egan, *The Immortal Irishman,* p. 167.

133 *"street cleaners, bricklayers":* Egan, *The Immortal Irishman,* p. 177.

These men played fiddles: Richard F. Welch, "Why the Irish Fought for the Union," *Civil War Times Magazine,* October 2006, reprint at Historynet.com.

"the noble sons of Erin": Egan, *The Immortal Irishman,* p. 215.

"God bless the Irish flag": Egan, *The Immortal Irishman,* p. 215; O'Dowd, *Lincoln and the Irish,* p. 62.

"replenishing streams": O'Dowd, *Lincoln and the Irish,* p. 45.

photographer Mathew Brady: O'Dowd, *Lincoln and the Irish,* p. 9. Brady didn't claim Irish heritage.

"We did not cause this": Egan, *The Immortal Irishman,* p. 248.

"clique of abolitionists": Egan, *The Immortal Irishman,* p. 217.

"the greatest event in": Egan, *The Immortal Irishman,* p. 245.

134 *"to the national cause"*: Egan, *The Immortal Irishman,* p. 192.
  days-long rampage: Loughery, *Dagger John;* O'Dowd, *Lincoln and the Irish;* Elizabeth
  Mitchell, "The Real Story of the 'Draft Riots,'" *NYT,* February 21, 2021; *ARCH,*
  vol. 2, p. 708; Draft Riots page at Tenement.org.
  A federal investigation: "Court Cases Related to the New York City Draft Riots,
  1864," Historical Society of the New York Courts, history.nycourts.gov; also Draft
  Riots page at Tenement.org.
135 *"great injustice done":* O'Connor, *Fitzpatrick's Boston,* p. 210.
  killing at least six: Stevens, *Hidden History,* p. 95. Possibly many more were killed.
  "complied with the order": O'Connor, *Fitzpatrick's Boston,* p. 212.
  Irish-blooded soldiers: Egan, *The Immortal Irishman,* p. 266.
136 *"War-battered dogs":* Emily Lawless, "Clare Coast," *With the Wild Geese.* London: Ibis-
  ter, 1902.
  "This is the only nation": Egan, *The Immortal Irishman,* p. 194.
  Eben Jordan had installed: Edwards, *Tales of the Observer,* pp. 16, 48–49; "Memorial
  Tributes: Eben D. Jordan, born Oct. 13, 1822—died Nov. 15, 1895," *BG,* November 15, 1895, reprint at archive.org; Sammarco, *Jordan Marsh,* p. 29.

12. BRIDGET THE GROCER

138 *"A man would hardly":* Duis, *The Saloon,* p. 65.
  "Liquor is food": Duis, *The Saloon,* p. 96.
  "Not to be drunk on": Introduction, Liquor License Records, Massachusetts State Archives.
140 *"a penniless boy":* NYT, November 16, 1895.
  a reputation for helping: BG, "Memorial Tributes: Eben D. Jordan."
  "Jordan imbued every associate": BG, "Memorial Tributes: Eben D. Jordan."
  "Adam-less Eden": Erin Blakemore, "How 19th-Century Women Used Department
  Stores to Gain Their Freedom," November 22, 2017, History.com.
  women's suffrage movement: Marlen Komar, "Department Stores Are Basically the Reason Women Were Allowed in Public," February 9, 2018, Racked.com.
  "leads to slang, bold talk": Komar, "Department Stores."
141 *"open shops and set up":* Eliza Lynn Linton, "Wild Women as Social Insurgents," *The
  Nineteenth Century,* October 1891, pp. 596–605.
  "Shop by Kennedy": Boston Business Directory, 1870.
  According to some: KMMS, p. 13.
  might've had to return: US Census, 1870. Bridget's work is listed as "house keeping."
142 *"the first Irishman that ever":* BP, October 10, 1851.
  fired, then reinstated: Stevens, *Hidden History,* p. 45.
  no Irish person had served: Stevens, *Hidden History,* p. 44.
143 *Katharine Conway:* Paula M. Kane, "The Pulpit of the Hearthstone: Katharine Conway and Boston Catholic Women, 1900–1920," *US Catholic Historian,* vol. 5, no.
  3/4, Women in the Catholic Community (Summer–Fall, 1986), pp. 355–70.
144 *ethnically and culturally:* Osofsky, "Abolitionists, Irish Immigrants."
  suburbs or their country estates: Goodwin, *The Fitzgeralds and the Kennedys,* p. 53.
  kept out of certain jobs: Thomas O'Connor, "How the Civil War Changed Boston,"
  Boston Globe Magazine, August 14, 2011.

first Black police officer: Anthony W. Neal, "Sergeant Horatio J. Homer: Boston's First Black Police Officer," *Bay State Banner,* February 4, 2016.

"hub of the solar system": Goodwin, *The Fitzgeralds and the Kennedys,* p. 46.

more like America's Dublin: Okrent, *The Guarded Gate,* p. 47 (per Theodore Parker).

"bright and twinkling": Goodwin, *The Fitzgeralds and the Kennedys,* p. 48.

"Boston is what I": Dickens, "American Notes"; Maria T. Olia and Kerren Barbas Steckler, *The Little Black Book of Boston.* White Plains, NY: Peter Pauper Press, 2010, p. 23.

opposition to Christmas: "Charles Dickens Brings 'A Christmas Carol' — and Christmas — to Boston," New England Historical Society, 2020.

"The city has increased": *New York Daily Tribune,* December 3, 1867.

145   *more tobacco, rum, and bitters:* Sample grocer's ledger from diary of C. S. Johnson and Company, MHS.

"being right in the middle": Goodwin, *The Fitzgeralds and the Kennedys,* p. 17.

"among the many redeeming": Reprint in *East Boston Ledger,* January 9, 1849.

could not easily become: Marian L. Smith, "Women and Naturalization, ca. 1802–1940," *Prologue,* Summer 1998, vol. 30, no. 2, archives.gov.

13. P.J. THE RASCAL

150   *One of the jobs Bridget:* PJKB.

"smashed his brains out": *New England Farmer,* August 7, 1852.

free ride to the city: Bunting, *Portrait of a Port,* p. 154.

skipped school to play: Goodwin, *The Fitzgeralds and the Kennedys,* p. 23.

"Boston Harbor was": Bunting, *Portrait of a Port,* p. 154.

drowned after climbing: BP, August 18, 1849.

151   *"His recovery is considered":* BP, September 25, 1858.

"ill-dressed and ill-mannered": Buckley, "Thoreau and the Irish"; *The Journal of Henry David Thoreau,* vol. 2, pp. 341–42, 1851, Walden.org.

"sins of young men": BP, December 4, 1858.

"deserving young woman": BP, July 15, 1854.

152   *Our Lady of the Isle:* BP, January 15, 1859; author's communication with Nancy C. Barthelemy, archivist at the Sisters of Notre Dame de Namur.

not listed as graduates: Nancy C. Barthelemy, archivist at the Sisters of Notre Dame de Namur.

sisters in the workforce: US Census, 1870.

often whipped or expelled: Cullen and Taylor, *The Story of the Irish in Boston,* pp. 137–38.

"Nothing that was Catholic": Goodwin, *The Fitzgeralds and the Kennedys,* p. 29.

153   *"damn Yankee prayers":* *Boston Courier,* March 24, 1859.

former Know Nothing: ARCH, vol. 2, p. 590.

the "persecuting bigots": ARCH, vol. 2, p. 595.

more palatable to Catholics: ARCH, vol. 2, p. 595.

"disposed of by the Civil War": BP, March 1, 1862.

154   *served only girls:* Archdiocese of Boston, Catholic School Directory, 1866; Nancy C. Barthelmy, archivist at the Sisters of Notre Dame de Namur.

named for a proslavery: Henry P. Bowditch, "Theodore Lyman," *Proceedings of the American Academy of Arts and Sciences,* vol. 34, no. 23, June 1899.

the first "branch" library: Sammarco, *East Boston.*

"attractive baritone": PJKB.

A classmate's diary: Diary of Arthur Rogers, MHS.

155   *castaways and delinquents:* Welch, "Why the Irish Fought for the Union."

"riotous proceedings": BP, September 8, 1849.

Boston's House of Reformation: Kenneth R. Geiser, *Reform School Reform: The Nature of Change in a Social Policy Biography,* doctoral dissertation, Massachusetts Institute of Technology, 1977, p. 38; Richard G. Hewlett, "Josiah Quincy: Reform Mayor of Boston," *New England Quarterly,* vol. 24, no. 2, June 1951.

156   *"most original and daring":* Gustave de Beaumont and Alexis de Tocqueville, *On the Penitentiary System in the United States and Its Application in France.* Carbondale: Southern Illinois University Press, 1979. Originally published in French in 1833.

"a wanton and lascivious": Geiser, *Reform School Reform,* p. 38.

only meager attempts: Geiser, *Reform School Reform,* p. 130.

facilities were dangerously: City of Boston, Annual Report, Board of Directors for Public Institutions, 1869–70, 1870–71.

sometimes held in an attic: City of Boston, Annual Report, Board of Directors for Public Institutions, 1870–71.

when a boys' dormitory: Robert S. Pickett, *House of Refuge: Origins of Juvenile Reform in New York State, 1815–1857.* New York: Syracuse University Press, 1969, pp. 97–98.

"contiguity of paupers and prisoners": City of Boston, Annual Report, Board of Directors for Public Institutions, 1869–70, p. 27.

"I struck her with all": BP, January 9, 1864.

"a pauper and penal colony": BP, August 18, 1849.

Protestants running institutions: BP, August 6, 1853.

157   *Irish "street boys":* BP, August 6, 1853.

In 1870, one of those: US Census, 1870.

logbook of lawbreakers: Suffolk County Sheriff's Records, FamilySearch.com.

was merely a truant: Author's interview with Chris Carter, Massachusetts Judicial Archives.

"Some of these boys": BP, January 9, 1864.

158   *playing cards on a Sunday:* BG, November 12, 1878.

"engaging in a prize fight": Suffolk County Sheriff's Records, FamilySearch.com.

a few months to two years: Fourteenth Annual Report of the Board of Public Institutions of the City of Boston, 1870–71; Thirteenth Annual Report, 1869–70; First Semi-Annual Report of the Inspectors of Prisons, 1870; Suffolk County Sheriff Records.

sentenced to nine years: BP, February 12, 1870.

"happen to be called": BP, June 18, 1870.

to pardon O'Brien: Bridget took in an Irish-born boy named Michael O'Brien after Patrick's death in 1858, and years later, P.J. would share an apartment with a Michael O'Brien. Because the name O'Brien was so common, it is impossible to prove a clear connection between the families.

159   *to conclude his schooling:* Some accounts claim P.J. briefly attended one of East Boston's other parochial schools, Assumption or Sacred Heart, both run by the Sisters of Notre Dame (and later by the Xaverian Brothers). However, neither had opened by the time P.J. reached the magical age of fourteen, when he could leave school and work

the docks. Also, Sacred Heart was a girls-only school (until the 1890s). He could've stayed in school beyond fourteen and perhaps attended another school, but based on the family's limited income and his own restless inclinations, it's unlikely.

14. P.J. THE LONGSHOREMAN

160   *"pursue some honest calling"*: *BP,* December 4, 1858.
  "Boys," one article read: BP, December 4, 1858.

161   *Men regularly fell through: BP,* September 16, 1871.
  "The affair was exceedingly": BP, November 27, 1858.
  hit his head on the way down: BG, December 15, 1880.
  and sent bodies flying: BG, June 30, 1885.
  "tearing away one side": East Boston Argus-Advocate, October 4, 1873.
  thirty to fifty cents: "The Longshoremen," *BG,* November 17, 1878.

162   *on strike in 1872: BG,* July 22 and 27, 1872.
  A longshoremen's union: "The Longshoremen," *BG,* November 17, 1878.
  "If we wish to be considered": BG, June 12, 1878.
  Daniel Skerry: BG, February 24, 1878.

164   *"muffled roar of the loom":* Jack London, "The Apostate," *The Works of Jack London.* New York: The Review of Reviews Company, 1917, p. 67.

165   *"All his bones ached":* London, "The Apostate."
  "the black, shapeless mass": "Pemberton Mill Collapse, 1860," CelebrateBoston.com.; "The Fall of the Pemberton Mill," *NYT,* April 18, 1886.
  written to her family: Author's interviews with Phyl and Michael Conway; Maier, *The Kennedys,* p. 50. Those letters were known to survive well into the twentieth century, kept in a box in a family closet, but they apparently were burned after P.J. died.

166   *the series of fires:* "Great Fires in Boston," *New York Herald,* July 26, 1870.

167   *"our already sadly burdened":* "A Great Fire," *BG,* August 1, 1873.

168   *23 and 25 Border Street:* Boston City Tax Records; Massachusetts State Census, 1865; US Census, 1860.
  P.J. would stop by: KMMS, p. 15.
  "piles of cabbages, potatoes": George G. Foster, *New York by Gas-Light: With Here and There a Streak of Sunshine.* Oakland: University of California Press, 1990. Originally published in 1850.

169   *a "strong, cheerful woman":* Davis, *The Kennedys,* p. 24.
  "a generous heart": Leamer, *The Kennedy Women,* pp. 19–20.
  "a determined woman": Author's interview with Celestine Murphy.
  scrappy businesses: East Boston Argus-Advocate, June 16, 1888; Boston City Directory, 1870, 1885.
  "Pure Rye Whiskey": East Boston Argus-Advocate, June 16, 1888.
  Bridget's shop became: Nasaw, *The Patriarch,* p. 8; Maier, *The Kennedys,* p. 36.
  "Irish women and sluttish": Foster, *New York by Gas-Light,* p. 60.

170   *"extreme and unusual": Boston Post,* April 4, 1867.
  "fatal to any liberty": Boston Post, April 4, 1867.
  "drive it out of sight": Boston Post, February 21, 1867.
  "prosecute the parties": BP, August 2, 1873.

171   *paid for their licenses:* Suffolk County liquor licenses, 1868–69, Massachusetts State
      Archives.
      "ancient temples remodeled": Dineen, *Ward Eight,* p. 61.
      police regularly raided: BG, September 30, 1881, and August 4, 1876.
      "oppressive and excessive": BG, December 15, 1884.
172   *"Married Women Doing Business":* Boston City Archives.
      "Tomatoes 8c per can": East Boston Argus-Advocate, June 16, 1888.
      none were female-owned: Cullen and Taylor, *The Story of the Irish in Boston.* This book
      lists occupations in Boston, based on the 1885 census.
      deeper into the workforce: "Raising a Glass to Irish American Women," National Wom-
      en's History Museum.
173   *"What Women Are Doing": BP,* September 16, 1871.
      "there are hundreds of women": BP, September 16, 1871.
      "New avenues for higher": Denise Kiernan, *We Gather Together.* New York: Penguin,
      2020, p. 179.

15. P.J. THE BARTENDER

175   *"among the best known": Boston with Its Points of Interest.* New York: Mercantile Illustrat-
      ing Company, 1894, p. 170; ad, Boston City Directory, 1875.
      their own union: BG, June 29, 1882, and April 12, 1882; *Fall River Daily Herald,* June
      29, 1882.
      the auction of Hayward's: BG, July 11, 1879.
      owner had been arrested: BG, July 20, 1876.
176   *"the lifeless body": BG,* May 10, 1879.
      Class 4 liquor license: Liquor license records, 1879–80, Boston City Archives.
      Bridget and P.J.'s sisters: PJKB.
      annoying new "screen law": Boston Post, April 7, 1880.
      "foolish" and "cowardly": BG, April 19, 1881.
      "While it is claimed": BG, July 25, 1881; Annual Report from the Board of Police
      Commissioners, 1881.
177   *"respectable" and "has paid":* R.G. Dun & Co. credit report volumes, Massachusetts,
      Volume 75, Baker Library, Harvard Business School, p. 287.
      "Keeps well covered up": R.G. Dun & Co. credit report volumes, Massachusetts, Volume
      75.
      one saloon per 245 residents: "Drinking Saloons and Population," *BG,* September 24,
      1882.
      "East Boston. For sale": Ad, *BG,* April 26, 1885.
      roughly $25 a month: Ad, *BG,* July 16, 1888.
178   *landowner named Treadwell: The Spirit of '76,* vol. 2. New York: Spirit of '76 Publish-
      ing Company, 1895, p. 321.
      P.J. signed the papers: Liquor license records, 1883–84, Boston City Archives; Boston
      City Directory, 1882.
      Rueter often lobbied: "Brewer's Argument before joint special commission on the Liquor
      Question," Printed at the Job Room of the *Boston Post,* 1878, archive.org; "Brewer's
      Convention," *St. Louis Globe Democrat,* June 5, 1879; Miller, *Boston Beer,* p. 42.

"Instead of refusing": "Brewer's Argument before joint special commission on the Liquor Question."

popular high-alcohol: Schorow, *Drinking Boston,* p. 163. The brew was 15 percent alcohol.

179   *"The committee is confident":* "Brewer's Argument before joint special commission on the Liquor Question."

to quote Benjamin Rush: Schorow, *Drinking Boston,* p. 78; Emma Green, "Colonial Americans Drank Roughly Three Times as Much as Americans Do Now," *Atlantic,* June 29, 2015.

"taken in small quantities": Benjamin Rush, "An Inquiry into the Effects of Ardent Spirits on the Human Mind and Body," pamphlet, 1784; Green, "Colonial Americans Drank."

"good, wholesome" lager beer: Boston City Directory, 1882.

German immigrant proprietors: Boston City Directory, 1879.

free or cheap snacks: Schorow, *Drinking Boston,* p. 59.

180   *two dozen liquor licenses:* Gallus Thomann, *Colonial Liquor Laws: Part II of "Liquor Laws of the United States."* New York: The United States Brewers' Association, 1887, p. 28; Schorow, *Drinking Boston,* pp. 28–29.

Cotton Mather complained: Samuel Adams Drake, *Old Boston Taverns and Tavern Clubs.* Boston: Cupples, Upham, and Company, 1917, p. 14.

roughly 850 licensed: Goodwin, *The Fitzgeralds and the Kennedys,* p. 16.

"the great Apostle": BP, August 11, 1849.

181   *"The epidemic has driven":* BP, August 11, 1849.

the rare moral cause: Thomas Lester, "The Temperance Movement in 19th Century Boston," *BP,* June 21, 2019.

"grieved, humbled, and mortified": Liam Hogan, "Frederick Douglass's Journey from Slavery to Limerick," *The Irish Story,* September 29, 2014.

all sorts of public behavior: Duis, *The Saloon,* p. 8.

Quigleys, O'Connors, Finnerties: Suffolk County liquor license records, 1868–69, Massachusetts State Archives.

182   *for the next five years:* Duis, *The Saloon,* p. 11.

One crafty proprietor: BG, July 20, 1876.

P.J.'s "Elbow Street store": Letter from James T. Fitzgerald, PJKP.

183   *"well-muscled":* Whalen, *The Founding Father,* p. 13.

184   *"somewhat larger than":* PJKB, p. 6 (also "rosy complexion" and "well-shaped head").

"adding to his air of composure": John F. Kennedy Library Foundation, *Rose Kennedy's Family Album,* p. 20.

"rarely seen lifting a glass": Whalen, *The Founding Father,* p. 21.

"only on the most festive": Horowitz and Collier, *The Kennedys,* p. 14.

be so "straight": Bill Duncliffe, "Joseph P. Kennedy: His Life and Times," *Boston Record American,* January 7, 1964.

"news, gossip, celebrations": John F. Kennedy Library Foundation, *Rose Kennedy's Family Album,* p. 20.

185   *"In this short time":* Fourteenth Annual Report of the Board of Public Institutions of the City of Boston, 1870–71, p. 41.

"almost invariably fall into": Fourteenth Annual Report of the Board of Public Institutions of the City of Boston, 1870–71, p. 47.

Daniel Skerry, the longshoreman: BG, February 24, 1878.

186   *fines of one to three dollars:* East Boston Free Press, May 1, 1886.

       "An unusually large number": East Boston Argus-Advocate, May 1, 1886.

       "a dangerous condition": BG, December 27, 1886.

       Anheuser Busch beers: Schorow, Drinking Boston, p. 59; BG, September 21, 1886.

       Sullivan ran his own: "John L. Sullivan's Saloon," New York Sun, December 24, 1884; Christopher Klein, "It's Time for Boston to Honor Its First Irish Superstar," WBUR, March 13, 2014; NYT, August 2, 1915.

187   *a man called Hastings:* BG, May 25 and September 22, 1881.

       "He hears the best": John Koren, "Social Aspects of the Saloon," in *The Economic Aspects of the Liquor Problem.* An investigation made for the Committee of Fifty under the direction of Henry W. Farnam. Boston: Houghton Mifflin, 1889, p. 215.

188   *"Predictably, he became":* John F. Kennedy Library Foundation, Rose Kennedy's Family Album, p. 21.

16. P.J. THE DEMOCRAT

189   *"one of the most agreeable":* BG, April 23, 1878.

190   *Other Ward 2 operators:* Cullen and Taylor, The Story of Irish in Boston; BG, October 30, 1880.

       "read some resolutions": Boston Transcript, February 17, 1881.

       P.J.'s "efficient" efforts: BG, December 29, 1883.

191   *"extend our heartiest sympathies":* BG, May 26, 1881.

       "every son of Erin": BG, October 17 and 18, 1881.

       a prolific letter-writer: PJKB.

192   *More than 100,000:* McCourt, Malachy McCourt's History of Ireland, p. 201; "The Irish Atlantic," Chronology, MHS, https://www.masshist.org/irish-atlantic/chronology.

       P.J. helped organize: BG, May 26, 1881.

       88 percent of the land: Costigan, A History of Modern Ireland, p. 237.

193   *"destroy the system":* Maier, The Kennedys, p. 46.

       Bridget's in-laws became: Maier, The Kennedys, pp. 46–47; Sean Pierce, self-published manuscript.

       "Now there is an Irish": Costigan, A History of Modern Ireland, p. 239.

       "righteous struggle": BG, October 21, 1881.

       "the most enthusiastic": BG, October 21, 1881.

       "the first important meeting": BG, October 18, 1881.

194   *P.J. was tapped to run:* BG, April 1, 1882.

       Ward 2 caucus elections: BG, October 30, 1880.

       to deliver fifty votes: Ainley, Boston Mahatma, p. 57.

       the Ward 2 caucus: BG, December 3, 1883.

       more party responsibilities: BG, October 17 and 23, 1885.

195   *John H. Sullivan:* Cullen and Taylor, The Story of Irish in Boston, p. 391.

196   *"a social force in":* Koren, The Economic Aspects of the Liquor Problem, p. 216.

       "the liquor dealer is": Anbinder, City of Dreams, p. 164.

       "the proprietor of the social": Duis, The Saloon, p. 126.

       Lawrence Logan emigrated: Ryan, A Journey Through Boston Irish History, pp. 85–86; Cullen and Taylor, The Story of the Irish in Boston, p. 369.

James William Kenney: Ryan, *A Journey Through Boston Irish History*, p. 85.

197 *"Your saloon's on fire!":* Duis, *The Saloon*, p. 141.

"half starved Irishmen": BP, December 17, 1853.

Boston's annexation of suburbs: O'Connor, *The Boston Irish*, p. 115.

198 *the first Irish mayor:* "Boston Swears in First Irish-born Mayor," MassMoments.org.

200 *"a perfect uproar":* BG, March 29, 1884.

candidate, P.J. Kennedy: BG, March 12, 1884; April 26, 1884; October 31, 1885; November 4, 1885.

201 *the top vote-getter:* BG, November 4, 1885.

doorkeeper Captain Tucker: Massachusetts General Court, "Bird Book," 1892.

his seat, number 85: Massachusetts General Court, "Bird Book," 1886.

202 *"Democratic Improvement":* BG, November 4, 1885.

"Battle of New Orleans": BG, January 8 and 9, 1885.

donkey as its mascot: James McWilliams, "How the Battle of New Orleans Birthed the American Character," *The New Yorker,* January 8, 2015.

"disciples of the great": BG, January 8, 1886.

17. P.J. THE LEGISLATOR

205 *"young Democracy of":* BG, July 3, 1886.

"Who Will Control": BG, October 11, 1886.

"in the liquor business": BG, October 11, 1886.

"Genial and popular": East Boston Argus-Advocate, October 2, 1886.

206 *receiving more votes:* BG, November 2, 1886.

"altogether a glorious day": BG, November 2, 1886.

"Democracy stronghold": East Boston Argus-Advocate, October 2, 1886.

Board of Metropolitan Police: Duis, *The Saloon*, p. 13.

liquor licenses in Boston: Schorow, *Drinking Boston*, p. 50.

separating drinking from voting: Duis, *The Saloon*, p. 131.

207 *"natural rights of man":* Schorow, *Drinking Boston*, p. 88.

"one of the most popular": BG, December 7, 1888.

208 *"not large enough to hold":* PJKB.

209 *province of Newfoundland:* East Boston Argus-Advocate, May 1, 1886; US Census, 1910.

J.J. Quigley had parlayed: Boston City Directory, 1885.

James T. Fitzgerald: Letter from James T. Fitzgerald, December 15, 1937, PJKB.

211 *real money: $650:* KMMS, p. 25.

brewery salesmen and liquor: Letter from James T. Fitzgerald, PJKB.

"bordering on the puritanical": Sean Pierce, "The Kennedys Who Left and the Kennedys Who Stayed," p. 10.

He called her "Mame": Horowitz and Collier, *The Kennedys*, p. 14.

"never had a romance": Leamer, *The Kennedy Women*, p. 94.

"no time for girl friends": Leamer, *The Kennedy Women*, p. 94.

212 *"set her cap":* KMMS, p. 26.

Mary was the eldest: Massachusetts State Census, 1865; US Census, 1870, 1880, 1900; marriage, birth, and death records, Ancestry.com and FamilySearch.com.

ran a construction business: Davis, *The Kennedys,* p. 26, which states that Hickey was a "well-off saloonkeeper." Other biographers describe him as a prosperous businessman (Horowitz) and a contractor (Nasaw) but don't mention his saloon.

Irish maid of their own: Davis, *The Kennedys,* p. 26.

Charles and James, after working: US Census, 1880.

effective cough medicine: KMMS, p. 28.

"an amazingly quick-witted": Goodwin, *The Fitzgeralds and the Kennedys,* p. 227.

213 *"going to be a marvelous":* Leamer, *The Kennedy Women,* p. 93.

they were married: KMMS; *East Boston Argus-Advocate,* November 26, 1887.

214 *a bowl of chowder:* Mary Lou McCarthy, oral history, 1977, JFKL.

"very firm and very severe": Mary Lou McCarthy, oral history, 1977, JFKL.

"the power behind the throne": Leamer, *The Kennedy Women,* p. 101.

Democratic National Convention: BG, June 2, 1888.

215 *his new friend, Rosnosky:* BG, May 1, 1888.

to bestow congratulations: East Boston Free Press, September 8, 1888.

"no little P.J.'s running": Horowitz and Collier, *The Kennedys,* p. 20.

216 *lived past age six:* ELG; US Census, multiple years. Per ELG (and the 1900 US Census) Bridget may have had as many as twenty-eight grandchildren, thirteen of whom died by age six. Two of her daughters' children may have died in childbirth.

"The contest was the most": BG, November 3, 1888.

party for Mary and P.J.: East Boston Argus-Advocate, December 1, 1888.

217 *Bridget wasn't able:* Leamer, *The Kennedy Women,* p. 23; Davis, *The Kennedys,* p. 26; *East Boston Argus-Advocate,* December 29, 1888; BG, December 24, 1888.

218 *space at the family plot:* Leamer, *The Kennedy Women,* p. 24.

"a well-known and charitable": East Boston Argus-Advocate, December 29, 1888.

"a woman of many noble": BG, December 24, 1888.

"determined" and "resourceful": Author's interview with Celestine Murphy, 2020.

"one of the most successful": Leamer, *The Kennedy Women,* p. 19.

valued at $2,200: Probate records; Davis, *The Kennedys,* p. 26.

"Wanted: strong girl": BG, December 29, 1888.

219 *"a large quantity of malt":* BG, July 23, 1889.

"virtuous old-fashioned": Kane, "The Pulpit of the Hearthstone," p. 364.

"lead useful, pleasant lives": Louisa May Alcott, *Little Women.* Ware, UK: Wordsworth Editions, 1993, p. 97. Originally published in 1868.

"busy, useful, independent": Louisa May Alcott: Her Life, Letters, and Journals. Boston: Roberts Brothers, 1889, p. 197.

220 *Bridget and perhaps:* Author's interviews with Sean Pierce, 2006; *The Wexford People,* October 26, 1887; "Eviction at Foley's Fort," Scoil Mhuire, at Horeswood; Maier, *The Kennedys,* pp. 46–48; KMMS.

18. P.J. THE SENATOR

221 *to the house five times:* BG, October 8, 1891.

"packed to suffocation": BG, October 18, 1889.

"Stormy Caucus in Ward 2": BG, October 18, 1889.

"It takes the citizens": BG, October 18, 1889.

"one of the largest": East Boston Free Press, July 13, 1889.

222   *that "popular Democrat":* East Boston Argus-Advocate, July 20, 1889.
      "contest of opinion": Lepore, These Truths, p. 165.
      Boston Electric Elevated: Journal of the House, 1889.
      Jeffries Yacht Club: Petitions, Journal of the House, 1888; BG, February 2, 1888.

223   *past thirty thousand:* BG, February 9, 1887.
      An East Boston bridge: Journal of the Senate, June 1892.
      P.J. never managed: BG, February 9, 1887; Argus-Advocate, November 26, 1887; East
      Boston Free Press, April 23, 1887.
      came at hiring time: BG, February 9, 1888.
      changes that could've doomed: Journal of the House (January 1886, February 1886,
      March 1886); House Bill No. 534 (1889); Journal of the Senate (March 1893).

225   *"rum shop" on pilings:* East Boston Argus-Advocate, June 16, 1888.
      out of business: Duis, The Saloon, p. 31; various BG stories.
      "bartenders will carry": BG, April 28, 1889.
      the number of licenses: Duis, The Saloon, p. 31.
      brought in $336,000: House Auditor abstract, December 31, 1888.

226   *always made the cut:* Boston liquor license records; annual BG stories.
      "relic of the puritanical": Duis, The Saloon, p. 53.
      overturned in 1891: Duis, The Saloon, p. 55.
      Louis D. Brandeis: BG, March 13, 1891.
      begun sending "spotters": Proceedings of the Sixth Annual Meeting, Citizens' Law and
      Order League of Massachusetts, 1888.

227   *"look after business interests":* East Boston Free Press, September 8, 1888.
      accept the nomination: BG, November 21, 1890.
      "It's impossible for me": BG, September 16, 1890.
      state senate candidate: BG, October 8, 1891.
      "one of the best-known": BG, October 8, 1891.

228   *"prosperous advancement":* BG, October 11, 1891.
      "I assure you that": BG, October 11, 1891.
      "There is not another man": BG, October 8, 1891.
      "there should be no doubt": Boston News, February 2, 1892.
      "We will make him senator": BG, October 8, 1891.
      Holy Cross Cemetery: Undertaker Report; Massachusetts death registry.

229   *"unexpected . . . senseless":* KMMS, p. 37; Goodwin, The Fitzgeralds and the Kennedys, p.
      227.
      $5,275 at an estate sale: Leamer, The Kennedy Women, p. 96.

230   *Roughly 70 percent:* Okrent, The Guarded Gate, p. 48. The statistic is from 1900.
      "guard our civilization": Okrent, The Guarded Gate, pp. 35–36, 50–51.
      P.J. cast one of ten: Journal of the Senate, 1893.
      "hard-drinking, idle": Okrent, The Guarded Gate, p. 62.

231   *ice cream and salad:* BG, October 4, 1892.
      "Shall we permit these": Okrent, The Guarded Gate, p. 58.
      "a wild and motley throng": Okrent, The Guarded Gate, p. 64.

232   *John F. Fitzgerald:* Journal of the Senate, January 1893. Fitz sat in number 7, P.J. in
      number 8.
      died of a heart attack: Goodwin, The Fitzgeralds and the Kennedys, p. 59. It's possible
      that she was forty-five.

"Oh, Gawd, here goes": Bill Duncliffe, "Joseph P. Kennedy: His Life and Times," *Boston Record American,* January 7, 1964 (part of a twenty-one-part series that ran in early 1964).

"his own greatest admirer": Dineen, *The Kennedy Family,* p. 6.

233   *"They are a stupid, sodden":* Okrent, *Last Call,* p. 46; O'Dowd, *Lincoln and the Irish,* p. 35.

saloonkeepers, politicians: Joanna Scutts, "The Cartoonist Who Drew America Dry," talesofthecocktail.org, October 30, 2015.

"I 'spose you can": Okrent, *The Guarded Gate,* p. xiv.

234   *"monkey on an organ":* Cutler, *Honey Fitz,* p. 66.

"It is fashionable today": Goodwin, *The Fitzgeralds and the Kennedys,* p. 102.

"an impudent young man": Cutler, *Honey Fitz,* p. 64.

"salt of the earth": Koskoff, *Joseph P. Kennedy,* p. 5.

235   *"He is genial and popular": East Boston Argus-Advocate,* July 20, 1889.

"In your prayers you": Letter, PJKP.

ten hours or less: Index, Journal of the House, 1888.

"Bill to provide for": Journal of the Senate, May 1893.

"The liquor interest": BG, December 16, 1891.

236   *"to promote temperance":* Journal of the Senate, June 1892.

legislative "mischief": Journal of the Senate, June 1892.

House Bill 420: "Bill to Incorporate the Columbia Trust Co.," Journal of the Senate, 1892, chapter 400 of Acts.

237   *"no aspirations to leadership":* PJKB.

"a familiar figure in that": Robert Cantwell, "Mr. Kennedy, The Chairman," *Fortune,* September 1, 1937.

19. P.J. THE BOSS

238   *P.J. stood at the bow: BG,* September 24, 1892.

exploring these islands: For more on Quigley's boat and excursions, see PJKP; PJKB; *BG,* July 29 and September 24, 1892; ad, *BG,* April 13, 1893.

239   *work on Quigley's boats:* Whalen, *The Founding Father,* p. 30.

"Everyone in the party": BG, September 24, 1892.

he'd name Eleanor: KMMS; Cutler, *Honey Fitz,* p. 74.

240   *as "a shrine":* Whalen, *The Founding Father,* p. 31; Nasaw, *The Kennedys,* p. 16.

"Bridgie" came to Boston: Passenger list, *Cephalonia;* US Census, 1900; Letter, 1907, PJKP.

241   *vacationing "gentlemen": BG,* August 11, 1896.

"It has men of every station": BG, July 30, 1895, and August 25, 1897.

burned to the ground: BG, September 12, 1896.

P.J. became better acquainted: PJKP at JFKL.

hundred miles on horseback: BG, August 15, 1896.

242   *Redberries also gathered: Boston Post,* July 26, 1895.

The Redberries once: BG, April 25, 1895.

a rowdy sendoff: Boston Post, December 1, 1895.

"My playgrounds were": Cutler, *Honey Fitz,* p. 39.

"the only field where": Maier, *The Kennedys,* p. 53.

"I suppose they must": John F. Kennedy Library Foundation, *Rose Kennedy's Family Album*, chapter 1.

243   *"aliens" and "enemies"*: BG, August 5, 1895.

Rioters fired shots: BG, July 5 and 6, 1895.

"We are one people": BG, August 5, 1895.

"a magical place": Goodwin, *The Fitzgeralds and the Kennedys*, p. 124.

exploding soda tank: PJKP; *Boston Post*, April 7, 1895.

244   *Fitz as a buffoon*: Dineen, *The Kennedy Family*, p. 8. P.J. also considered Fitz "insufferable."

"the pink-cheeked youngster": Goodwin, *The Fitzgeralds and the Kennedys*, pp. 96–98.

"Now that the fight": Goodwin, *The Fitzgeralds and the Kennedys*, p. 98.

as Fitzgerald recovered: Fitzgerald and P.J. in Asheville from Goodwin, *The Fitzgeralds and the Kennedys*, p. 100; *Asheville Citizen-Times*, January 24, 1982; PJKP; and subsequent news photos found at JFKL.

245   *P.J. took over as president*: Senate "Bird Book," 1892–93, p. 124.

P.J. bought and sold: Sean Pierce, self-published manuscript, p. 10; assorted BG stories (e.g., August 14, 1908, and February 24, 1909); *Boston Traveler*, June 29, 1891; July 8, 1891; July 6, 1892.

Thomas J. "T.J." Lane: Obituary, BG, August 11, 1906.

"organization of prominent": Obituary, BG, August 11, 1906.

246   *"cliques and factions"*: BG, April 29, 1892.

He could be "ruthless": Kessler, *The Sins of the Father*, p. 9.

247   *Suffolk Coal Company*: Cutler, *Honey Fitz*, p. 73.

lucrative city contracts: BG, April 3, 1903.

J.J. Cotter had died: *Boston Post*, August 14, 1894.

began adding Mary's name: BG, April 1, 1899, and July 23, 1919.

wood-handled corkscrews: Horowitz and Collier, *The Kennedys*, p. 14.

"celebrated rock cordials": Ad, BG, June 18, 1881; ad, *Boston Post*, April 3, 1880; *Boston and Bostonians*, p. 163.

"standard remedy for lung": *Boston and Bostonians*, p. 163.

"Fairbanks Rock Cordial": Ad, BG, December 20, 1914.

liquor stores and druggists: *Boston and Bostonians*, p. 163.

through Thomas Barron: KMMS, p. 52.

one of the city's most: BG, November 17, 1890; December 10, 1890; December 16, 1890.

248   *P.J. installed Barron*: KMMS, p. 32; Sean Pierce, self-published manuscript.

two large oxen to tow: Cutler, *Honey Fitz*, p. 74.

249   *Democratic National Convention*: *Boston Post*, July 12, 1896.

Maguire's funeral arrangements: BG, November 30, 1896.

"an owl in a hole": BG, October 20, 1898.

250   *the Board of Strategy*: John T. Galvin, "Patrick J. Maguire: Boston's Last Democratic Boss," *New England Quarterly*, vol. 55, no. 3, September 1982.

"The great mass of people": Dolan, *The Irish Americans*, p. 151.

Lomasney had concocted: Most of the details of this incident come from BG, October 20 and 21, 1898.

251   *the papers were filled*: BG, October 20 and October 21, 1898.

252   *"gentlemen conversant with"*: BG, November 18, 1899.

253   *"done: his days are numbered"*: Ainley, *Boston Mahatma,* p. 84.

      "No man can surpass": Ainley, *Boston Mahatma,* p. 82.

      "Mr. Kennedy is said to": BG, November 18, 1899.

      "He is classed among": BG, November 18, 1899.

      "undisputed leader of": BG, November 18, 1898.

254   *1899 he shot himself: Sacred Heart Review,* April 15, 1899; *BG,* April 10 and 11, 1899.

      "an ideal citizen": BG, April 10, 1899.

      "seriously embarrass": BG, April 11, 1899.

255   *"one of the older generation"*: BG, December 22, 1899.

      a $3,500 salary: BG, November 1, 1900.

      "promptness, honesty": BG, November 1, 1900.

20. P.J. THE AMERICAN

256   *"The Irish immigration here"*: Letter to cousin Jim Kennedy, PJKP.

257   *Italian and Hebrew:* BG, November 14, 1903.

258   *Tammanyization of Boston:* BG, November 14, 1903.

      His first official act: BG, January 6, 1902.

      he declined the offer: BG, March 17, 1902.

259   *had become "inseparable"*: Goodwin, *The Fitzgeralds and the Kennedys,* p. 228; KMMS, p. 37.

      the family's Saint Bernard: KMMS, p. 44.

260   *Friday night card games:* PJKP; photo at JFKL.

      seeking the "personal favor": Letters, 1903, PJKP.

      Fitzgerald, who was more showy: Cutler, *Honey Fitz,* p. 53.

      "We never sat down": Duncliffe, "Joseph P. Kennedy."

      "tell them we're eating": Leamer, *The Kennedy Women,* p. 99.

      "All I could see": Goodwin, *The Fitzgeralds and the Kennedys*, p. 229.

261   *the boy, Johnny Ryan:* Duncliffe, "Joseph P. Kennedy."

      "I shall pass through": KMMS, p. 33.

      "Everyone knew that P.J.": BG, October 20, 1898.

      "Who has controlled Boston": BG, November 14, 1903.

      "Don't make mistakes": Dineen, *The Kennedy Family,* p. 6.

262   *"remarkably unsullied"*: Duncliffe, "Joseph P. Kennedy," p. 6.

      He didn't curse: Boston Record American, January 7, 1964.

      "not even his bitterest": Boston Record American, January 7, 1964.

      came home and collapsed: BG, July 20, 1905.

263   *died of Bright's disease:* BG, November 23, 1900.

      producing tears on demand: Cutler, *Honey Fitz,* p. 53.

      New England Seamless Casket: The Directory of Directors in the City of Boston and Vicinity, 1911, p. 212.

      "not on terms of intimacy": BG, March 26, 1905.

      "crying and weeping": BG, November 11, 1905.

264   *"no statement to give"*: BG, October 25 and 29, 1905.

      thirty-eighth mayor of Boston: "Boston's 'Honey Fitz' Fitzgerald Elected to Congress," MassMoments.org.

      Democrats spent $30,000: BG, January 12, 1906.

"wasteful and unnecessary": Goodwin, *The Fitzgeralds and the Kennedys*, p. 137.

found himself under scrutiny: Goodwin, *The Fitzgeralds and the Kennedys*, p. 120; Connolly, *The Triumph of Ethnic Progressivism*, pp. 85–90.

265 *patronage and corruption*: Goodwin, *The Fitzgeralds and the Kennedys*, p. 136; Connolly, *The Triumph of Ethnic Progressivism*, pp. 85–90.

"Alleged Fraud in the City Coal": BG, September 7, 1907; Connolly, *The Triumph of Ethnic Progressivism*, pp. 87–88, 99.

damning investigative reports: Goodwin, *The Fitzgeralds and the Kennedys*, p. 136; Connolly, *The Triumph of Ethnic Progressivism*, p. 80.

Whenever P.J. saw: KMMS, p. 64.

266 *"I don't know, Pat—"*: KMMS, p. 64.

"one of East Boston's best": BG, March 30, 1907.

the SS Ivernia: BG, May 23, 1907; letters, PJKP.

267 *"fleeing to this country"*: BG, March 29 and September 12, 1907.

photographs had been: Letter to cousin Jim Kennedy, PJKP.

268 *a "royal welcome"*: BG, May 23, 1907.

was "far from good": BG, May 24, 1907.

"You remember me speaking": Letter to cousin Jim Kennedy, PJKP.

269 *street commissioner*: BG, January 8, 1908.

"The great surprise of": BG, November 20, 1908.

"Mr. Kennedy, who is": Nasaw, *The Patriarch*, pp. 26–27.

the "poorer choice": Goodwin, *The Fitzgeralds and the Kennedys*, p. 231.

"hope for a long continuance": BG, December 2, 1908.

his father grieved: Goodwin, *The Fitzgeralds and the Kennedys*, p. 231.

270 *"I believe you can get"*: Letter from John A. MacDonald, PJKP.

"Never was there a single": Goodwin, *The Fitzgeralds and the Kennedys*, p. 228.

EPILOGUE: JOE AND JOHN

272 *"The wisest Americans"*: John F. Kennedy, *A Nation of Immigrants*. Introduction by Robert F. Kennedy. New York: Harper and Row, 1964.

Joe tried to influence: Kessler, *The Sins of the Father*, p. 22.

273 *"ultimate defeat is inevitable"*: Goodwin, *The Fitzgeralds and the Kennedys*, p. 230.

274 *"glad to learn of his"*: BG, December 18, 1913.

of "intense interest": BG, October 7, 1914.

276 *"He wouldn't let us cut"*: Cutler, *Honey Fitz*, p. 245.

"Joe Kennedy inherited": Koskoff, *Joseph P. Kennedy*, p. 13.

praised in the headlines: P.J.'s obituaries and other stories, BG, May 20 and 21, 1929; BG, July 13, 1929.

277 *"Mr. Kennedy was a remarkable"*: BG, May 20, 1929.

"Pat gave away two fortunes": Koskoff, *Joseph P. Kennedy*, p. 5.

278 *"Saloon Keeper's Son to"*: Kessler, *The Sins of the Father*, p. 5.

279 *"This is not the land"*: "A Journey Home: John F. Kennedy in Ireland," remarks at reception in Limerick, Ireland, June 29, 1962, JFKL.

"No country in the world": John F. Kennedy, remarks at Dublin Airport, Ireland, June 1963, JFKL.

280   *"sail across dark seas"*: Kennedy, *A Nation of Immigrants*, p. 5.
281   *"my great-grandfather left here"*: John F. Kennedy, remarks at New Ross, June 27, 1963, JFKL.

ACKNOWLEDGMENTS AND AUTHOR'S NOTE

284   *"All of us are immigrants"*: Steve Earle, "City of Immigrants," *Washington Square Serenade*, 2007.

SELECT BIBLIOGRAPHY

Ainley, Leslie G. *Boston Mahatma.* Boston: Bruce Humphries, 1949.

Anbinder, Tyler. *City of Dreams: The 400-Year Epic History of Immigrant New York.* Boston: Houghton Mifflin Harcourt, 2016.

———. *Five Points: The Nineteenth-Century New York City Neighborhood.* New York: Free Press, 2012.

Barrett, James R. *The Irish Way: Becoming American in the Multiethnic City.* New York: Penguin, 2012.

Beaumont, Gustave de. *Ireland.* London: Harvard University Press, 2007. Originally published 1839.

Blight, David W. *Frederick Douglass: Prophet of Freedom.* New York: Simon and Schuster, 2020.

Bunting, W. H. *Portrait of a Port: Boston, 1852–1914.* London: Harvard University Press, 1994.

Coffey, Michael, and Terry Golway, eds. *The Irish in America.* New York: Hyperion, 2000.

Connolly, James J. *The Triumph of Ethnic Progressivism: Urban Political Culture in Boston, 1900–1925.* Cambridge, MA: Harvard University Press, 2009.

Considine, Bob. *It's the Irish: The Story of the Irish in Ireland and America.* New York: Doubleday, 1961.

Coogan, Tim Pat. *The Famine Plot: England's Role in Ireland's Greatest Tragedy.* New York: St. Martin's, 2012.

———. *Wherever Green Is Worn: The Story of the Irish Diaspora.* London: Head of Zeus, 2015.

Costigan, Giovanni. *A History of Modern Ireland: With a Sketch of Earlier Times.* New York: Pegasus, 1969.

Cullen, James Bernard, and William Taylor, eds. *The Story of the Irish in Boston:*

Together with Biographical Sketches of Representative Men and Noted Women. Boston: J. B. Cullen and Company, 1889.

Cutler, John Henry. *"Honey Fitz": Three Steps to the White House — The Life and Times of John F. (Honey Fitz) Fitzgerald.* Indianapolis: Bobbs-Merrill, 1962.

Davis, John H. *The Kennedys: Dynasty and Disaster.* New York: S.P.I., 1993.

Dezell, Maureen. *Irish America: Coming into Clover.* New York: Knopf Doubleday, 2002.

Dineen, Joseph Francis. *The Kennedy Family.* Boston: Little, Brown, 1959.

——— . *Ward Eight.* New York: Harper and Brothers, 1936.

Diner, Hasia R. *Erin's Daughters in America: Irish Immigrant Women in the Nineteenth Century.* Baltimore and London: Johns Hopkins University Press, 1983.

Dolan, Jay P. *The Irish Americans: A History.* New York: Bloomsbury, 2010.

Dudden, Faye E. *Serving Women: Household Service in Nineteenth-Century America.* Middletown, CT: Wesleyan University Press, 1983.

Duis, Perry. *The Saloon: Public Drinking in Chicago and Boston, 1880–1920.* Champaign: University of Illinois Press, 1999.

Egan, Timothy. *The Immortal Irishman: The Irish Revolutionary Who Became an American Hero.* Boston: Houghton Mifflin Harcourt, 2016.

Elly, Sandham. *Potatoes, Pigs, and Politics, the Curse of Ireland, and the Cause of England's Embarrassments.* London: Kent and Richards, 1848.

Evans, E. Estyn. *Irish Folk Ways.* Mineola, NY: Dover Publications, 2000. Originally published in 1957.

Gallagher, Thomas. *Paddy's Lament: Ireland, 1846–1847 — Prelude to Hatred.* New York: Harcourt Brace Jovanovich, 1987.

Gibney, John. *A Short History of Ireland, 1500–2000.* New Haven, CT: Yale University Press, 2018.

Glazier, Michael. *The Encyclopedia of the Irish in America.* Notre Dame, IN: University of Notre Dame Press, 1999.

Goodwin, Doris Kearns. *The Fitzgeralds and the Kennedys.* New York: Simon and Schuster, 1987.

Handlin, Oscar. *Boston's Immigrants, 1790–1880: A Study in Acculturation.* 4th ed. Cambridge, MA: Belknap Press of Harvard University Press, 1991.

Holloran, Peter C. *Boston's Wayward Children: Social Services for Homeless Children, 1830–1930.* Madison, NJ: Fairleigh Dickinson University Press, 1989.

Horowitz, David, and Peter Collier. *The Kennedys: An American Drama.* New York: Warner Books, 1985.

John F. Kennedy Library Foundation. *Rose Kennedy's Family Album: From the Fitzgerald Kennedy Private Collection, 1878–1946.* Foreword by Caroline Kennedy. New York: Grand Central Publishing, 2013.

Kelly, John. *The Graves Are Walking: The Great Famine and the Saga of the Irish People.* New York: Henry Holt, 2012.

Keneally, Thomas. *The Great Shame: And the Triumph of the Irish in the English-Speaking World.* New York: Knopf Doubleday, 2010.

Kennedy, Edward M., ed. *The Fruitful Bough.* Privately published.

Kennedy, Edward M. *True Compass: A Memoir.* New York: Grand Central Publishing, 2009.

Kennedy, John Fitzgerald. *A Nation of Immigrants.* New York: Harper and Row, 1986. Originally published in 1958.

Kessler, Ronald. *The Sins of the Father: Joseph P. Kennedy and the Dynasty He Founded.* New York: Grand Central Publishing, 2012.

Kinealy, Christine. *This Great Calamity: The Irish Famine, 1845–1852.* Dublin: Gill and Macmillan, 2006.

Kinealy, Christine, Ciarán Reilly, and Jason Francis King, eds. *Women and the Great Hunger.* Hamden, CT: Quinnipiac University Press, 2016.

Kinsella, Anna. *County Wexford in the Famine Years, 1845–1849.* Enniscorthy, Ireland: Duffry Press, 1995.

———. *Women of Wexford, 1798–1998.* Dublin: Courtown Publications, 1998.

Klein, Edward. *The Kennedy Curse: Why Tragedy Has Haunted America's First Family for 150 Years.* New York: St. Martin's, 2004.

Kline, Christina Baker. *Orphan Train: A Novel.* New York: HarperCollins, 2019.

Koskoff, David E. *Joseph P. Kennedy: A Life and Times.* Englewood Cliffs, NJ: Prentice-Hall, 1974.

Land, Stephanie. *Maid: Hard Work, Low Pay, and a Mother's Will to Survive.* New York: Hachette Books, 2019.

Laxton, Edward. *The Famine Ships: The Irish Exodus to America.* New York: Henry Holt, 1998.

Leamer, Laurence. *The Kennedy Men: 1901–1963.* New York: William Morrow, 2011.

———. *The Kennedy Women: The Saga of an American Family.* New York: Villard Books, 1996.

Lee, Erika. *America for Americans: A History of Xenophobia in the United States.* New York: Basic Books, 2019.

Lee, J. J., and Marion Casey, eds. *Making the Irish American: History and Heritage of the Irish in the United States.* New York: NYU Press, 2007.

Lepore, Jill. *These Truths: A History of the United States.* New York: W. W. Norton, 2018.

Lord, Robert H., John E. Sexton, and Edward T. Harrington. *History of the Archdiocese of Boston in the Various Stages of Its Development, 1604 to 1943.* 3 vols. New York: Sheed and Ward, 1944.

Loughery, John. *Dagger John: Archbishop John Hughes and the Making of Irish America.* Ithaca, NY: Cornell University Press, n.d.

Lynch-Brennan, Margaret. *The Irish Bridget: Irish Immigrant Women in Domes-

tic Service in America, 1840–1930. Syracuse, NY: Syracuse University Press, 2014.

Maier, Thomas. *The Kennedys: America's Emerald Kings — A Five-Generation History of the Ultimate Irish Catholic Family.* New York: Basic Books, 2003.

Marchi, Regina. *Legendary Locals of East Boston.* Mount Pleasant, SC: Arcadia Publishing, 2015.

McCourt, Malachy. *Malachy McCourt's History of Ireland.* Philadelphia: Running Press, 2004.

Meagher, Timothy J. *The Columbia Guide to Irish American History.* New York: Columbia University Press, 2005.

Miller, Kerby A. *Emigrants and Exiles: Ireland and the Irish Exodus to North America.* Oxford, UK: Oxford University Press, 1988.

Miller, Kerby, and Patricia Mulholland Miller. *Journey of Hope: The Story of Irish Immigration to America.* San Francisco: Chronicle Books, 2001.

Miller, Kerby, and Paul Wagner. *Out of Ireland: The Story of Irish Emigration to America.* Boulder, CO: Roberts Rinehart, 1997.

Miller, Norman. *Boston Beer: A History of Brewing in the Hub.* Charleston, SC: History Press, 2014.

Mitchel, John. *The Last Conquest of Ireland (Perhaps).* https://www.libraryireland.com/Last-Conquest-Ireland/Contents.php.

Mitchell, Arthur. *JFK and His Irish Heritage.* Dublin: Moytura Press, 1993.

Most, Doug. *The Race Underground: Boston, New York, and the Incredible Rivalry That Built America's First Subway.* New York: St. Martin's, 2014.

Nasaw, David. *The Patriarch: The Remarkable Life and Turbulent Times of Joseph P. Kennedy.* New York: Penguin, 2013.

O'Connor, Thomas H. *Bibles, Brahmins, and Bosses: A Short History of Boston.* Boston: Trustees of the Public Library of the City of Boston, 1984.

———. *The Boston Irish: A Political History.* New York: Little, Brown, 1997.

O'Connor, Thomas H., David C. Baldus, Charles A. Pulaski Jr., and George G. Woodworth. *Fitzpatrick's Boston, 1846–1866: John Bernard Fitzpatrick, Third Bishop of Boston.* Boston: Northeastern University Press, 1984.

O'Dowd, Niall. *Lincoln and the Irish: The Untold Story of How the Irish Helped Abraham Lincoln Save the Union.* New York: Skyhorse Publishing, 2018.

Okrent, Daniel. *The Guarded Gate: Bigotry, Eugenics, and the Law That Kept Two Generations of Jews, Italians, and Other European Immigrants Out of America.* New York: Scribner, 2020.

———. *Last Call: The Rise and Fall of Prohibition.* New York: Scribner, 2010.

O'Neill, Gerard. *Rogues and Redeemers: When Politics Was King in Irish Boston.* New York: Crown Publishers, 2012.

Ó Tuathaigh, Gearóid. *Ireland Before the Famine: 1798–1848.* Dublin: Gill and Macmillan, 2007.

Peterson, Mark. *The City-State of Boston: The Rise and Fall of an Atlantic Power, 1630–1865.* Princeton, NJ: Princeton University Press, 2019.

Poirteir, Cathal. *Famine Echoes.* Dublin: Gill and Macmillan, 1995.

Price, Michael, and Anthony Mitchell Sammarco. *Boston's Immigrants, 1840–1925.* Mount Pleasant, SC: Arcadia, 2000.

Puleo, Stephen. *A City So Grand: The Rise of an American Metropolis—Boston, 1850–1900.* Boston: Beacon Press, 2011.

———. *Voyage of Mercy: The USS* Jamestown, *the Irish Famine, and the Remarkable Story of America's First Humanitarian Mission.* New York: St. Martin's, 2020.

Quinlin, Michael. *Irish Boston: A Lively Look at Boston's Colorful Irish Past.* Guilford, CT: Globe Pequot, 2013.

Rachlin, Harvey. *The Kennedys: A Chronological History, 1823–Present.* New York: World Almanac, 1986.

Railey, Julia Houston. *Retail and Romance.* Boston: Walker Lithograph and Publishing Company, 1926.

Reedy, George E. *From the Ward to the White House: The Irish in American Politics.* Toronto: C. Scribner's Sons, 1991.

Ryan, Dennis P. *A Journey Through Boston Irish History.* Mount Pleasant, SC: Arcadia, 1999.

Sammarco, Anthony Mitchell. *East Boston.* Mount Pleasant, SC: Arcadia, 2004.

———. *East Boston Through Time.* Charleston, SC: America Through Time, Arcadia Publishing, 2020.

———. *Jordan Marsh: New England's Largest Store.* Mount Pleasant, SC: Arcadia, 2017.

Schorow, Stephanie. *Drinking Boston: A History of the City and Its Spirits.* Guilford, CT: Globe Pequot, 2019.

Schwarz, Ted. *Joseph P. Kennedy: The Mogul, the Mob, the Statesman, and the Making of an American Myth.* Hoboken, NJ: Wiley, 2003.

Shannon, William V. *The American Irish: A Political and Social Portrait.* Amherst: University of Massachusetts Press, 1989.

Smith, Jean Kennedy. *The Nine of Us: Growing Up Kennedy.* New York: Harper, 2016.

Stevens, Peter F. *Hidden History of the Boston Irish: Little-Known Stories from Ireland's "Next Parish Over."* Mount Pleasant, SC: Arcadia, 2008.

Sumner, William Hyslop. *A History of East Boston: With Biographical Sketches of Its Early Proprietors and an Appendix.* Bristol, CT: Higginson Book Company, 1858.

Tóibín, Colm, and Diarmaid Ferriter. *Irish Famine: A Documentary.* London: Profile Books, 2004.

Vowell, Sarah. *Lafayette in the Somewhat United States.* New York: Riverhead Books, 2015.

————. *The Wordy Shipmates.* New York: Riverhead Books, 2009.

Wagner, J. B. (Joseph Bernard). *Cooperage: A treatise on modern shop practice and methods; from the tree to the finished article.* Yonkers, NY: J. B. Wagner, 1910.

Whalen, Richard J. *The Founding Father: The Story of Joseph P. Kennedy—A Study in Power, Wealth, and Family Ambition.* Washington, DC: Regnery, 1993.

Whyte, Robert. *The Ocean Plague; or, A voyage to Quebec in an Irish emigrant vessel.* Boston: Coolidge and Wiley, 1848.

————. *Robert Whyte's 1847 Famine Ship Diary: The Journey of an Irish Coffin Ship.* Cork, Ireland: Mercier Press, 1994.

Woodham-Smith, Cecil. *The Great Hunger: Ireland, 1845–1849.* London: Hamish Hamilton, 1962.

Work, Henry H. Wood. *Whiskey and Wine: A History of Barrels.* London: Reaktion Books, 2014.

INDEX

African Americans
  African American women, Boston and, 52,
    115
  Boston locations/populations, 52, 130,
    144, 257
  Fourteenth and Fifteenth Amendments,
    143
  integration/American cities, 130
  See also Civil War (US); Irish-African Amer-
    ican relations; slavery
alcohol consumption/establishments
  American history/laws and, 180
  beer popularity, 178–79, 182
  "blind pigs"/establishments on pilings,
    Boston, 225
  fermented beverages vs. distilled spirits
    debate/laws, 178–79
  German immigrant proprietors, Boston,
    179
  immigrants and, 179, 180–81
  laws, Boston area, 138, 169–71, 176, 177,
    180, 181–82, 187, 196, 206–7, 219,
    223–26, 235–36
  licenses and, 138, 171, 176, 178–79, 180,
    181–82, 206, 224, 225–26
  popularity, Boston area, 169, 177, 179
  prohibition, Massachusetts, 177, 181
  Republican views, 195
  role of saloons for immigrants, 183
  states drinking more than Massachusetts,
    179
  temperance movement/activists and,
    59–60, 169–70, 179, 180–81, 186,
    201, 206, 224–25, 235, 274–75
  turnover in saloon business, 177

vigilante groups and, 226
  See also specific individuals/establishments
alcohol/P.J.
  Cotter & Kennedy liquor store, 207–8,
    209, 226
  focusing on retail/wholesale shops, 226–27
  Kennedy & Quigley liquor store/saloon
    and, 208–9, 226
  licenses and, 226
  P.J. Kennedy and Company, 247, 248,
    274–75
  P.J. listing occupation, 225
  profits, 211
  Prohibition and, 274–75
  as state representative and, 223–25,
    235–36
alcohol/P.J. as bartender proprietor
  dark side of drinking and, 185–86
  Democratic Committee Headquarters
    location and, 187–88
  description/character, 177, 183–85
  Elbow Street saloon/beer, 178, 179,
    182–83, 186–88, 208, 226
  Hayward's saloon, 176, 177, 186–87
  laws/license and, 176, 182
  listening/learning and, 184–85, 187
  other investments/establishments, 186–87
  R. G. Dun & Co./agent report, 177
Alcott, Louisa May, 41, 42, 97, 120, 151, 219
Aldrich, Thomas Bailey, 231
Almanac (Know Nothing publication), 87
almshouse, Deer Island, 39, 114, 156
amendments to the Constitution, 135, 143
American Party, 87, 88, 89
American Woman Suffrage Association, 143

Andrew, John, 132, 170
Anthony, Susan B., 175
anti-Catholicism attitude/actions
    Broad Street Riot, 73, 81–82
    conspiracy/burning of convent, 73, 81–82
    education and, 81
    history/"witches," 79–80
    orphanages/institutions and, 111–13, 115
    overview, 2, 43, 51–52, 73, 79–82, 83–91,
        100, 152–53, 243
    See also Know Nothings; *specific individuals/
    groups*
anti-immigration attitude/actions in America,
    80, 81–82
    See also discrimination/violence against
    Irish immigrants; *specific groups*
Anti-Saloon League, 233
Aspell, Nicholas, 23–24, 70
Aspell, Richard, 23–24
Atlantic Monthly (magazine), 143–44, 231

Baltimore American (newspaper), 89
banking/P.J.
    Columbia Trust Company, 236, 245–46,
        255, 273, 277
    Sumner Savings Bank, 246, 277
Barron, Bridget, 75
Barron clan
    Bridget's relatives and, 15, 23–24, 63
    family in Boston, 23–24, 75
    Mary (Bridget's mother) and, 15, 23, 63
Barron, Edward, 77
Barron, James/John, 15, 23–24
Barron, Johanna, 23–24, 70
Barron, Mary, 23–24, 77, 117, 119
Barron, Patrick
    background/death, 15, 23–24, 61, 263
    becoming naturalized citizen/right to vote,
        78, 90
    Bridget/Patrick and, 2, 55, 61, 63, 70, 75,
        110
Barron, Patrick, Sr., 15, 23–24, 77
Barron, Thomas, 247–48
Barton, Jabez, 117, 118
baseball, Boston, 259–60
Battle of New Ross, 57
Beard, Frank, 233
Beecher, Lyman, Reverend, 74, 79, 81, 85
Bible Riots of 1844, Philadelphia, 82
Bly, Nellie, 173

Board of Alderman, Boston, 142, 178–79,
    194, 195, 198, 199, 206, 252, 268
"Board of Strategy"
    after Sullivan's death, 254–55
    exposé/backlash against, 252, 259, 261
    meeting attendees/goals, 248–52, 254–55
    name and, 248, 249–50
    P.J. and, 248–55, 258, 259
    Quincy House meetings, 248–50, 254–55
    replacing Maguire/infighting and, 249–52
Boston
    antislavery organizations/individuals, 52,
        118, 130–31
    Black maids and, 52
    "Brahmins"/names, 43, 54, 82, 108, 117,
        143–44, 172, 182, 198, 199, 202, 230,
        256, 272, 281
    Catholic school system development, 81
    crime rates (through late 1840s), 39
    description (at time of Bridget's arrival),
        20, 22–23, 37, 42–43
    description/economy (postwar), 139, 144
    ethnic makeup (early 1900s), 256–57, 267
    immigrant businesses/examples, 138,
        141–42
    Irish policemen, 142, 163, 198
    population/Irish immigrants and, 51, 75,
        77–78, 119
    poverty and, 39
    pre-/post–American Revolution descrip-
        tion, 42
    as shaped by Irish, 256
    subway system, 257
    See also East Boston
Boston Asylum, Deer Island, 114
Boston Beer Company, 196
Boston Globe (newspaper), 140, 162–63, 167,
    171, 175, 176, 185, 189, 190, 192,
    193, 200, 202, 205, 206, 207, 216,
    218, 221, 225, 227, 243, 245, 246,
    251–52, 253, 255, 259, 261, 266, 267,
    268, 269, 274
Boston Herald (newspaper), 84, 231
Boston Journal (newspaper), 135, 165
Boston News (newspaper), 228, 235
Boston Pilot (newspaper)
    advice to Irish, 41, 76, 78, 84, 128, 151,
        160, 180–81, 187
    Deer Island institutions and, 156–57, 158,
        170

Boston Pilot (newspaper) (*cont.*)
  on discrimination against Irish, 84, 85,
    87–88, 89–90, 91, 116, 153, 170–71,
    197
  "Information Wanted" section/"Search for
    Missing Friends" ads, 35–36
  Irish soldiers/Civil War and, 132, 133
  letters from maid and, 53–54
  name/founders and, 76, 81, 129
  orphans/adoption, 113, 115
  praise from, 123–24, 126, 142
  reporting deaths, 16, 21, 38–39, 93–94,
    108, 161
  urging immigrants to move on/dangers,
    37–40, 41, 42, 68–69, 78
  women in workforce/first female editor and,
    143, 172–73
  See also Donahoe, Patrick
Boston Post (newspaper), 112, 170
Boston Record American (newspaper), 281
Boston Tea Party, 20
Boston Transcript (newspaper), 82, 190
Boycott, Charles, 192
"boycott" term origins, 192
Boyse, Jane Colclough/Thomas, 32–33
Brace, Charles Loring, 113
Brandeis, Louis D., 226
Brando, Marlon, 163
Brass-finisher work, 174–75
brass-manufacturing history, Boston, 175
breweries/distilleries, New Ross, 59
Brian Boru, King, 58
"Bridget" name, 14–15
Brontë, Emily, Anne, Maria, Elizabeth, 107
Brothers Grimm, 50–51
Bryan, William Jennings, 249
Bulfinch, Charles, 62, 201
Bumstead, Jeremiah, 180
Burke, Charles, 275
Burke, William J., 190
Burns, Jack ("Dock Parson"), 268

Carbee, Milo, 174–75
Carlyle, Thomas, 10
Cass, Thomas, 132
Cathedral of the Holy Cross, Boston, 62–63
Catholic Total Abstinence Union, 223–25
Caulfield, John, 210
Cavendish, William ("Billy"), 279
Cherry Brothers Brewery, 59–60

Cherry, Richard/William, 59
Cheverus, Jean-Louis Lefebvre de, Bishop, 62
Children's Aid Society, 111, 113
Chinese Exclusion Act, xiv, 230
Chinese immigrants/anti-Chinese attitudes
  and actions, xiv, 116, 230, 233
cholera, 8, 16, 30, 36, 37, 39, 68, 107
cholera infantum, 2, 92, 94, 216
Christmas Carol, A (Dickens), 144
Christmas holiday, 79, 144
Churchill, Pamela, 279
Church of the Sacred Heart, 213
Cinderella (Brothers Grimm), 50–51
Citizens' Law and Order League, 226
Civil War (US)
  African American soldiers, 134–35, 144
  Confederate States of America formation,
    131
  Fifty-Fourth Massachusetts Regiment/Fort
    Wagner, 134–35, 144
  Irish and draft riots, 134–35
  Irish soldiers, 132–34, 135–36
  Irish wavering on, 127–30
  slavery and, 127–30
Clarendon, Lord, 19
Cleveland, Grover, 197, 215, 231, 234
coal/Suffolk Coal Company, 246–47, 265
Colclough, Caesar, 32
Collins, Hannah, 116
Collins, Patrick A.
  background/description, 197, 258, 262
  as mayor, 255, 258
  P.J. and, 214–15, 230–31, 258, 262, 263
  politics/Board of Strategy and, 194, 195,
    197–98, 202, 214–15, 230–31, 254,
    255, 258, 261
Colored Orphan Asylum, New York, 134
Common Council, Boston, 142, 190, 194,
    195, 197, 198, 199, 200, 206, 207,
    208, 232, 252, 268
Connelly, George, 275
consumption
  consequences, 1, 2, 39, 68, 102–3, 104,
    107–8, 121, 244, 268
  recovery and, 103, 244, 247, 273–74
  "vampires" and, 107–8
Conway, Katharine, 143, 144
coopering, 65–66, 101
Corbett, Joseph J., 248–49, 254, 258
Corcoran, Michael, 132, 133

Cotter, John J. (J.J.)
  background/description, 207, 247
  Cotter & Kennedy liquor store, 207–8, 211
  P.J. and, 207–8, 211, 213, 217
Cromwell, Oliver, 28, 79, 153
Curley, James, 211

Daniel Francis Cooperage and Brass Foundry,
    65
Davitt, Michael, 192
Declaration of Independence, America, 80,
    139, 179, 240
Deer Island
  facilities for orphans/criminals, 114–15,
    155–58, 163, 171, 185
  quarantine hospital and, 114, 156
  reputation/description, 114–15, 156
Dickens, Charles, 42–43, 114, 144
diphtheria, 165, 216, 228, 229
discrimination/violence against Irish immi-
    grants
  anti-Catholicism and, 2, 43, 51–52, 73,
    79–82, 83–91, 100, 152–53, 243
  anti-immigration/Irish stereotypes and,
    3, 73–75, 78–79, 80–81, 83–91, 100,
    107, 111, 131
  Beard's cartoons, 233
  Bloody Monday, 89
  Boston, 1–2, 40, 41–42, 43, 72–75,
    78–79, 81–82, 83–86, 87–88, 90, 93,
    105–6
  brutal deaths as entertainment, 108
  excluding Irish work applicants, 48,
    51–52, 115–16, 122
  following Famine/pre–Civil War (summa-
    ry), 142
  funerals/gravesites and, 1–2, 3, 93, 105–6
  Know Nothings/proposed laws, 85–91,
    132, 142, 153, 197
  maids and, 48, 51–54, 116
  Orr/mobs, 83–85
  paramilitary clubs, 83–84
  Penal Laws, 80–81, 93
  riots/shootings (1895), 243
  tar/feathering priest, 85
  Theodore Roosevelt and, 233
Doherty, Cornelius, 190
Donahoe, Patrick
  Boston Pilot publisher/opinions, 37–38, 40,
    78, 85, 102–3, 113, 128, 153, 167

Deer Island/public institutions and, 156–57
orphans/adoption, 113
recruiting Irish soldiers/Civil War (US),
    132
selling/buying back *Boston Pilot,* 167
wife's death/burial, 102–3, 105
  See also Boston Pilot (newspaper)
Donovan, James ("Smiling Jim"), 222,
    248–49, 250, 251, 252, 258, 269
Douglas, Stephen, 131
Douglass, Frederick
  background, 127
  Emancipation Proclamation and, 133
  Father Matthew and, 181
  Irish and, 127–28, 129–30
  sons/Civil War and, 135–36
Dred Scott Supreme Court decision, 101, 128
Dublin Pilot (newspaper), 129
Dunn, James H., 269

East Boston
  children playing at waterfront/dangers and,
    150–51
  development/businesses, 63–64, 76, 100
  fire (1908), 270
  fires/rebuilding (early 1870s), 166–67
  history, 63
  population/growth, 63, 64–65, 223
  shipbuilding industry boom/bust, 95,
    100–102, 149–50
  *See also specific components; specific individuals/
    groups*
East Boston Advocate/Argus-Advocate (newspa-
    per), 100, 141, 186, 205–6, 213
East Boston Ledger (newspaper), 141
East Boston Ferry Company, 64, 88, 124
education, Boston area
  girls vs. boys, 152
  Irish immigrant children and, 155–56
  parochial school beginnings, 153–54
  Protestant teachings and, 152–54
  See also specific individuals/institutions
Eleanor (yacht), 239–40, 267
Elgee, Jane Francesca, Lady, 12
Eliot School, 152–53, 154
Emancipation Proclamation, xiv, 133
Emerson, Ralph Waldo, 42, 240
Emigrant Savings Bank, 40
England-Ireland relationship
  English landlords/rents, 58, 191, 192

England-Ireland relationship (*cont.*)
  English rule over Ireland and, 132, 153,
    191
  evictions of Irish and, 7, 17, 30, 38, 191,
    192, 219–20
  Great Irish Potato Famine and, 8–10,
    11–12, 28–30, 31
  Irish reform efforts/revolution and, 31, 57,
    129, 132, 191–93
  See also specific individuals
Excelsior Associates, 189, 193, 209, 238, 245,
    262, 266

Farm School for Indigent Boys, Deer Island,
    112–13, 114
Fenwick, Benedict J., 76, 81
ferry system
  bridge/tunnel between Boston and East
    Boston vs., 223, 235, 257
  description, 124, 222–23
  "free" system and, 223
Field, Marshall, 125
Filene, Edward, 140
Filene's Basement, 140
Fisher and Fairbanks liquor company, 247–48
Fitton, James, Father, 2, 105
Fitzgerald, James, 200–201, 209, 244
Fitzgerald, John F. ("Honey Fitz")
  anti-Catholic riots/shootings (1895) and,
    243
  background, 184, 232, 242
  consumption/recovery, 244, 273–74
  descriptions/character, 232, 242, 244, 258,
    260, 279
  grandchildren and, 276, 279, 280
  investigations into, 264–65
  P.J. and, 232–33, 242, 244, 263, 264, 265,
    269, 273–74, 276, 277, 280
  politics/reputation and, 209, 222, 232–33,
    234, 237, 244, 252, 253, 255, 258,
    259, 263, 264–65, 268, 269, 273
Fitzgerald, Rosanna Molly ("Rose") Cox, 232
Fitzgerald, Rose, 184, 242, 243, 265, 273
  See also Kennedy, Joseph Patrick/Rose;
    Kennedy, Rose
Fitzgerald, Thomas, 232
Fitzpatrick, John Bernard, Father/Bishop, 76,
    77, 89, 105–6, 128, 135, 153, 154
Flying Cloud clipper, 100–101
Flynn, Nick, 189, 200, 201, 213, 261

Forbes, Robert Bennet, 73
*Foreign Conspiracy Against the Liberties of the
    United States* (Morse), 81
Fortune (magazine), 237
Franklin, Ben, 80
Freeman's Journal (newspaper), 17, 33
Fuller, Margaret, 42

Garfield, James, 189
Garrison, William Lloyd, 128–29
Geary Act (1892), 230, 233
German immigrants, 48, 178, 179, 180
Glascott, William/Glascott family, 58
Glover, Ann ("Goody"), 79
Godey's (magazine), 173
Grainger, William, 260
Great Boston Fire (1872), 167
Great Irish Potato Famine
  beginnings/Wexford farmer findings,
    26–27
  Boston/other US cities helping Irish,
    73–74
  conditions/death, 7, 30–31, 32, 34, 60
  England's response, 28–30, 31
  immigration to America and, 16–17, 23,
    33–34
  locations, 7, 31, 60
  mythology, 33
  potato crop failure (1845, 1846, 1847),
    27–28
  soup kitchens/conditions for getting food,
    29–30, 58
  stealing food/consequences, 31, 32
  women's empowerment and, 33
Great Republic (ship), 101
Greeley, Horace, 169
Grey, Earl, 28
grocery business
  all-purpose establishments described/
    names, 137–38, 168–69
  liquor sales and, 138, 139, 171, 181–82,
    224
  turnover, 141
grocery shop/Bridget Kennedy
  Bridget claiming occupation as baker, 172
  description/items for sale, 137–38
  as family business, 145, 167
  liquor and, 138, 139, 171–72
  location (original), 144–45
  managing sales/accounts, 138–39, 145

relocations/Border Street, 167
significance for Bridget Kennedy, 138, 139,
    141–42, 145–46
surrounding businesses, Border Street, 169
versions of beginnings/other work and,
    140, 141

Hale, Sarah Josepha, 173
Hall, Prescott, 231
Hall, Samuel (shipbuilder), 64, 88
Hall, Samuel W., 88
Hancock House, 171
Hancock, John, 171, 201, 207
Hancock, Winfield Scott, 189
Harper's/Harper's Weekly (magazine), 48, 53,
    54, 116
Harrison, Benjamin, 215
Haskins, George, Father, 113–14, 115, 153,
    170
Hawthorne, Nathaniel, 10, 42
Hayward's saloon, 175–76
Hickey, Catharine ("Katie"), 212, 213, 275
Hickey, Charles, 212, 213
Hickey family, 212, 213
Hickey, James, 212, 213, 263
Hickey, James (Sr.), 212, 245
Hickey, John, 212
Hickey, Margaret, 212
Hickey, Margaret ("Martha"), 212
Hickey, Mary Augusta
    background/education, 211
    descriptions/character, 211, 212–13
    pursuing P.J., 211–12
    See also Kennedy, Mary Hickey; Kennedy,
        P.J./Mary
Highland Spring Brewery, 178
Hillard, George S./wife, 118
History of the Archdiocese of Boston (Catholic
    Church), 128
Holmes, Oliver Wendell, 43, 143–44
Holy Cross Cemetery, Malden, 217–18, 228,
    262, 277
Home Rule Party, 192
House of Correction, Deer Island, 114, 156
House of Industry, Deer Island, 114, 156
House of Reformation for Juvenile Delin-
    quents, Deer Island
    beginnings, 114, 155–56, 157–58, 253
    P.J. and, 157–58, 160, 185, 187, 253
    reform goals/conditions, 155–56, 157–58

House of the Angel Guardian, 113, 114
housing/Irish immigrants
    Boston landlords/evictions, 71–72
    descriptions/costs, 67–68, 71, 72
    disease/deaths and, 67, 68, 92, 102–3, 216,
        228, 229
    health officials and, 68, 72
Howe, Samuel, 42
Hughes, John, Bishop, 82, 128
Hugo, Victor, 107
Hyannis Port and Kennedys, xi–xii, 276, 282

Illustrated London News (newspaper), 17
immigrants/America
    in 1890s, 229–30
    anti-immigration sentiments/examples, xiv,
        91, 230–31, 231, 233, 234
    by late 1870s, 164
    See also discrimination/violence against
        Irish immigrants; *specific acts; specific
        individuals/groups*
Immigration Act (1917), 230
Immigration Restriction League, xiv, 231
Indigenous people and Puritans, 80
"intelligence offices," 41–42, 120
Ireland
    abstinence movement, 59–60
    peat fires, Irish homes, 25, 49, 56–57
    revolution/consequences (1848), 31–32,
        129, 132
    See also England-Ireland relationship; *specific
        events/individuals*
Irish–African American relations
    draft riot, New York City, 134
    economic competition and, 52, 127, 128
Irish-American (newspaper), 17
Irish Emigrant Society, 38, 40
Irish immigrants
    in 1870s/1880s, 192
    assimilation and, 78–79
    churches nationwide (by mid-1800s), 78
    deaths/causes, Boston, 38–39, 67, 68,
        165–66
    deportation to Ireland and, 90
    Irish-heavy cities (other than Boston), 196
    men's status/life span and, 54, 66–67, 104,
        111
    post–Civil War change, Boston, 142–43
    women delaying marriage/children, 48,
        165

Irish immigrants (*cont.*)
    See also discrimination/violence against
        Irish immigrants; housing/Irish immi-
        grants; orphanages/institutions; *specific
        components; specific individuals/events; work
        of Irish/Irish immigrants*
Irish immigrants/trip to America
    American vs. British ships, 18–19
    arrival (Boston), 19–23
    conditions vs. promises/Atlantic crossing,
        13–14, 17–19
    disasters/Atlantic crossing, 15–16, 17, 19
    disease/deaths, 13–14, 17–18, 19
    doctors inspecting passengers, 13–14
    encouragement to leave Ireland, 11
    encouraging relatives to come to America/
        overpromising, 36–37
    pamphlets for immigrants, 9, 20
    port physicians/health inspectors, 21, 23
    ships used, 15–16, 17, 18
    statistics on, 23, 51
    women and, 11–12, 24, 33–34, 51
    working-class people/starving people,
        16–17, 61
    See also Great Irish Potato Famine; Liver-
        pool; *specific individuals*
Irish National Land League/clubs, 192, 193,
    197
Italian immigrants/communities, 43, 115,
    163, 164, 180, 230, 234, 256, 257, 267

Jackson, Andrew, 103, 202
Jefferson, Thomas, 80, 222
Jewish immigrants/communities, 43, 77, 106,
    115, 164, 230, 234, 256, 257, 267, 272
Jordan, Eben Dyer, 124–25, 126–27, 136,
    139–40
Jordan, Marsh and Company, 125
Jordan Marsh Store
    Bridget Kennedy/hair styling, 124–26,
        136, 137
    Civil War and, 136
    descriptions/innovations, 124, 125, 126,
        127, 137, 139
Joyce, Ambrose death/poem, 94–95
Joyce, James, 11

Kane, Lawrence, 210, 223, 239, 262
Kane, Martin, 210, 223
Kazan, Elia, 163

Keany, Matthew, 232
Keliher, John A., 248–49
Kelley, D. D., 197
Kelly, Daniel F., 190
Kennedy, Bobby, 281, 282
Kennedy, Bridget (P.J.'s cousin), 240–41
Kennedy, Bridget Murphy
    accomplishments (summary), 168
    burying husband, 1–2, 106–7
    buying property, 168
    commute to Jordan Marsh, 124, 139
    death/wake and burial, 217–18
    descriptions/character, 7, 24, 59–60, 124,
        126, 169, 180–81, 217, 218, 219
    estate/worth, 218
    extended family and, 210–11, 213, 216
    grandchildren losses (summary), 216
    as hairdresser/learning and, 124–27,
        139–40
    helping nephews in Ireland, 219–20
    Kennedy legacy and, 282
    letters to relatives in Ireland, 77, 166, 191
    life as widow (summary), 4
    maid work/Maverick House (Sturtevant
        House), 116–17, 119, 120–21
    monetary worth on paper (around 1860),
        119
    move after fires/rebuilding, 167
    moves, 119, 167
    P.J.'s politics and, 189–90, 199–200
    plan to leave service, 120–21, 122
    renting building next door, 168
    situation following husband's death,
        110–11
    "widow" status and, 172, 218
    See also grocery shop/Bridget Kennedy;
        Murphy, Bridget
Kennedy, Bridget/Patrick
    children at time of Patrick's death, 2,
        104–5
    children's births, 69–71, 99
    children's godparents/help with, 70–71
    death/burial of John (son) and, 92–93
    family burial plot, Cambridge, 3, 93, 106,
        165, 217–18
    homes/moves, 62, 63, 67, 71, 72, 75, 99
    life together (summary), 1
    naturalized citizenship and, 78, 90
    wedding, 62–63
Kennedy, Eunice, 281

Kennedy, Francis Benedict (P.J./Mary child),
    228–29
Kennedy, James (Patrick's brother), 56, 59,
    111, 192
Kennedy, James (Bridget's nephew), 219–20
Kennedy, Joanna (Bridget/Patrick child)
    birth/childhood, 2, 70, 72, 77, 104, 151,
        152, 167
    death, 275
    marriage/children and, 165–66, 210, 239
    work, 164
    See also Mahoney, Humphrey/Joanna
Kennedy, John (Patrick's brother), 56, 59,
    111, 192
Kennedy, John (Bridget/Patrick child), 2, 3,
    70, 77, 92–93, 106
Kennedy, John F., 107, 274, 278, 279–81, 282
Kennedy, John, Jr.
    description, xii
    plane crash and, xi, xi–xii, xii, 282
Kennedy, Joseph, Jr., 274
Kennedy, Joseph Patrick (P.J./Mary child)
    birth/baptism, 215, 217
    careers/adult life, 271, 273, 276, 277–78
    descriptions, xiii, 229, 276, 277, 278, 280
    father and, 259, 260–61, 270–71, 276
    Fortune magazine profile, 237
    Irish heritage/ancestors and, xiii, 278
    name selection and, 215–16
    Rose Fitzgerald and, 243, 265
    schools/schooling and, 240, 272
    working with Quigley/boat tours, 239
Kennedy, Joseph Patrick/Rose
    children, 274, 275
    homes/locations, 274, 276
    in London, 278
    summers/Hyannis Port, 276
    wedding, 274
Kennedy, Kathleen ("Kick"), 279
Kennedy, Margaret (Bridget/Patrick child)
    birth/childhood, 2, 70, 77, 92, 151, 152
    death, 275
    1870s and, 164
    marriage/children and, 165–66, 210, 216
Kennedy, Margaret (P.J./Mary child), 240,
    260, 274, 275
Kennedy, Mary (Bridget/Patrick child)
    birth/childhood, 2, 70, 77, 104, 151, 152,
        167
    death, 275

marriage/children and, 165, 166, 210, 223,
    239, 262
work, 164
See also Kane, Lawrence
Kennedy, Mary Hickey
    death, 275
    life/reflections on life, 275
    P.J.'s breaks/vacations and, 265–67
    See also Hickey, Mary Augusta; Kennedy,
        P.J./Mary
Kennedy, Mary Johanna, 56, 63
Kennedy, Mary Loretta (P.J./Mary child), 229,
    274, 275
Kennedy, Patrick (Ann Murphy's husband),
    25, 166
Kennedy, Patrick (Bridget's nephew), 219–20
Kennedy, Patrick (Sr.), 56
Kennedy, Patrick (America)
    burial/site, 1–2, 3–4, 106, 107
    employment/cooper work and, 55, 61, 64,
        65, 66, 69, 95, 100, 101, 102
    illness/death and mass, 2, 95, 100, 103,
        104, 105
    See also Kennedy, Bridget/Patrick
Kennedy, Patrick (Ireland)
    as cooper trainee, 59, 60
    description, 56
    family land/home, 57–58, 219–20
    famine and, 55, 57, 58
    "Kennedy" name evolution, 59
    life/schooling, 57–58
    parents/siblings, 56, 58–59
    reasons for leaving Ireland, 58, 59
    ship/travels to America and, 60–61
Kennedy, P.J. (Patrick Joseph)
    anti-Catholic riots/shootings (1895) and,
        243
    coal/Suffolk Coal Company, 246–47, 265
    commissioner of wires/salary, 258–59, 264
    death/funeral, 276–77
    descriptions/character, 163, 237, 242, 243,
        246, 260–61, 276, 277, 281
    Eleanor (yacht) and, 239–40, 267
    European tour following wife's death, 275
    European tour/visiting Ireland and, 266–68
    Excelsior Investment Company, 245
    family life, 259–60
    Fitzgerald and, 232–33, 242, 244, 263,
        264, 265, 269, 273–74, 276, 277, 280
    grandchildren and, 274, 275–76

Kennedy, P.J. (Patrick Joseph) *(cont.)*
    health issues, 264, 268, 276
    helping at family grocery store, 168
    housing arrangements, 167, 175, 209–10
    Kennedy legacy and, 282
    letters to relatives in Ireland, 191
    as longshoreman/stevedore, 160, 161, 162,
        163, 168, 173
    losses of, 262–63
    making money and, 240, 244–45
    Quigley/yacht and, 238–40
    running for office (early 1900s) and, 268–69
    status/clubs and, 241–42
    See also alcohol/P.J.; banking/P.J.; poli-
        tics/P.J.
Kennedy, P.J. (Patrick Joseph) childhood
    attention/women relatives and, 173, 229
    birth/baptism, 99–100
    as Bridget/Patrick child, 99
    description, 154
    House of Reformation for Juvenile Delin-
        quents and, 157–58, 160, 185, 187, 253
    losing father/peers losing fathers and, 108–9
    Michael O'Brien and, 119
    play/activities, 149, 150, 154–55, 242
    school and, 149, 152, 154, 159, 160
    at time of father's death, 2, 104, 105
Kennedy, P.J./Mary
    children's births, 215–16, 228, 229, 240
    family life, 259–60
    grandchildren and, 274, 275–76
    homes/locations, 214, 229, 269–70
    honeymoon, 213–14
    marriage, 214, 215
    meeting and, 213
    neighbor's son and, 261
    party for first anniversary, 216–17
    P.J. Kennedy and Company, 247, 248,
        274–75
    P.J.'s breaks/vacations and, 265–66
    status/"lace curtain" and, 240–41
    summers/Maine, 229, 241–42, 265
    wedding/guests and, 213
    Winthrop move and, 269–70
    See also Hickey, Mary Augusta; Kennedy,
        Mary Hickey
Kennedy, Rose, 188
    See also Fitzgerald, Rose; Kennedy, Joseph
        Patrick/Rose
Kennedy, Rosemary, 274

Kennedy, Ted, xii, xiii, 281
Kenney, James William, 196
Kerouac, Jack, 186
Kilmainham Jail, Ireland, 192
King James Bible, 81, 90, 152
King, Martin Luther, Jr., 81
Know Nothings
    background, 85–86
    description/anti-Catholicism, xiv, 85–88,
        90–91, 106, 131, 132, 142, 153, 197
    elections/fraud and, 88–91
    laws proposed, 90–91, 100
    social clubs/print material, 86

Labor Day as national holiday, 235
Lady's Book (magazine), 173
Lally, Frank/sisters, 266, 267
Land Purchase Act (1903), 220
Lane, Thomas J. ("T.J."), 245, 262
Lazarus, Emma, 231
Leaves of Grass (Whitman), 106
Les Misérables (Hugo), 107
Liberator (newspaper), 128, 129
lice, 8, 17
Lincoln, Abraham
    Civil War and, 132, 133, 135
    Emancipation Proclamation/slavery and,
        xiv, 81, 133
    Irish and, 91, 131, 133
    presidential election (1860) and reelection,
        131, 135
    Thanksgiving and, 173
Linton, Eliza Lynn, 140–41, 142
liquor. *See alcohol*
Little Women (Alcott), 120, 151, 219
Liverpool description (mid-1800s), 8–10
Liverpool Mail (newspaper), 10
Liverpool Mercury (newspaper), 17
Lodge, Henry Cabot, 230–31, 234, 280
Logan, Lawrence, 196
Lomasney, Martin ("the Mahatma")
    descriptions, 249–50, 253, 258, 263–64
    on marriage, 211
    politics and, 211, 222, 249–52, 253, 259,
        263–64, 268, 269
    replacing Maguire and, 250–52
    on Sullivan, 254
London, Jack, 164–65
Longfellow, Henry Wadsworth, 42, 209,
        238–39

longshoremen
    origins of term, 160
    P.J. as, 160, 161, 162, 163, 168, 173
    union/strikes and, 162
    work description/conditions, 160–62, 163
Lord's Prayer, 152
Louisville Daily Journal (newspaper), 89
Louisville Times (newspaper), 89
Lowell mills, 164
Lunatic Hospital, Deer Island, 114, 156
Lyceum Hall, 117, 190, 191, 193
Lyman School, 149, 153, 154, 159, 160, 178, 200
Lyman, Theodore, 78–79

Magdalene asylums/laundries, 33
Maguire, Patrick, 195, 197, 198, 214–15, 249
Mahoney, Humphrey/Joanna, 165, 167, 175, 210, 239
Malden, Karl, 163
"Married Women Doing Business" certificate, 172
Marsh, Benjamin, 125
Marsh, Charles, 125
Mather, Cotton, 79, 180
Mathew, Theobald, Father, 59–60, 180–81
Maverick House, 117–18
    See also Sturtevant House Hotel
Maverick, Samuel, 80, 117
Maverick Square, 67, 75–76, 80, 83, 117, 141, 144–45, 154, 164, 167, 182, 257
May, Abigail, 41, 120
M. Carbee and Company, 174–75
McCarthy, Lawrence, Father, 217
McCarthy, Mary, 36–37
McEnaney, Thomas O., 245
McGee, Thomas D'Arcy, 38, 87
McGinniskin, Barney, 142, 198
McGowan, Ann, 63
McKay, Donald, 64
McKay's shipyard/record ships, 100–101
Meagher, Thomas Francis, 31, 132–34, 136
Melville, Herman, 10
Mitchel, John/sons, 29, 129, 131
Mitchell, Charles, 257
Monroe, James, 103
Morse code, 81
Morse, Samuel F. B., 81, 101
Most Holy Redeemer Church, 2, 99–100, 105, 119, 135, 152, 199, 215, 217, 262

Murphy, Ann, 25, 166, 210, 262–63
Murphy, Bridget
    character, 7–8
    farm life/family, 25–26
    See also Kennedy, Bridget Murphy; Kennedy, Bridget/Patrick
Murphy, Bridget/America arrival and early days
    arrival/Boston, 19–23
    Barron family and, 15, 36, 55, 63
    employment and, 43, 51, 55
    occupation declaration, 21–22
Murphy, Bridget/travels to America
    crossing the Atlantic, 10–11, 13–14
    description (time of travels), 7, 24
    escape reasons, 7–8, 11, 24, 33–34
    Liverpool trip/stay, 8, 9–10
    theories on vessel taken, 15–16
Murphy, Catherine, 25, 102, 166, 262–63
Murphy, Edward, 25
Murphy family
    decision to keep land, 30
    land/crops, 25, 27
    landlords, 32–33
    potatoes/potato famine and, 27–28, 30
    as tenant farmers, 25, 27, 28, 32–33
Murphy, James, 25
Murphy, Johanna, 25, 166
Murphy, Margaret, 25, 71, 102, 210
Murphy, Mary, 25, 63
Murphy, Richard, 25, 27

Nation (magazine), 196
National Woman Suffrage Association, 143
Nation of Immigrants, A (John Kennedy), 280
Native American Party, 87
    See also American Party
Naturalization Act (America/1798), 78
"New Colossus, The" (Lazarus), 231
New-England Primer, 81
New Ross, 57–58, 58
New York Irish-American (newspaper), 90
New York Times (newspaper), 101, 123, 133, 139–40
New York Tribune (newspaper), 169
Noodles Island
    history, 63–64, 80
    See also East Boston
North American Review (magazine), 230
Notre Dame Academy, 211

O'Brien, Hugh, 195, 198–99, 202, 206, 252
O'Brien, Michael, 119, 158, 261
O'Brien, William Smith, 31
O'Connell, Daniel, 31, 129
O'Connor, T. P., 193
Old Orchard Beach, Maine
    activities, 229, 241–42, 243–44
    fire, 243
    Fitzgerald/family, 241, 242, 265
    P.J./family, 229, 241–42, 265
    Redberry Club, 241–42
    Rose Fitzgerald/Joe Kennedy and, 245, 265
O'Neil, Joseph, 244
On the Waterfront (film), 163
O'Reilly, John Boyle, 143
orphanages/institutions
    anti-Catholicism and, 111–13, 115
    Catholic priests/Irish charitable organiza-
        tions and, 113–14
    orphan trains, 111–12
    overview/description, 111–15
    See also specific groups/institutions
Orr, John/mob, 83, 84–85
Our Lady of the Isle school, 152

Panic of 1857/consequences, 101–2, 115,
    118
Parker, Theodore, Reverend, 81
Parnell, Charles Stewart, 191–93, 219–20,
    227–28
Parnell, Fanny, 192
Passenger Acts, British, 13
"Patrick" name, 60
Paul Revere House, 171
Peabody, Ephraim, 72–73
Pemberton Mill implosion/fire, 165
Pepper, George, 87
Pilot. See Boston Pilot (newspaper)
Pius XI, Pope, 275
Polish immigrants, 43, 115, 230
politics (Boston/East Boston)
    "bolters" and, 194, 200–201
    career pattern and, 196–97, 199
    Democratic Party and, 189–91, 193–95,
        197–202
    Irish independence and, 191, 192, 193
    Irish politicians significance/backlash,
        257–58
    wards/system, 190
    See also specific individuals

politics/P.J.
    ascent after elected office, 253, 255
    attempt to retire from elected office,
        227–28
    Board of Election Commissioners/salary
        and, 255
    campaigning/winning Massachusetts
        House, 199–202
    civic/political activities background, 189
    descriptions/character, 199, 205, 206,
        222, 227, 228, 234–35, 253, 255,
        260–62
    Irish independence and, 192, 193
    leaders recognizing, 189–90, 193
    lessons learned from elections, 205
    saloons and, 195–96
    strengths/weaknesses, 190, 193, 222, 223,
        253
    as ward leader/responsibilities, 194–95
    See also "Board of Strategy"
politics/P.J. as state representative
    assignment/orientation, 201
    decision to step back/focus on business,
        221–22
    Democratic National Convention, St. Louis
        and, 214–15
    ferry system issue and, 222–23, 235
    liquor issues and, 223–25, 235–36
    reelections/terms, 205–6, 216, 221–22
    salary, 211
    working man/unions and, 235
politics/P.J. as state senator
    Columbia Trust Company creation, 236
    election and, 227–28
    leaving, 233, 236–37
    reputation, 234–35
    voting/Fitzgerald and, 233
    workingman and, 228
Poor Laws, 31
"Pope Night" parties, 79
potato famine. *See* Great Irish Potato Famine
Prince of Wales, 132
Profiles in Courage (John Kennedy), 280
Prohibition Party, 179, 195–96, 200
Puck (magazine), 121
Punch (magazine), 28–29
Puritan religion, 79, 80

Quakers, 80
Quigley, Charles, 208, 209

Quigley, John J. ("J.J.")
    background, 209
    boat tours/*Excelsior* yacht and, 209,
        238–40
    Kennedy & Quigley liquor store/saloon
        and, 208–9, 211, 238
    P.J.'s return from Europe and, 267
    P.J.'s wedding/party and, 213, 217
Quincy House, Boston, 241–42, 248–50,
    254–55
Quincy, Josiah, 88
Quincy, Josiah, VI, 252–53, 254

Reagan, Ronald, 74
Redberry Club, 241–42
Redburn: His First Voyage (Melville), 10
Republic (newspaper), 198
Reuter, Henry, 178–79
Revere, Paul, 171, 175, 201, 240
Revolutionary War (America), 63
Robinson, George D., 202
Roche, Mary (Bridget's niece), 102, 166
Roche, Nicholas, 25, 102
Rogers, Aaron/diary, 158
Roosevelt, Theodore, 233, 278
Rosnosky, Isaac, 214, 215
Rourke, Daniel, 250, 251
Rush, Benjamin, 179, 182
Russell, William, 226, 236, 249
Ruth, Babe, 186

Saint Brigid of Kildare, 14, 47
Saint Brigid's Day, 47
Saint Patrick, 60
St. Augustine Cemetery, 3, 105–6
St. Brigid's Church, 60
St. Brigid's Well, 60
St. Nicholas Church
    building use/school, 152
    history, 76, 88
    Kennedys/community, 70, 75–76
    Orr/mob and, 84–85
    replacement, 99–100
St. Petersburg (ship), 15–16, 17, 21, 64
Salem mills, 164
Santa Claus, 76
scarlet fever, 39, 107
scurvy, 17
Sewall, Arthur, 249
Sheridan, Frank, 225

shipbuilding industry
    boom/bust, 95, 100–102, 149–50
    steam-powered ships beginnings/conse-
        quences, 101, 149–50
Shipping and Commercial List (newspaper),
    198
Sisters of Notre Dame, 152, 163–64
Skerry, Daniel, 162–63, 185
slavery
    abolishment, 135, 144
    antislavery organizations/individuals, 52,
        118, 130–31
    Boston and, 80, 117
    Constitution argument/idiocy and, 128
    Dred Scott Supreme Court decision, 101,
        128
    Emancipation Proclamation, xiv, 133
    as focus in US, 91
    lie that Black people were better off, 128,
        129
    Missouri Compromise/consequences,
        101
    Puritans and, 80
    Thirteenth Amendment and, 135
    See also Civil War (US); *specific individuals*
slums. *See* housing/Irish immigrants
smallpox, 2, 17, 68, 107
Special Olympics, xiii–xiv, 281
SS *Ivernia,* 266, 267
Stanton, Elizabeth Cady, 173
Statue of Liberty, 231
Steffens, Lincoln, 197, 257
stevedore
    description/work and, 161–62
    origins of term, 160–61
    P.J. as, 163, 173
Stowe, Harriet Beecher, 74, 107
Sturtevant House Hotel
    description/founder, 118–19, 122
    Noah Sturtevant's death and, 123–24
    See also Maverick House
Sturtevant, Noah, 118–19, 123–24
Sullivan, John H.
    attempt to retire from politics, 227
    background, 195
    Columbia Trust Company, 246
    death/funeral, 253, 254, 262
    P.J. and, 195, 205, 213, 227, 228, 246,
        249, 253–54
    politics and, 195, 205, 213, 227, 228